Mathematics Is a Verb

Mathematics Is a Verb

Options for Teaching
A Book of Readings

Edited by

C. W. SCHMINKE
University of Oregon

WILLIAM R. ARNOLD
Colorado State College

THE DRYDEN PRESS INC.
Hinsdale, Illinois

PREFACE

Not solely an eclectic reader nor simply a collection of discrete teaching "gimmicks," this is a professional book for teachers and prospective teachers. It is at once mathematical and pedagogical, designed primarily as a supplemental reader for use in methods courses for prospective teachers as well as in-service courses for experienced professionals. It is especially appropriate for those classes where the collective desire is to reinforce or update basic knowledge while giving appropriate attention to concomitant instructional practices. Simply stated, the purpose of the book is to provide the teacher with a functional, substantive, and pedagogical reference for those concepts children must learn in elementary school mathematics.

This book possesses several outstanding features as a result of the unique criteria used for the selection and organization of its content.

Initially, the seven sections may be seen to constitute a sequential order closely paralleling topics from the most widely used professional texts in the teaching of elementary school mathematics:

Section I — Mathematics and Learning: Developing a Rationale for Teaching

Section II — Basic Mathematical Language: Constructing Ideas Symbolically

Section III — Relationships and Properties: Developing an Understanding of Structure

Section IV — Basic Operations: Utilizing Forms of Composition and Decomposition

Section V — Geometry: Examining Spacial Relationships

Section VI — Problem Solving: Motivating Ability to Reason and Inquire

Section VII — The Case for Teachers: Facilitating Professional Decisions

Beyond functional criteria for organization, the book is equally concerned with growth toward mathematical maturity in a substantive sense. Beginning with the assumption that mathematical ideas are abstract, the student's first step must be to acquire a knowledge of the language of mathematics. As he does so, understanding develops through a knowledge of fundamental relationships. In order for number systems to be useful, computational procedures must be learned. Numerical ideas are expanded by relating them to the physical world of geometry. Finally, the student

v

should acquire the ability to solve problems. It is axiomatic to note that the sequence above can be placed in one-to-one correspondence with Sections II through VI.

The desire to provide elementary school teachers with the opportunity to gain increased confidence in their ability to learn mathematics and, consequently, to teach mathematics more effectively to children provides a basis for the second outstanding feature of this book. Within each of the separate Sections II through VI the substantive aspects of mathematics basic to contemporary elementary school programs are reinforced with a series of carefully chosen, mathematically-oriented selections. At the same time these selections may be used by the teacher as the basis for translating topics and concepts into functional instructional settings for children. For representative articles an illustrative flow-chart lesson is provided to suggest to the teacher how this may be done. Thus, each selection within a given Section is a unique resource with two distinct but related purposes. First, each selection is self-contained in nature. That is, the content of the article has sufficient clarity to provide the teacher with considerable closure in relation to a basic concept in mathematics. Second, each article, either explicitly or implicitly, contains the basis for a teaching strategy. The teacher can, with little cost in material and time, translate these mathematical concepts into direct lessons for children.

The presentation of mathematical content to teachers or prospective teachers is not sufficient to insure good teaching. While all good teaching needs to be functional in nature, to be really effective and consistent it must find its basis in knowledge of learning theory and child development. This knowledge must relate to how mathematical concepts are formed, the purposes of instruction, and their implications for developing teaching strategies. Active engagement of children in learning mathematics is the principle concern of this book. Section I establishes this focus.

Section VII anticipates the decisions teachers must make daily regarding the welfare of children actively engaged in learning mathematics. Five crucial areas of decision making are identified, and information is provided which will serve to guide classroom teachers in making professional decisions each day.

The final unique feature derives from the authors' original contributions. An "Introduction" to each section creates and maintains a philosophical position related to learning and teaching, with special reference to subsequent articles. In turn, "Before You Read" sections provide a support function for interpreting each article, as well as a basis for extending considerations from the Introduction. Each "Before You Read" concludes with explicit statements which maintain focus and suggest purpose for study.

In conclusion, we wish to restate that our total object has been to provide teachers and prospective teachers with a supplemental, substantive, and pedagogical guide which can contribute substantially to improved teaching of elementary school mathematics. At the same time we wish to express our thanks to the authors, editors, publishers, and organizations which gave permission to reprint the material in this book.

Eugene, Oregon   —C.W.S.
Greeley, Colorado   —W.R.A.
November 1970

PROLOGUE

ANGELS ON A PIN

Alexander Calandra

Some time ago, I received a call from a colleague who asked if I would be the referee on the grading of an examination question. He was about to give a student a zero for his answer to a physics question, while the student claimed he should receive a perfect score and would, if the system were not set up against the student. The instructor and the student agreed to submit this to an impartial arbiter, and I was selected.

I went to my colleague's office and read the examination question: "Show how it is possible to determine the height of a tall building with the aid of a barometer."

The student had answered: "Take the barometer to the top of the building, attach a long rope to it, lower the barometer to the street, and then bring it up, measuring the length of the rope. The length of the rope is the height of the building."

I pointed out that the student really had a strong case for full credit, since he had answered the question completely and correctly. On the other hand, if full credit were given, it could well contribute to a high grade for the student in his physics course. A high grade is supposed to certify competence in physics, but the answer did not confirm this. I suggested that the student have another try at answering the question. I was not surprised that my colleague agreed, but I was surprised that the student did.

I gave the student six minutes to answer the question, with the warning that his answer should show some knowledge of physics. At the end of five minutes, he had not written anything. I asked if he wished to give up, but he said no. He had many answers to this problem; he was just thinking of the best one. I excused myself for interrupting him, and asked him to please go on. In the next minute, he dashed off his answer which read:

"Take the barometer to the top of the building and lean over the edge of the roof. Drop the barometer, timing its fall with a stopwatch. Then, using the formula $S = \frac{1}{2}at^2$, calculate the height of the building."

At this point, I asked my colleague if *he* would give up. He conceded, and I gave the student almost full credit.

In leaving my colleague's office, I recalled that the student had said he had other answers to the problem, so I asked him what they were. "Oh, yes," said the student. "There are many ways of getting the height of a tall building with the aid of a barometer. For example, you could take the barometer out on a sunny day and measure the height of the barometer, the length of its shadow, and the length of the shadow of the building, and by the use of a simple proportion, determine the height of the building."

"Fine," I said. "And the others?"

"Yes," said the student. "There is a very basic measurement method that you will like. In this method, you take the barometer and begin to walk up the stairs. As you climb the stairs, you mark off the length of the barometer along the wall. You then count the number of marks, and this will give you the height of the building in barometer units. A very direct method.

"Of course, if you want a more sophisticated method, you can tie the barometer to the end of a string, swing it as a pendulum, and determine the value of 'g' at the street level and at the top of the building. From the difference between the two values of 'g,' the height of the building can, in principle, be calculated."

"Finally," he concluded, "there are many other ways of solving the problem. Probably the best," he said, "is to take the barometer to the basement and knock on the superintendent's door. When the superintendent answers, you speak to him as follows: 'Mr. Superintendent, here I have a fine barometer. If you will tell me the height of this building, I will give you this barometer.' "

At this point, I asked the student if he really did not know the conventional answer to this question. He admitted that he did, but said that he was fed up with high school and college instructors trying to teach him how to think, to use the "scientific method," and to explore the deep inner logic of the subject in a pedantic way, as is often done in the new mathematics, rather than teaching him the structure of the subject. With this in mind, he decided to revive scholasticism as an academic lark to challenge the Sputnik-panicked classrooms of America.

CONTENTS

Mathematics Is a Verb

Mathematics and Learning: Developing a Rationale for Teaching

"There are two ways to teach mathematics. One is to take real pains towards creating understanding—visual aids, that sort of thing. The other is the old British system of teaching until you're blue in the face."

—James Newman, New York *Times*, September 30, 1956

Introduction

1. Irvin H. Brune, *Learning Theory: Historical Perspective*

2. Norbert Maertens, *Piaget, Children, and Mathematics*

3. Zoltan P. Dienes, *Some Basic Processes Involved in Mathematics Learning*

4. Edward G. Buffie, Ronald C. Welch, and Donald D. Paige, *Mathematics: Strategies of Teaching*

5. Paul C. Burns, *Common Elements of Method*

6. William R. Arnold, *Flow Charting the Components of Teaching Strategy*

INTRODUCTION

There has been much dialogue regarding how one learns mathematics and how one teaches mathematics. Too often these areas have not been considered simultaneously. For example, mathematics has been and in many cases is still being taught by a logical expository approach wherein concepts are explained to pupils during a fixed period of time. Following this, pupils complete some type of textbook assignment to reinforce the learning.

Recent discoveries in the areas of developmental psychology have shown that pupils do not always learn mathematics logically or topically; and they may not learn best those concepts which are only explained. These discoveries have caused some educators to swing completely away from didactic and Socratic approaches in teaching toward more exploratory methods wherein pupils discover mathematical concepts. If one can assume that learning principles exist, it seems appropriate to assume that as new principles of learning are discovered, methods of teaching should be modified to accommodate the new discoveries. Present principles of learning support the notion that singular approaches to teaching elementary school mathematics are unlikely to produce optimal results.

Two notions related to contemporary mathematics are implicit in the paragraph above. The first is that as psychologists have observed children in order to determine *how* they learn, they have discovered *what* children learn. For example, in their play very young children form sets of objects, work with one-to-one and other correspondences, and talk about various relationships from this prospective. Modern mathematics can be a product. It is a body of ideas for elementary school children to learn on an interrelated rather than a logical or topical basis.

A second notion is that psychologists have come to understand much about how children learn. In this respect, consider two dimensions of learning. One deals with level of learning. Memorizing information is considered a lower level of learning than synthesizing concepts. There is a vast difference between expecting a pupil to memorize addition facts and expecting him to understand the operation of addition as the union of disjoint sets. A second dimension deals with the stage of a child's mental development as he attempts to learn. Regardless of the terminology used by the psychologist, it is known that a young child understands few ideas in mathematics apart from how he perceives physical objects. As he grows older he understands an idea in relation to some semiabstract referent. Later, the child can make conjectures that are purely abstract. Thus, modern mathematics has come to be a process; as such, it is the manner in which a child attempts to learn at a given point in time. It is not until the teacher thinks of contemporary mathematics as both a product and a process that he can begin to formulate effective teaching strategies.

ACTIVE LEARNING

What is advocated throughout this book is that both child and teacher become actively engaged in the process of learning mathematics. To facilitate active teaching and, consequently, active learning the teacher (1.) must be informed and reflective concerning the unique behavioral characteristics of children in regard to mathematics, (2.) must know the mathematics that children are to learn, and (3.) must possess a knowledge of diverse and functional instructional settings and teaching strategies for developing mathematical ideas.

The conditions for active learning are met by (1.) creating an opportunity for communication, (2.) maintaining a conscious awareness of mathematics in the environment, and (3.) setting the stage for observing relationships and making mathematics useful. The following examples should provide a clear notion of the interrelatedness of these conditions.

Children have a natural proclivity for communication. This tendency provides an opportunity to foster language development actively and at the same time create an interest in the quantitative world. When a small group of children is given some new instructional materials with which to experiment, for example, Cuisenaire Rods, they may ask, "Why is this one longer?" or "Are all the yellow ones the same size?" Nondirective teacher response can elicit discovery and encourage new questions. Additional opportunities for discussion might arise in connection with plane figures that have been painted on a surface play area. Guided discussion can lead to such inquiries as, "Are all the shapes in four-square the same?" "Is the ball field a true rectangle?" Or, "How many steps will it take to cross the court?" As questions arise from common experience they can lead to new lines of mathematical investigation by children.

Creating and maintaining a conscious awareness of the mathematics of the school environment can be further generated within the framework of routine classroom business. Recording birth dates, noting time, maintaining attendance and monetary records, weather charts, and personal growth and achievement records are but a few examples. Others may involve noting relationships between dimensions of windows and doors or between heights and shadows. Certainly the preceding, when considered collectively, set the stage for discovering relationships in a meaningful manner, and provide ample opportunity for children to use and enjoy mathematics.

All teachers encounter children who do not appear to understand or do not look beyond the simple mechanics of an activity. For example, consider the recording of numerals on a height-weight chart. As an active partner with children in the educational process, the teacher must not permit instruction to become ritualistic. Teachers need to make subtle inquiries which demand further evaluation of obtained data, suggest alternate procedures for recording this data, or require the acquisition of additional relevant data. All contribute to active learning. These are key teacher behaviors which encourage children to participate in further activity and develop new insights.

In this Section you will be introduced to selections which form the basis for active learning. Professor Brune provides perspective through some historical antecedents of current learning theory. Although not generating a totally unified theory of instruction, Norbert Maertens' analysis of Piaget and Professor Dienes' selection which follows, contain the genesis for active learning. Buffie, Welch, and Paige identify both sources and types of goal-oriented instruction, and describe an hierarchical nature for goals in such a way that they may be seen as compatible with the sequential nature of concept development. Using "situation specific" examples, Paul C. Burns translates some pedagogical implications from learning theory into illustrative procedures for teachers.

With the final contribution Professor Arnold provides a model which assists teachers in generating active learning as they plan mathematics lessons. The model does not purport to be a "method" of teaching mathematics, nor is there a single theory of learning involved. Rather, it is a model for creating the conditioned climate within which active learning may take place. Equally important, however, it may be used as a guide to the development of lessons for children for all the articles in this book.

I LEARNING THEORY: HISTORICAL PERSPECTIVE

Irvin H. Brune

BEFORE YOU READ   Throughout man's recorded history theories of learning have risen and fallen. Unfortunately, the fact that some of the theories had their genesis in pure speculation did little to deter philosophers, psychologists, and educators from applying the conclusions to human learning. In this article Professor Brune describes features of some learning theories that have influenced mathematics methodology over the years. The teacher should notice that a particular theory of learning is based upon knowledge as it exists and is structured for a given time. What educators tend to do is translate each new theory into a set of guidelines for the teaching of mathematics. Professor Brune points out that while teachers have always been concerned about having children understand mathematics, it is only recently that learning theories have emerged which provide more comprehensive ways in which this can be accomplished.

There are some interesting parallels between today and yesterday. Professor Brune quotes E.H. Moore (1903) ". . . every result of importance should be obtained by at least two distinct methods and thus the student is made independent of all authority." This statement is certainly not antagonistic to the contemporary learning theories postulated by Piaget and Dienes, and provides a very early rationale for the "multiple approaches to learning" considered by Paul C. Burns in "Common Elements of Method."

As a result of reading this article the teacher should be able to identify the essential characteristics of several early learning theories, describe their influence on instructional practice, and contrast that practice with current thought.

How do people learn mathematics?

One of the very first considerations in mathematical teaching is *thoroughness*. In the past the *lack* of thoroughness has poisoned the minds of

---

Reprinted from *Mathematics Education K-8: Considerations in Learning Theory: A Second Look*, E.B. Wickes and Thomas C. Gibney, editors (Toledo, Ohio: University of Toledo, 1965), pp. 5–13. Professor Brune of Bowling Green State University has served as Editor and Chairman of the Editorial Board of *The Mathematics Teacher*.

the American youth with an utter dislike and a bitter hatred of mathematics. Whenever it *is* well understood, it is generally liked.[1]

> It is to be hoped that the near future will bring reforms in the mathematical teaching in this country. We are in sad need of them. From nearly all our colleges and universities comes the loud complaint of inefficient preparation on the part of students applying for admission: from the high schools comes the same doleful cry. Errors in mathematical instruction are committed from the very beginning in the study of arithmetic.[1]

These remarks have a modern ring—they sound almost contemporary. Yet they first came to light in 1890. Moreover, the conviction that competence in mathematics stems from *understanding* mathematics probably arose earlier than that. And it probably did not dawn suddenly on any single observer. Surely at least a few perceptive people must have detected that overworking a pupil's memory and ignoring his reasoning powers fell short. However that may be, an attempt to fix the exact date when teachers first realized that understanding underlies learning need not concern us here. For our purposes it suffices to note that Cajori deplored a lack of understanding some seventy-five years ago.

Shortly after Cajori's report in America, Felix Klein in Germany wrote that:

> The presentation in the schools · · · should be psychological and not systematic. The teacher, so to speak, must be a diplomat. He must take account of the psychic processes in the boy in order to grip his interest; and he will succeed only if he presents things in a form intuitively comprehensible.[2]

Almost simultaneously John Perry in England declared that "the study of mathematics began because it was useful and continues because it is useful, and it is valuable to the world because of its results."[4]

Still another voice, that of E.H. Moore, added that "every result of importance should be obtained by at least two distinct methods, · · · and thus the student is made independent of all authority."[3]

The gist of the messages from men such as these has lasted through the years. Mathematics best serves useful ends, its learners profit through self-reliance, and its teachers very likely succeed in accordance with their use of psychology.

But even though pedagogic principles such as these have endured, the means to implement them have shown considerably less longevity. Theories of learning have risen, shone, and faded. Klein, except for urging that mathematics be presented "in a form intuitively comprehensible," did not spell out the details of what he meant by a psychological approach. And some other writers conceived several approaches without enunciating a lasting theory. In fact, psychology came into being relatively recently in the history of thought, and it therefore surprises few teachers, if any, that theories of learning came and went.

In the paragraphs that follow we shall look at a few approaches. In retrospect their ascending and descending provide more than a little edification. Moreover, although the art and science of teaching strides onward, we still have much to learn about how people learn mathematics.

LEARNING THEN AND NOW

A look at theories of learning could carry us back all the way to the dawn of prehistory. Man slowly and painfully developed concepts of number and form and transmitted them orally to his children. Gradually specialists, possibly scribes among priests, invented symbols for preserving knowledge. Their theory of learning emphasized memory work and apprenticeship. Thales and Pythagoras, for example, went from Greece to Egypt, became priests, learned the closely-guarded secrets of the caste, and eventually returned to Greece to establish secret societies of their own. Apparently lectures, questions and answers, and laborious copying of manuscripts implemented their theories of learning.

The dialogues of Plato brought out the Socratic Method, a system of questionings eliciting a series of answers comprising a logically developed body of knowledge. The method persists even today, although pupil-teacher ratios of, say, thirty-five to one, tend to discourage its use.

Dickens' *Nicholas Nickleby* brought out Squeers' Method, which in more recent times was too distasteful and too brutal for even the most ardent advocate of rigorous mental discipline, stern classroom discipline, or memorized mathematics as a scholastic discipline.

Every teacher, whether he professes it or not, has his own philosophy of education, based, at least implicitly, on his own theory of learning. From earliest history to the present moment teachers reveal by their methods what they believe about learning. Pythagoras as a type, Socrates as a type, and Squeers as a type have appeared over and over. Some aura of secrecy, some feeling of belonging, and some element of hero worship have even caused some of the camps marshalled into the modern mathematics movement at least faintly to resemble Pythagorean brotherhoods. At any rate it seems clear that only the initiated have dared to lecture, lead discussions, and copy the script. Socrates reappears in numerous contemporary systems of heuristic discovery, or directed discovery, even though, as suggested earlier, today's huge enrollments tend to hamper this kind of approach. Squeers enjoyed his heyday when mental discipline was the popular theory of learning. Yet, from what one notes even today in some quarters (pupils harassed by accelerations effected prematurely, by abstractions proffered prematurely, and by poorly-taught courses altered only in that they are set before ever younger children) it seems that academic misguidance has not entirely vanished.

MENTAL DISCIPLINE

When Cajori wrote his memorable report in 1890 some changes had occurred and other changes were arising. Geometry had served until the middle of the nineteenth century chiefly as a college subject. Demonstrations, based mostly on Euclid, usually were memorized by the students. A bit of doggerel, quoted by Cajori, suggested by sarcasm that mental discipline predominated:

> The Mathematics too our thoughts employ,
> Which nobly elevate the Student's joy.
> The little Euclids round the table set
> And at their rigid demonstrations sweat!

But that had changed. At least the subject, and possibly along with it some of the methods posited on the theory of mental discipline, had moved to preparatory schools and high schools. In the grade schools, textbooks in arithmetic had long since replaced the copybooks that had met with considerable favor in schools during our nation's early days. Of one such early textbook in widespread use Cajori wrote:

> The whole book is nothing but a Pandora's box of disconnected rules. It appeals to memory exclusively and completely ignores the existence of reasoning powers in the mind of the learner.[1]

The foregoing examples of geometry and arithmetic taught for memorization indicate what we mean by the theory of mental discipline. The theory held that the mind, like a muscle, developed with exercise. And, just as the weight lifter progressively adds weights to develop his muscles still further, so mental tasks were to become more and more arduous, the better to develop the mind. The multitudinous facts of arithmetic, plus the numerous theorems of geometry, plus the innumerable manipulations of algebra provided a rich source of exercise for pupils' minds. Distaste engendered by such tasks disturbed teachers not at all: a life of discipline presumably led to numerous rewards.

Implicit faith in mental discipline, however, ebbed considerably by Cajori's time, even though some allied, albeit vague, notions of mathematical benefits endured well into the twentieth century. Also the term "cultural values" persisted, as we read from D.E. Smith:

These three phases of the cultural side of arithmetic, the side of mental discipline, will then suffice for our present purpose, which is to show that such a side exists: (1) the contact with absolute truth; (2) the acquisition of helpful forms of analytic reasoning; (3) the acquisition of certain habits that "carry over" into related fields of work.[5]

Eventually, clearer ideas about the nature of mathematics put the concept of absolute truth in mathematics to rout. Similarly, the results of teaching helpful forms of analytic reasoning applied to non-mathematical situations shifted the emphasis on that phase of mental discipline. Likewise, experimentation with the transfer of training put a teaching-for-transfer twist on yet another aspect of mental discipline. The net result of these developments was to discredit the theory.

CONNECTIONISM

One reason why mental discipline was weakened lay in a new theory. Roughly coeval with an epoch of time studies, rates, and measures of efficiency in industry, the idea of subdividing the subject matter of arithmetic into tiny portions—the better to learn them—struck an especially responsive chord.

The key assumption in connectionism is that learning is the forming of connections—bonds between stimuli and responses. This idea appealed to teachers, who long since had felt misgivings about mental discipline, the doctrine that the specifics of a subject do not matter, as long as they are not too easy. Since the way to acquire connections (as habits rather than as neural bonds) lay in memory work and since the emphasis in arithmetic as mental discipline lay in memory work, the transition proceeded smoothly.

Further aspects of connectionism lent plausibility to it as a theory of learning. Separating arithmetic into bits—bits to make a day's lesson, bits to make a week's work, and bits to constitute the program for a year—reassured teachers; they knew exactly what their responsibilities were; only get the pupils to master the facts, recite the rules, and do the operations, and one's work met success. Directing pupils to establish only correct bonds also meant directing them to avoid incorrect bonds. Hence the teacher would select the fact, the correct rule, and the efficient operation, present them in concise (and adult) form, and thus *prevent* mistakes. What an efficient way it was that kept misconceptions and mistakes from ever entering children's minds!

Accompanying this theory, which has also been known as the drill theory, yet another development occurred. We referred to the efficiency movement in industry. A similar movement arose in education. It stemmed from ever more objective ways to measure pupils' progress. Scientific testing (and apparently the adjective was forced in some instances) stimulated teachers and pupils to more and more drill. Thus one's class could achieve higher scores and outrun one's competitors in other buildings, other towns, and other counties.

Edward L. Thorndike in 1922 published the classic in this field.[6] He wrote descriptions (at first called laws) of learning. Contrary to what some of his followers emphasized, he had an interest in pupils' learning organized,[7] related,[8] and applicable knowledge.[6] The net effect, however, was that teachers seized upon speed, one-hundred-per-cent accuracy, and "do it my way." They tended not to permit, on the other hand, such things as crutches, unorthodox algorisms, and novel solutions.

The upshot of teachers' embracing the drill theory did not dawn on people for some years. The pupils computed well, even though they seldom understood much about what the various operations would do to help solve problems. Makers of tests seemed to cooperate well, in that they emphasized computations and contrived so-called "problems" which were little more than further drill couched in words. As long as pupils made high scores, they, their teachers, and above all their principals (whose ambition often seemed to reside in records of high achievements in the "scientific tests") felt good.

Unfavorable reactions, however, did worm their way in. Realists in the profession eventually detected a much overworked emphasis on certain numerals. Why all the fuss about I.Q.'s, achievement scores, and gain scores? Granted that objective tests were furnishing precise measures, had anyone ever wondered whether the skills thus measured deserved such precision? What was the use of the skills? Did the skills help children to live better lives?

THEORY OF INCIDENTAL LEARNING

We indicated that reactions to tell-and-show teaching and also to drill-and-test procedures in arithmetic set in. One such reaction to connectionism acquired status just before World War II. Mathematics, some people reasoned, arose in the first place to help man solve problems. The traditional procedures, mathematics for discipline and mathematics for skill, merited only a hard look, with a view to replacement. A better approach, these people continued, would be to let daily problems dictate what mathematics to teach. Just immerse children in some genuinely compelling situations, and the children will feel an urge to learn the necessary arithmetic. The theory ostensibly brought some motivation to bear, and motivated children tended to learn. The opposite statement came in handily, too: unmotivated children tended not to learn.

Proponents of the child-centered school, teachers of the whole child, and advocates of meeting the child's felt needs embraced incidental learning as a theory rather enthusiastically. They were willing to experiment; they desired to devise better programs. Mental discipline had long since died (at least in theory) and the onus of tell-drill-test, repeat tell-drill-test, and repeat some more, wore connectionism quite thin. Pupils who knew how to divide, but who didn't know when to divide, could hardly bring satisfaction to their teachers (and principals) in the long run.

So there arose a strong swing toward broad problems that cut across subject lines. Should the children choose to study Indians (and children often did choose to study Indians) they would encounter problems in geography, history, language, science, art, music, geometry, arithmetic, and possibly other subjects. Master teachers indubitably led pupils through outstanding experiences in such an approach. An emphasis which clearly failed to appear in arithmetic as drill, namely, the social application of mathematics, got a life here. People rightfully study arithmetic so that they can solve problems.

The theory of incidental learning, however, waned more rapidly than it waxed. It, like its predecessors, lacked something. Whereas it emphasized how to apply arithmetic to problems that arose, it failed to provide all the problems that should arise. Mathematics develops as a system with a structure. But to locate broad problems, that entail the items that belong in the system, in the order in which they belong, proved to be all but impossible. To cause just the right concept to arise at the proper time defeated even the master teachers. The fault lay, not in the teachers, but in the theory. It glorified social uses at the cost of neglecting mathematical structures.

BALANCE

Theories of learning have risen and fallen because they lacked balance.

Mental discipline remained alive only so long as the selected few pupils who stayed in school found satisfaction in mathematics despite the way it was taught. The hardy intellects who succeeded were resourceful enough to apply what they had memorized—after they had wrested meaning from what they had memorized.

Connectionism failed partly because it emphasized skills and how to acquire skills, and partly because its practitioners overlooked the organization, interrelatedness, and meanings of items in arithmetic. E.L. Thorndike himself did not neglect meanings, relations, and structures in arithmetic. But his followers apparently missed his message. Accordingly, his theory perished because in practice it stressed skills and neglected applications.

Incidental learning came mightily to the rescue of the uses that had been all but lost in the drill theory. Yet its practitioners could not continue indefinitely to contrive situations in a sequence essential to pupils' learning arithmetic as a system of ideas.

WHAT IS AN IDEAL THEORY?

Accordingly, we note that a theory should be somewhat comprehensive. It should provide for pupils learning meanings, skills, relations, structures, and applications. It should stress the mathematical side of arithmetic (meanings, relations, structure), the social side of arithmetic (meanings, skills, application), and the psychological side of arithmetic (meanings, skills, problem solving). For the mathematical side we seek an understanding of facts, principles, rules of arithmetic; for the social side we seek an understanding of how to use arithmetic; for the psychological side we seek an understanding of children's minds as they study arithmetic. We have found the going to be difficult whenever we taught skills isolated from applications, or skills and applications isolated from psychology.

THE GROWTH OF PSYCHOLOGY

Indeed, much of the progress achieved in the twentieth century stemmed from the efforts of people who worked in both mathematics and psychology. For a while the latter of these had to bide its time. For it could develop only after physiology had made adequate progress. Physiology, in turn, grew in a matrix of adequate biology. Similarly, before biology there had to be chemistry, and before chemistry, physics, which in turn depended upon mathematics. Probably the only way one could extend the chain of dependence still farther would be to admit that, except for man's interest in heavenly bodies, precious little mathematics would have developed, and that astronomy is the basic ne plus ultra. The point, however, remains that psychology could not, in the nature of events, have arisen much earlier.

Accordingly, when Cajori deplored the state of affairs in mathematics education in 1890, there was little in the way of established psychology either to refute or support the theory of mental discipline. E.L. Thorndike's work, however unfortunate the results of its use and misuse may appear to us now, did open the way for other theories of learning to emerge from studies in the new area, psychology. In the long run psychology had to be in the act, despite some misconceptions about stimulus-response that lasted several decades too long.

The difficulty lay in too much analysis, too much atomization. Arithmetic analyzed to bits, operations imitated as steps, and problems approached as types defeated the major purpose for teaching arithmetic, namely, problem solving. Fortunately, a new psychology appeared.

THE THEORY OF MEANING

Although it developed slowly and its history was long, the new psychology came to the fore about 1935. It opposed dissection theories diametrically. Problems impel people to think, and learning stems from thinking rather than recalling. Instead of cutting up the problem situation in a search for familiar (presumably memorized) bits, the learner studies the context in its entirety. This undergirds the newer theories: *consider the whole situation.* Knowledge of facts germane to the situation can do no harm; it may, however, also do little good. The *relatedness* of the facts in the total situation provide the key. A challenging problem stems from an unstructured situation; studying the whole of it affords a structuring—a solution. When the relation of parts to whole becomes clear, the learner achieves insight—the goal in meaningful learning.

A simple example will help us here. Pupils look for a pattern in the start of an array:

```
    1  2  3  4  5  6  7
 1  2  3  4  5  6  7  1
 2  3  4  5  6  7  1  2
 3  4  5  6  7  1  2  3
 4
 5
 6
 7
```

What design does it have? Or what is the rule? The pattern resembles a table of addition facts, yet some of the entries seem strange. But if we label the numerals in the left column as "Days After" and the numerals in the top row as "Days of the Week," then three days after Friday (6) means Tuesday (2) and addition of this sort does make sense. Seeing the details as related to the whole arrangement affords insight. Arithmetic abounds in simple structures; so does algebra.

Geometry also provides patterns. Consider perpendicular radii $\overline{OA}$ and $\overline{OB}$ in the accompanying figure.

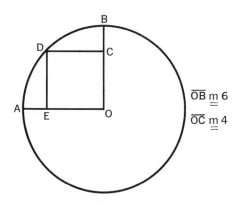

$\overline{OB} \underset{=}{m} 6$

$\overline{OC} \underset{=}{m} 4$

Figure 1.1

These radii measure six units. At C, four units from O, draw $\overline{CD}$ perpendicular to $\overline{OB}$, calling D the point where the perpendicular meets the circle. Then draw $\overline{DE}$ perpendicular to $\overline{AO}$. The question is, How long is $\overline{EC}$? Pupils conditioned by connectionism tend to try to apply the Theorem of Pythagoras—they see a right triangle EOC, a leg $\overline{OC}$, the hypotenuse $\overline{EC}$. Seldom does this succeed. A look at the total situation, however, does lead to a solution. The missing item in the momentarily unstructured situation falls into place. The Gestalt (German for 'form') appears. Insight ensues.

DISCOVERY

In practice, the theory of meaning, based on gestalt psychology, thrives on situations that encourage pupils to discover relatedness among the parts and the whole. Accordingly, the teacher takes his job to be the contriving of situations, the composing of problems, and the framing of questions. The pupil's responsibility, accordingly, is to find answers, discover relations, appreciate patterns, discern structures, and state his findings, probably crudely at first, but nonetheless insightfully. This task may loom large, but it is more realistic than the ever-mounting loads that memory work formerly heaped on innocent children.

MODERN MATHEMATICS

During the past forty-five years organizations such as the National Council of Teachers of Mathematics have pioneered in the work of improving the teaching of mathematics. During the past ten years, the number of such groups has increased. Since Sputnik I (October 4, 1957) the total public apparently has caught the spirit. However questionable the term 'modern mathematics' may be, part of the current extra effort comes to bear in the better application of today's improved knowledge of how people learn mathematics. Insight rates first as an objective. Drill on the operations of arithmetic and algebra, provided that the pupils first have understood why the operations work, has a proper place. The transfer of mathematical ways of thinking, using undefined terms, definitions, postulates, and logic, gets attention. The careful use of precise language comes through as an extra benefit. Some questions about reviving stimulus-response psychology via the use of some sorts of programmed materials have reared their disconcerting heads, but, having already exceeded our space, we cannot debate the issue here.

CONCLUSION

We have seen that theories of learning have risen and fallen. Mental discipline, the learning of difficult assignments (often through sheer memorization) to strengthen the minds of the learners, had its protracted inning.

Connectionism, also called here 'stimulus-response psychology,' seemed for half a century just as plausible. Gaining ascendancy (however slowly) during the past thirty years, the theory of meaningful learning stemmed from gestalt psychology, which emphasizes learning via problem solving via structuring situations that appear (at least mildly and at least momentarily) frustrating. Helping pupils to face up to genuine problems, to discover relations in the problems, and to gain understanding uniquely their own makes today's teacher's task rewarding. Fortunately for pupils of yesterday, today, and tomorrow, however, few teachers cleave to any one single theory of learning alone. And it is heartening to note that teachers help pupils more and more to see the power of the proverb, "With all thy getting, get understanding."

REFERENCES

1 Cajori, Florian. *The Teaching and History of Mathematics in the United States.* Washington: Government Printing Office, 1890.
2 Klein, Felix. *Elementary Mathematics from an Advanced Standpoint* (English translation by E. R. Hedrick and C. A. Noble). New York: The Macmillan Company, 1932.
3 Moore, E. H. "On the Foundations of Mathematics," *Bulletin of the American Mathematical Society.* IX (May, 1903).
4 Perry, John. "Discussion on the Teaching of Mathematics," *Report of the British Association at Glasgow.* New York: The Macmillan Company, 1901.
5 Smith, David Eugene. *The Teaching of Arithmetic.* Boston: Ginn and Company, 1911.
6 Thorndike, E. L. *The Psychology of Arithmetic.* New York: The Macmillan Company, 1922.
7 Thorndike, E. L. *The New Methods in Arithmetic.* New York: Rand-McNally Company, 1921.
8 Thorndike, E. L. *The Principles of Teaching Based on Psychology.* Syracuse: Mason-Henry Press, 1906.

2 PIAGET, CHILDREN, AND MATHEMATICS

Norbert Maertens

BEFORE YOU READ   Psychological investigations of learning encompass at least two dimensions: one dealing with learning theory, the other with child development. Too often teachers make the assumption that children can and do learn in the same manner as adults. The work of psychologists such as Piaget has shown that this assumption may not be valid. It appears there are some gross differences between adults and children in regard to how concepts are learned and how these can be represented at a given time. These gross differences are both subtle and crucial.

This article by Professor Maertens describes the manner in which children develop an ability to understand mathematics according to the age-norm basis for intellectual growth defined by Piaget. The "Piagian psychology" may be new to the reader, yet, it has definite historical antecedents. Consider Dr. Brune's quotation from Felix Klein (Germany, 1932): "The presentation in the schools . . . should be psychological and not systematic. The teacher, so to speak, must be a diplomat. He must take account of the psychic processes in the boy in order to grip his interest . . ."

Piaget's work supports a growing belief that human learning passes through certain sequential stages, which parallel the growth of the ability in children to deal with the abstractions of mathematics in a logical fashion. Recognition of the developmental stages does not imply that progress through them can be affected by factors within the control of the teacher.

As a result of careful study of this article the reader should be able to describe Piaget's levels of intellectual growth and translate the general significance of each into a functional referent for teaching behavior.

Simply stated, the purpose of this article is to provide a descriptive account of how children mature in their ability to understand mathematics. Through

---

This article is a portion of a chapter from *Elementary Mathematical Methods* by C.W. Schminke, William Arnold, and Norbert Maertens (Hinsdale, Ill.: The Dryden Press Inc., 1971). Professor Maertens is at the University of Oregon, Eugene, Oregon.

years of painstaking observation and record-keeping the eminent Swiss psychologist, Jean Piaget, identified certain broad stages of intellectual development through which every child must pass. He found that a child's evolution to maturity is marked by a series of progressively more sophisticated levels of intellectual growth—growth to which he attached approximate chronological labels. These labels, although not infallible, give a teacher a basis on which to make educated decisions concerning the teaching of children. Understand that the time at which a child passes through a level varies in relationship to his experiences, ability, and education; however the sequence remains invariant.

This article does not claim to exhaust the implications for teaching suggested by Piaget. To do so would be presumptuous. Instead, readers are urged to reflect upon the material presented in the following pages, and indeed to take issue with it. In so doing, perhaps a new awareness of children will be formed, a new sensitivity developed, a new thirst for understanding acquired. An attempt is made to translate Piaget's theory into classroom exemplars. Examples are given not as inclusive but as suggestions of applications to be made in the future. The reader should consider the contents of this article in the light of his own experience, and reflect upon its relevance.

LEVELS OF INTELLECTUAL DEVELOPMENT—PIAGET'S THEORY

A child's first years (0–2 years)   Much of a child's first two years are spent in sensing and manipulating. Such activities shape his perception of his environment. He sees order and pattern in his world and is impressed by it.

A child's first perception of the world about him might be the ordered spacing of the bars on his crib or the rectangular proportions of the perimeter of the crib. By the end of his first month of life not only can he perceive relatively minor differences in the objects he views but he also shows a preference for complex patterns over simple, homogeneous stimuli.[1] For example, when presented with two rectangular frames of equivalent size, where one has a simple cross-hatched design on its interior, the very young child will make definite movements toward the more complex rectangle.

His early relationships with others are likely to involve a one-to-one correspondence between his mouth and a baby bottle or his mother's breast. This early introduction to one-to-one correspondence is later strengthened when his mother places a rattle in his hand or a teddy bear in his crib.

[1] Paul Mussen, John Conger, and Jerome Kagen, *Child Development and Personality* (New York: Harper & Row, 1963) pp. 87–126.

Early in the child's first year of life he learns that certain acts will produce specific responses; they become intentional. He knows that if he shakes his crib in a certain fashion a rattle or other object will move. He defines the bars on his crib in terms of the action he has taken toward them. The bars are to shake or his pacifier is to suck. He is unaware of those things in which he is not involved. If an object is removed from his sight it ceases to exist for the child.

Toward the end of the child's first years of life an impressive change begins to take place. The child's ability to perceive the world gradually expands so that he does not have to be involved in an act to be impressed by it. Objects develop permanence—they still exist whether or not they are in sight. When an object is removed, the child can form a mental image in his construction of space.

The child who is almost two years old loves to imitate both human and nonhuman objects. Sometimes his imitation occurs with the person he is imitating, but not necessarily. He has the ability to defer his imitation to other time periods. This is seen in the child's play. Whereas the younger child merely played games requiring simple motor skills, the child who is nearly two may imitate Mother or Father, and he may use dolls or other concrete objects as representations for his brothers and sisters. These early experiences enable the child to build a cognitive framework; a framework which makes it possible for him to consider his experiences, to assimilate them, and to make accommodations (reorganization of the mental structure) for later use—he has internalized them. He can now enter the world of make-believe. Without such a variety of experiences the child can become educationally retarded and unable to move to a more complex stage.

During these initial years the child has learned that objects have permanence, that symbols may be used to represent real objects, and that actions may be imitated and internalized. The child uses these early perceptions and imitations throughout his entire education, for without them he is incapable of understanding the abstract qualities of mathematics. The cumulative growth of a child's initial years, the sensorimotor period, forms the transition for that which Jean Piaget calls the "Concrete Operations Period."[2]

Concrete operations period (2–11 years) The elementary school child's path toward mathematical understanding takes him through the concrete operations period. Most elementary age children are found here and so are of particular importance to the elementary school teacher. The concrete operation period can best be understood by careful analysis of two easily discernible subperiods.

Preoperational subperiod (2–7 years) A child in the preoperational subperiod gains increasing ability to internalize symbols; he learns to

[2] John A. Flavell, *The Developmental Psychology of Jean Piaget* (Princeton, N.J.: D. Van Nostrand Company, Inc., 1963).

discriminate between words and the objects they represent. He is able to organize his behavior as it relates to a goal, trying alternate approaches rather than a single, rigid approach.

Whereas the sensorimotor child is limited to very brief internalizations of events from the recent past, the preoperational child can include past, present, and future representations of reality. He does not need continuous access to direct experience. Past events can be signified through words; and future events may be planned and described by using the same medium. Similarly, whereas the sensorimotor child was limited to the pursuit of concrete goals, the preoperational child is able to reflect upon the most efficient behavior needed by him to attain the goal. He is capable of being taught about objects not directly present. Consider how these capabilities develop.

The child of two–seven years of age gradually forms a vocabulary to express concepts of a particular object. At first, these ideas are bound to the actions he takes with objects. For example, the word "milk" may represent a two-year-old child's desire for a drink of milk, or for a drink of juice or water. He does not recognize the need for more discriminating vocabulary. During play, the child may use the same word when feeding her doll. Such beginning word concepts are typically broad, so that the word "milk" comes to represent anything which may be drunk. With growth, the child gradually refines his vocabulary to conform with the more precise definitions of the adult world. He understands that "milk" refers to the white liquid in the refrigerator, and that it is independent of other liquids or from his uses of it. He develops a new vocabulary to describe his intended use of the liquid. The ability to develop a precise vocabulary is essential to the learning of mathematics. A child must be able to understand that "five" represents a particular quantity, a quantity which exists independent of the operations that may be performed with it.

The thinking of the preoperational child is still characterized by his need for concrete objects. Although he can perform mental manipulations, he only manipulates what he can see concretely. His mental manipulations merely represent what he would actually be doing physically with objects. He is not capable of analyzing or synthesizing without objects. For this reason, primary grade teachers find it necessary to be very explicit in their instruction, and they must use a variety of concrete aids precisely to demonstrate desired actions.

Figure 2.1

The thinking of the preoperational child is also characterized by his inability to mentally reverse his actions. For example, consider two plasticene balls of equal size. Determine with the child that the balls are identical in size. Now, as he watches, roll one into a sausage shape. Then ask the child if the balls are still the same size or if one has more plasticene than the other. Usually, he responds that the sausage-shaped object has more plasticene than the round object. Sometimes he selects the round object, saying that it now has more plasticene. He is not able to mentally relate back to the point where the two balls were identical in size and shape. Although he saw that only the shape was changed, he still makes his decision on what is before him at the moment. His reasoning is perceptually rather than factually oriented.

Reversibility is an integral feature of mathematical operations. For example:

$$4 + 3 = 7$$
$$7 - 3 = 4$$

In this example, 3 was combined with 4, yielding the sum of 7. To reverse this operation, subtract 3 from 7, yielding the original quantity 4. For example, we increase the size of a group and then decrease it—a demonstration of reversibility.

A further illustration of the importance of reversibility to mathematics is shown below:

$$4 + 3 = 7$$

This is a statement of equality. To maintain this equality any changes made on one side of the equal sign must be compensated for by making equivalent changes on the other side.

$$(4 + 3) + 1 = 7 + 1$$

The statement was changed by adding 1 to the addends $4 + 3$. Having done this, the sum 7 must now be changed by also increasing it by 1.

What is apparent to an adult is incomprehensible to the child. To understand that adding a quantity on one side of the equality symbol requires the addition of an equivalent quantity on the other side the child must be able to think back to the starting point where both quantities were equal. Then, he must understand that adding 1 to one side of the equation destroys the equality, but only to the extent of the quantity added. In order to bring the statement back into "balance," he must now add 1 to the other side.

The concept of reversibility is not normally attained by the child until the end of the preoperational subperiod or early concrete operations subperiod, and teachers should be wary of rushing too quickly into mathematical operations requiring children to be able to reverse their actions, thereby relating two operations. This is easily demonstrated by having two equal piles of blocks and asking the child which has more. When he responds that the piles are equal, add 1 to one pile and ask him if they are still equal. Allow him to explain that by adding 1 to one pile the equality is destroyed. Relate this to the earlier mathematical statement. When the operation of addition is taught, for example, be aware of those children who don't seem to understand the relationships involved in combining and separating sets. For example, if a child cannot see that $4 + 3 = 7$ and $7 - 3 = 4$ are related in a unique way, then he cannot understand subtraction as the undoing of addition. For him, mathematics is becoming a series of disjoint operations. It is better to delay such teaching with this child and spend additional time on learning experiences which are subordinate to the algorithm.

Let the child have the experience of physically joining different sets. Allow him time to discover that joining a set of 5 objects with a set of 2 objects forms a set with a new cardinal. Let him describe his action by using the number sentence $5 + 2 = 7$. In the same manner encourage him to describe what happens when objects are removed. Continue such experiences until he demonstrates his awareness of the relationship of addition to subtraction.

Preoperational children tend to focus their attention on only one aspect of a total situation at a time. Whereas an adult might consider a string of brightly colored beads as gaudy and out of place on a black evening gown, a child considers each independently. The adult considers the total situation. The child considers only the bright object, noting its attractiveness. He attends to spatial problems in much the same way.

Consider Figure 2.2 below. While the child watches, equal quantities of water are added to container A and container B. The preoperational child is then asked if the containers have an equal quantity of water in them. Usually the child will say that container B has more water. Occasionally the child will choose container A. When asked to explain his answer the child choosing container B will usually indicate that the water level in B is higher than that in A. Those choosing A may indicate that the container for A is larger than B. They have centered their attention on only one item of the total situation, the width or height of the given container.

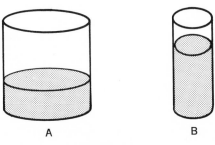

A   B

Figure 2.2

To understand the water-pouring problem, the adult is able to construct mentally the sequence of events which occurred. Seeing the containers filled with water, he visually reconstructs the transformation from these containers into the containers of differing shapes. The preoperational child cannot do this. His attention focuses independently upon each successive stage as it occurs. No relationship between stages is seen; and he cannot integrate the series of events into a logical whole. Further, when asked to explain the cause-and-effect relationship demonstrated by the addition of equal quantities of water to dissimilar containers, the pre-operational child has a strong tendency to break up the whole sequence into a series of fragmentary and incoherent statements. The order in which the events occurred is often confused, as are logical or causal relationships. The child prefers factual descriptions to cause → effect explanations. These limitations render the child incapable of making a coherent whole out of the explanation. Such a phenomenon is called juxtaposition.

It is only at the approximate age of seven to eight that a child begins to reflect and unify, as well as to avoid contradiction. At this time a child becomes conscious of the logic of his acts. He does not think deductively. The implications of this phenomenon for mathematics teaching are many.

Consider the addition sentence $4 + 3 = 7$. The child must be able to reconstruct in his mind the sequence of events beginning with a pile of 4 blocks, then physically joining 3 blocks to this to yield 7 blocks. The preoperational child probably cannot do this. His attention is likely to be focused upon either the 4 blocks, the 3 blocks, or the joining act, without achieving synthesis. The teacher must proceed cautiously at this point in time, observing carefully when a child appears to appreciate temporal, cause → effect, and logical relationships. To push ahead prior to such understanding only invites associative learning without understanding.

During the preoperational period many subtle changes have occurred in the child's thinking. Rather than being rigidly tied to specific objects or situations, he has acquired a more comprehensive ability to think. His ability to perform mental operations has improved considerably; and he has gradually developed a vocabulary to describe his actions. Despite these observable qualities of cognitive growth, the child's thinking remains quite immature. His conceptual understandings are still closely tied to concrete situations and are irreversible. He tends to view situations in parts rather than synthesizing these parts into a conceptual whole. He still lacks the ability to mentally restructure simple transformations into a composite showing an entire sequence of actions.

Concrete operations subperiod (7–11 years) In the initial subperiod the child was unable to perform operations requiring a simple one-to-one relationship. If several small boxes were placed in a row, and sticks were piled near them, the early preoperational child was unable to arrange the sticks so that they were in a one-to-one correspondence with the boxes.

Later on in the period he developed the ability to set up such a correspondence but could be misled into believing that the correspondence no longer existed if someone increased the spacing between the objects of one of the groups.

Once the child has entered the concrete operations subperiod, he will no longer be fooled. He understands that changing the order of objects does not affect their quantity. He no longer centers on a particular state of an action; and he is able mentally to reverse actions. He knows that objects which were in a one-to-one correspondence, as in this example, could again be placed into the same correspondence.

CONSERVATION OF QUANTITY, WEIGHT, AND VOLUME

Recall the experiment with the plasticene balls. The preoperational child could not reverse his thinking, and thus centered upon each state as an entity, comparing the transformed objects as they appeared to him at that time. Around the age of seven the child acquires the ability to think back to the starting point. He understands that changing the form of a substance does not change its quantity. His thinking is no longer dominated by his perception of the changed quantity.

The ability to conserve substance is essential for a full understanding of mathematical processes. When a child is able to conserve substance he can understand examples, such as the following:

> 7 bunnies are eating in Mr. Carter's field. After they finish eating, 3 lie down for a nap, while 4 play in another part of the field. How many bunnies are there in Mr. Carter's field now?

A correct answer of 7 indicates that the child realizes that $4 + 3$ is merely a change in the arrangement, not a change of substance. He has learned to conserve quantity.

Even though the child understands that changes in form do not change the substance of a material, he still does not understand that the weight or volume of the material is also unchanged. Conservation of weight occurs at about the age of nine, while conservation of volume doesn't occur until about the ages of eleven or twelve.

NUMBER

According to Piaget number is a synthesis of two operations: classifying or cardination and ordering. Late in the preoperational stage the child develops the ability to classify. He understands that 4 balls are equal in number to 4 trees, and so forth.

Items representing the class "4" are considered as numerically equal. The child has also developed the ability to order objects by size, from smallest to largest. He has not yet developed the ability to synthesize these two operations into a single, reversible operation.

Figure 2.3

Piaget performed a series of experiments using dolls and sticks. A child was given 10 dolls and 10 sticks varying in size (*see* Figure 2.4).

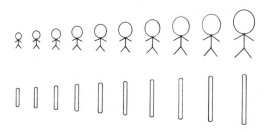

Figure 2.4

The child was told that the dolls were going for a walk and that he should arrange the dolls and sticks so that each doll could find his stick. Piaget then asked which stick will this doll take (while he pointed at one of the dolls)?

Typically, the beginning first grade child can construct a series and can match the dolls and sticks if they are arranged in the same order. If the order is reversed, as in Figure 2.5, he may no longer be able to match the correct stick to a given doll.

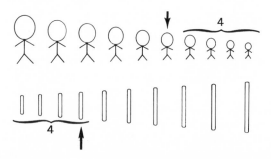

Figure 2.5

His behavior is something like this for the reversed setting. Those dolls which are smaller than the selected doll are placed in a separate collection, and he counts the elements of the set.

Instead of eliminating the same number of small sticks, the child remembers that there are 4 in the set and selects the fourth stick. He did not synthesize his classification of small dolls with a classification of small sticks, and so he selected an incorrect stick. By the time he enters the concrete operations stage he simply eliminates the set of small sticks corresponding to the set of small dolls and chooses the next higher of the remaining sticks. He has now attained the ability to number meaningfully. Knowledge of a child's development of meaningful numbering has direct application to teaching. Ability to label specific sets with certain numerical labels is essential to numeration, while the ability to arrange objects in some hierarchy is essential to an understanding of the ordinal property of numbers. A child who can synthesize the two can also solve such problems as those involving comparative subtraction:

Sally has 6 dolls, while Mary has only 4 dolls. How many more dolls does Sally have than Mary?

The child must classify the set of Mary's dolls as 4 and remove that amount from Sally's dolls. The remainder of the dolls left for Sally is the difference.

$$6 - 4 = 2$$

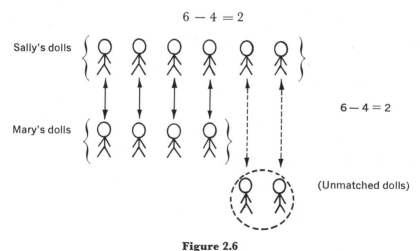

Figure 2.6

About the age of seven the concrete operations child develops the capability of assimilating another's viewpoint on matters which interest him. He develops a desire to play games involving rules, and is capable of co-operative endeavor with others. Mathematical games become interesting to him.

During the concrete operations period the child learns to perceive Euclidean space, time, movement, and velocity correctly. These perceptions are learned gradually throughout the period. Consider Figure 2.7.

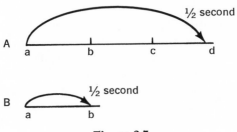

Figure 2.7

If an experimenter moves an object on line "A" from point a to d, and simultaneously moves an object on line "B" from point a to point b, the early concrete period child will probably say that it took longer for the object on line "A" because it is farther. He centers his attention on the spatial aspect of the situation. A correct response to this problem involves a synthesis of concepts involving spatial movement and velocity. Studies of this type have broad implications for teaching elementary school mathematics. It is common practice for teachers to use such aids as number lines and time lines in their teaching. Some children in the early concrete operations period, grades one and two, may still be perceptually tied to spatial factors centering on terminal position. Illustrations of $7 + 3$ and $4 + 3$ are shown in Figure 2.8.

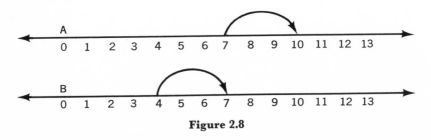

Figure 2.8

An addend in both situations is 3. The placement of the addend in line "A" is such that it might appear greater because it is positioned ahead of the addend in line "B."

At the very least Piaget's findings illustrate the need for careful drawing of the number line by the teacher so that equal distances between digits are maintained. Also, the preoperational child tends to confuse spatial representations; and it would seem wise to defer the use of the number line until well into the concrete operations period, about grade three.

During the concrete operations period children have learned to conserve substance, weight, and volume. In addition, they develop the ability to synthesize their concepts of classifying and ordering to form a concept of numbering. Their thinking has become less egocentric; and they are able to respond to others' views on a variety of matters. While the thinking of the concrete operations child is still tied largely to his own concrete experiences, he can make limited extrapolations from data available either from the current situation or from past situations which he remembers. It is here that the formal operations period begins.

Formal operations period (11 years)   Whereas the concrete operations child has the ability to form hypotheses and test them through an experiment, the formal operations child now develops the ability to assemble or synthesize the results of several experiments to form logical relationships. In essence, he restructures the operations; he forms a cognitive pattern which he may use to solve problems. Consider the problem $1/3 \div 1/7 = N$. To solve this problem the child must recognize many abstract concepts involving fractions and operations with them. A possible solution might involve thinking as follows:

$$1/3 \div 1/7 = N$$

I know that this is the same as:

$$1/3 = N \times 1/7$$

because I learned that

$$8 \div 2 = 4 \text{ is inversely related to } 4 \times 2 = 8.$$

I know that I can multiply both sides of the equal sign by 7 because I understand conservation equality over multiplication.

$$7 \times 1/3 = N \times 1/7 \times 7.$$

Now, simplifying, I find

$$7/3 = N \times 7/7 \text{ or } 7/3 = N.$$

Reducing, I find that

$$N = 2 \ 1/3.$$

With experience, the child's construction of reality becomes more precise and extended. He is able to fill in gaps between related events he sees by forming and testing hypotheses, sometimes without actually needing to manipulate any concrete objects.

The formal operations child is now capable of following a logical argument outside the context of the specific incident being cited. Phillips[3]

[3] John L. Phillips, Jr., *The Origins of Intellect, Piaget's Theory* (San Francisco: W. H. Freeman and Company, 1969), p. 103.

uses the following syllogism to demonstrate this idea:

> All children like spinach;
> Boys are children;
> Therefore boys like spinach.

The young child will likely make a response such as, "But I'm a boy, and I don't like spinach." The formal operations child, however, follows the logic of the argument because he is intrigued by it; he is impressed by its form. He solves mathematical problems because he enjoys finding the correct pattern.

During the formal operations period the child synthesizes operations into propositions which become a part of his cognitive structure. His thinking, although originally evolving from past experience, is no longer tied to it but rather to the "reorganization" within his own mental framework. The content of a problem has now become subordinate to its form.

COGNITIVE STRUCTURE

A careful study of the work of Piaget reveals that each new experience must be accommodated by the child in the light of his existing structure before it can be internalized. At the same time each new experience affects the child's existing cognitive structure for change in response to the new experience. From the early sensorimotor period, where actions are almost always overt, the child now organizes representations of concrete objects into propositions which underlie logical thinking. Each new structure depends upon and is made up of structures that were developed earlier.

Piaget's developmental theory provides the teacher with a vehicle whereby the teacher can analyze a child in terms of the operations of which he is capable at a particular time. Having done this, the desired task to be learned may then be analyzed to determine the operations required to perform it. In this fashion teachers can match desired learnings with "readiness," to produce a maximum outcome from instruction. The problem becomes one of sequencing and conducting effective instruction.

3 SOME BASIC PROCESSES INVOLVED IN MATHEMATICS LEARNING*

Zoltan P. Dienes

BEFORE YOU READ   When they are awake, children are active, seeking beings who desire new and changing stimuli. This exploration phenomenon is increasingly recognized as an integral part of any learning cycle and a necessary precondition to the meaningful development of mathematical ideas in children.

Professor Z. P. Dienes has contributed significantly to the expanding influence of the ideas of Piaget. Dr. Dienes lends considerable support to the notion of concrete experiences through manipulative materials, and equal support to the view that constructive thinking must come before analytical thinking, that is, exploration and experience before analysis and application. If one considers the materials available to children as comprising the "conditioned learning environment" established by the teacher, then it is logical to accept the crucial relationship in that environment of the interaction between child and materials. The author presents a rationale for the development of number ideas via that interaction.

At first children use a variety of materials in a relatively structured manner. Subsequently their actions become directed toward some end. Through constructing, ordering, and classifying a series of abstractions they form generalizations. Finally, after structural patterns and relationships are received, symbolic representation, including language, may be used in the production of new ideas.

As a result of reading this article the teacher should be able to identify the crucial function of continuous manipulative exploration, contrast the cyclical abstraction-generalization phenomenon, and describe the functional role of symbolic representation in learning mathematics.

---

* Inquiries should be addressed to International Study Group for Mathematics Learning, c/o Professor Zoltan P. Dienes, University of Sherbrooke, Sherbrooke, Quebec, Canada.

Reprinted with permission as excerpts from an article in *Research in Mathematics Education*, N.C.T.M., 1967. Professor Dienes is at the University of Sherbrooke, Quebec, Canada.

Mathematical play can be generated simply by providing children with a large variety of constructed mathematical materials. Suppose materials such as multibase arithmetic blocks, Cuisenaire rods, or various kinds of geometric materials that might induce them to learn about vector spaces, matrices, etc., have been made available. . . .

The *first* thing to do with these materials, of course, is to leave them around for the children to play with! Then one of two kinds of play usually takes place. In one, which might be called purely manipulative, the child tries to find out, almost consciously, how the material handles. He wants to know what kind of a tool he has. In the other, which might be called representational play, the child adds his imagination to the manipulation— he makes up all sorts of "cover stories" and uses the material to represent these ideas. . . .

Eventually, certain properties of the situation and other constraints will begin to make themselves clear to the exploring child. For example, the child may discover that some blocks do not stand up, that others do not fit alongside each other, that a triangle cannot be made out of squares or squares out of (some) triangles, and so on. The child, having realized the restrictions under which he is working and the possibilities that are open to him, will begin to ask questions concerning the conditions under which certain possibilities may be realized. For instance, can he build a certain kind of structure with a certain number of certain kinds of pieces? Is it possible to make windows in a certain part of the wall without causing the wall to collapse? Answers to such questions should be obtained rather easily by means of manipulating the material at hand.

ABSTRACTION

Abstraction is the gathering together of a number of different events or situations into a class, using certain criteria that must be applicable to all these events and situations. When we abstract we draw out from many different situations that which is common to them, and we disregard those things which are irrelevant to this common core.

If children are provided with a sufficient variety of mathematical materials, it will be more likely that the mathematical relationships determined during the course of their play with these materials will be abstract, rather than tied to certain particular situations. In effect, it is hypothesized that in mathematical learning abstraction will be more likely to take place if a multiple embodiment of a mathematical idea is provided, rather than a single embodiment such as Cuisenaire rods by themselves. Providing a number of embodiments enables the child to progress toward abstraction on a broad front. The more broadly based the abstraction, the more widely applicable will it be. In other words, if the abstraction is a result of gathering together the common properties of a large variety of situations, it is more likely that the final abstract concept will be applicable to a large variety of applications and situations.

The formation of abstract concepts seems to take place in cycles. The end point of each cycle can act as at least a partial beginning point of the next cycle. For example, the idea of natural number (or certainly of the cardinal aspect of natural number) is obtained partially by manipulating sets of objects, comparing them, and realizing that if two sets are in one-to-one correspondence then these sets are equivalent, i.e., have the same number of elements. When the order property is joined to this concept, the idea of natural number is made operational. This is the end point of a very long set of experiences in which the child finally realizes the irrelevance of various other properties of the sets and only the number property is retained. This child is probably unaware of this process, at least in the traditional educational setup. . . .

GENERALIZATION

By generating abstractions out of previously formed ideas we are moving along an abstraction dimension.

There are, of course, many other dimensions of mathematical thinking. One of the more important dimensions is generalization—something hinted at, but not made explicit, in the preceding section. Whereas an abstraction is created from elements by virtue of realizing some common property of the elements, generalization is the extension of an abstract class to a wider class of elements that possess the same properties as the original class, or, possibly, properties only similar to them.

One might, for example, generalize from the even-and-odd situation to the rules for adding numbers that are divisible by three, those that when divided by three leave a remainder of one and those that when divided by three leave a remainder of two. The resulting addition rules result in what is known as a modulo-three arithmetic. This table does not have the same properties as the other table (modulo two), but it has some similar properties. For instance, any two kinds of numbers, when added, result in one of the three kinds. In other words, the situation is "closed." Another feature common to the two tables is that in each kind of table there is a neutral element. The neutral element in the even-and-odd table is the class of even numbers and in the modulo-three table it is the class of those numbers that are divisible by three. . . .

Is it better to generalize on a narrow front and then abstract, or to abstract on a broad front and then generalize? In other words, is it better to restrict oneself to one or two situations to which the mathematical structure being learned is applicable, and at the same time pursue its mathematical generality as far as possible; or to look at a wide number of situations in which the structure is applicable, to encourage a broad abstraction of mathematics before extension of the mathematical structure itself is contemplated? Probably no easy answer is forthcoming. There might even be individual differences, and certainly the answer will depend at least in part on the type of mathematical situation being envisaged. . . .

SYMBOLISM

It is unclear what general laws govern the use of symbols in mathematical thinking. Until quite recently it had been taken for granted that the only way to learn mathematics is through symbols. Since it is now known that mathematics, even mathematics of quite sophisticated kinds can be learned via manipulative experiences with concrete objects, a question arises concerning the optimal use of symbols.

There seem to be some indications that a certain degree of abstraction is necessary before a symbol can effectively be used and applied in a wide range of situations. If symbolization takes place after only one embodiment has been introduced and children are asked certain questions to which the obvious answers (from the adult point of view) would be through the use of symbols, the children will almost invariably go back and manipulate the materials to provide the answers. On the other hand, if many different embodiments have been introduced and the symbols are beginning to mean for the children the common mathematical properties of these embodiments, then it becomes more likely that the children will use the symbols to provide the answer to a problem.

When a symbol to represent a certain situation has been either invented by a child or presented to him, it is always a problem to know what that symbol does, in fact, symbolize for that child. To what extent does the symbol denote that activity with those very things with which he is engaged, or to what extent does it denote a class of activities that he might engage in? It seems to be the hallmark of an intelligent child to think more in terms of classes of events than in terms of individual events.

Classifying events enables one to predict future events more accurately than regarding events simply as isolated individual occurrences. It seems a priori more probable that symbolization would be more effective after a high degree of abstraction has been achieved than if symbols are introduced at the very beginning.

Some people might argue that, on the other hand, introduction of the symbol would save a good deal of unnecessary work with concrete embodiments. Symbols are more easily transformable and manipulatable than concrete materials, so it is in a sense labor-saving to manipulate a symbol rather than an event. My reply to this criticism is that although it may be labor-saving, if the result of symbol manipulation is a knowledge only of how to manipulate further symbols it is of little use. At best, if the symbols denote one kind of activity then predictions regarding only that kind of activity will be possible as a result of manipulating the symbols. So it seems probable that the introduction of symbols *after* a variety of concrete experiences would be more effective than their introduction earlier—but just what variables are involved, only future research will determine.

SUMMARY

To sum up, the following observations are offered.

One, to encourage children to abstract (that is, to determine the elements common to a large number of different situations), a large number of different situations must be provided. This leads to the principle of *multiple embodiment* of mathematical concepts.

Two, to encourage children to generalize, one must try to vary the values of the mathematical variables that make up the mathematical concepts to be taught. An illustration is that of varying the mod value in modular arithmetic. This leads to the principle of *mathematical variability*.

Three, if children are to symbolize and use their symbols effectively, it is probably better to let them have a hand in the process itself. Children might want to change their symbols as they change their breadth of abstraction. They might not want to use the same symbols when two or three situations are pulled together into one. If they originally used the symbols to represent only one of these situations, they might want a different and possibly more concise symbolism when they realize that there could be literally hundreds of similar situations. The principle involved might be referred to as the principle of *dynamic symbolization*. Normally, symbols are static; but in this conception symbols take on a dynamic role and become an integral part indeed of the abstraction and generalization cycles.

Four, to encourage children to interpret, they might first be given some practice in making up imaginative stories to which their structures are applicable. Soon they will realize the kind of stories that are applicable and those that are not. So if children are allowed to take a hand in the process of interpretation they are more likely to understand the interpretation they have abstracted than if the teacher does all the interpreting for them. This leads to a principle that might be called the principle of *image construction*. Children should be encouraged to construct their own images.

4 MATHEMATICS: STRATEGIES OF TEACHING

Edward G. Buffie, Ronald C. Welch, and Donald D. Paige

BEFORE YOU READ   Most teachers would agree that children should be taught mathematics in accordance with our knowledge of how children form mathematical concepts. Generally, whether consciously or unconsciously, sound principles are used as guidelines for the development of specific learning activities. Often, however, the behaviors children are expected to demonstrate after they have participated in a learning activity are not specified. A significant dimension of teaching derives from mutual pupil-teacher awareness of the purposes which selected instructional activities are designed to fulfill. In this reading Glen Heathers' categories of goals—that is, content, process, and personal-social—establish an appropriate first step for the teacher who wishes to define desired goals in more specific terms. It should become clear that the determination of appropriate goals and specific behaviors cannot be independent of the processes involved in Professor Dienes' abstraction-generalization paradigm or the Piagian developmental stages as described by Professor Maertens. The unique role of goals in teaching and learning mathematics is best summarized by Dr. Brune's statement: "Mathematics best serves useful ends, its learners profit through self-reliance and its teachers very likely succeed in accordance with their use of psychology."

Upon completion of the following selection the teacher should be able to identify three major categories of goals and describe their significance in providing direction for goal-oriented instruction in mathematics.

GOAL-ORIENTED INSTRUCTION

For instruction to be of most benefit to pupils and most satisfying to teachers, it must be characterized by *goal-oriented experiences* in the classroom; that is to say, both teacher and pupils must be fully aware of the purposes which the instructional activity is designed to serve. Much controversy in education exists because of the vast difference between what we say we believe and what we actually do in terms of instructional practices.

Reprinted from Edward G. Buffie, Ronald C. Welch and Donald D. Paige, *Mathematics: Strategies of Teaching,* © 1968. Reprinted by permission of Prentice-Hall, Inc., Englewood Cliffs, N.J. Professors Buffie and Welch are at the College of Education of Indiana University in Bloomington, Indiana. Professor Paige is at Southern Illinois University, Carbondale, Illinois.

To noticeably reduce the gap between theory and practice is not an easy task. The first essential is a clear delineation of goals or purposes. Operational decisions—grouping patterns, selection of materials and content, and evaluation—should all be based upon the values we hold and the goals we seek. The making of these decisions can be simplified only if the purposes they are to meet are clear cut, not hazy and undefined.

To what source does one go for clarification of goals or purposes? Statements made by the Educational Policies Commission have long helped to perform this service. Few are the educators who are not familiar with statements of objectives relating to self-realization, human relationship, economic efficiency, and civic responsibility. While the Commission's 1938 statement centered around these ideas, it is particularly interesting to note the change in point of view as evidenced in the 1961 statement. The *central role of the rational powers* is stressed throughout. Such powers ". . . involve the processes of recalling and imagining, classifying and generalizing, comparing and evaluating, analyzing and synthesizing, and deducing and inferring. These processes enable one to apply logic and the available evidence to his ideas, attitudes, and actions, and to pursue better whatever ideas he may have."[1]

Though it is a relatively simple matter to achieve consensus on broadly stated goals, when it comes to interpretation of these goals with the anticipation of making resultant operational decisions, difficulties arise. What is really meant by rational powers, self-realization, civic responsibility? When we view goals as a basis for action decisions, it becomes distressingly clear that ambiguity and vagueness must move over and make room for painstakingly conceived specifics.

In a recent publication, Glen Heathers identified three major categories of goals which may help clarify our thinking:[2] content goals, process goals, and personal-social goals. The content goals, as these relate to any subject matter area, have to do with terminology, classification, information, explanatory theory, and technological application of information and theory. American education has typically emphasized the teaching of facts, although terminology and classification have also been stressed. It is this type of information-centered education that prompted Mortimer Adler to define formal education as "a process by which material passes from the notebook of the teacher to the notebook of the pupil, without passing through the head of either." At any rate, it is perfectly clear that an educated person is not one who merely has accumulated information—a walking encyclopedia. Facts are vehicles for the development of concepts and generalizations and, hence, rational thought. There has been relatively little concern for ". . . learning the general structure of ideas that orders knowledge of the

[1] The Educational Policies Commission, *The Central Purpose of Education* (Washington, D.C.: National Education Association of the United States, 1961), p. 9.
[2] Judson T. Shaplin and Henry F. Olds, editors, *Team Teaching* (New York: Harper and Row, 1964), pp. 349–351.

field and provides the basis for understanding that knowledge and for employing it to serve practical ends."[3]

The process goals relate to student ability to acquire, interpret, evaluate, and communicate knowledge as well as to develop basic fundamental skills. Educational reformers stress the point that a rapidly changing society must place a premium on one's ability to adapt to novel and unpredictable situations. Although there may not be complete agreement over what constitutes the process goals, Mr. Heathers' suggestions include: tool skills, critical and creative thinking, methods of inquiry, self-instruction, and self-evaluation. At the present time only the tool skills (reading, writing, counting, computing, etc.) seem to play a dominant role in American education.

Much controversy centers upon the *extent* to which the schools should assume responsibility for personality development, social behavioral patterns, and value formation. While goal emphasis is leaning more and more toward the development of intellectual powers, school must always be concerned with the personal-social goals because of the effect personal-social characteristics have upon learning. The development of an adequate and realistic self-concept is most important. Each child should be helped to develop a realistic understanding of both his strengths and weaknesses and then, more importantly, use his strengths to overcome his weaknesses when possible. As human beings strive toward selfhood, teachers have a responsibility to help children become increasingly more competent in self-direction, self-discipline, and self-evaluation. The responsibility for achievement of these particular goals, however, must be a shared one among home, church, and school.

As we continue to grow in our ability to state goals in more meaningful terms,[4] we will find ourselves drawn into closer confrontation with specific issues relating to goal accomplishment, i.e., grouping practices. If we accept the fundamental premise that our *over-all educational goal* is, indeed, the maximum development of the rational, creative being, every succeeding decision must find its roots in that acceptance.

If instruction is to be goal-oriented, one might quite logically inquire what all this suggests for the teaching of mathematics. The development of intellectual growth in mathematics, for example, is far too broad a goal for meaningful translation into action. Goals must be formulated and stated in more specific terms.

Years ago, the primary purpose of mathematics instruction was confined to developing computational skill in the fundamental arithmetical processes. Such an objective certainly would be categorized as a process

---

[3] *Ibid.*, p. 349.

[4] See Robert F. Mager's *Preparing Instructional Objectives.* Mager stresses the importance of stating objectives in behavioral or performance terms, such objectives being both observable and measurable. See also "Writing Instructional Objectives" by Thorwald Esbensen in the Jan. 1967 issue of *Phi Delta Kappan*, pp. 246–247.

goal (emphasis on the development of tool skills). Today our interpretation of process goals extends far beyond this very limited scope. In the past, the goal of computational facility greatly influenced the way in which the subject was taught, and emphasis was upon drill and practice. *Do not be misled; today such a goal is still important.* However, we would do well to recognize that today we have machines that can do calculations better and faster than any person. Some hand computers actually sell for less than a dollar. Therefore, other objectives must also serve as a focal point of instruction.

In the past decade or two, emphasis has been placed on the *why* as well as the *how* of computation. Mathematical understanding has taken its rightful place of major importance alongside the mechanics of arithmetical drill and skill. When understanding is firmly established, *then* drill and practice activities are capitalized upon to develop automatic mastery. Today's paramount concern for understanding has led to the identification of mathematical structures: those properties, principles, and laws which permeate all of mathematics. Who, today, has not heard of the commutative property, the associative property, the distributive property, or the identity elements? These ideas bind together the various elements of mathematics which are dealt with throughout the elementary school. A second major goal of instruction, then, is related to *understanding* mathematical content— the big ideas of mathematics as represented by the structure of the discipline. Another aspect of the content goals is an increased emphasis on related terminology. Much emphasis is placed upon learning and using proper mathematical vocabulary. As is true with all forms of language (and mathematics is a language), the more precise the vocabulary the greater is the possibility for effective communication and understanding. Once again, however, mere accumulation of information—understandings and termi-nology—could hardly be used *alone* to justify the teaching of mathematics (even if used in conjunction with the goal of computational efficiency). Content goals must be accompanied by still other goals.

As the case for a strong definition of content goals continues and strengthens, a parallel development is expected to evolve in evaluating and strengthening process goals. Emphasis in this area has traditionally centered on the fundamentals of computation. But today we are becoming equally concerned with helping children develop their rational powers and their ability to do critical and creative thinking. Teachers are capitalizing on the benefits of the inquiry, discovery, problem-solving approach to instruction, as well as techniques of self-instruction and self-evaluation.

Earlier, reference was made to "the development of rational power." Such a phrase has slightly different meanings depending upon the context in which it is found. In mathematics we are concerned with inquiry and creative thinking and problem-solving (all of which are process goals). Pupils are encouraged to approach problems or questions, each in his own unique way. A third major goal, therefore, is that divergent thinking be encouraged and its development deliberately sought. In the past, the usefulness of mathematics in practical matters was the most important factor in its vitality as a subject. *Even more important today than the inculcation of this practical handling of the basic facts and fundamentals is the kind of thinking we wish to encourage and the kind of mind we hope to cultivate.*

In order for pupils to become more creative in solving problems in unique ways, whether they be mathematical problems as illustrated below or mathematical problems in a social setting, they must develop an understanding of the structure of the discipline. It is this understanding and knowledge which makes possible unique and creative thought.

Picture this assignment: Solve the following problem and check it in as many different ways as possible:

$$n = 16 \times 25$$

Pupil solutions included:

25	16	25	16
16	25	16	25
150	80	150 (6 × 25)	80 (5 × 16)
25	32	250 (10 × 25)	320 (20 × 16)
400	400	400	400

$n = 16 \times 25$	$n = 16 \times 25$	$n = 16 \times 25$	$n = 16 \times 25$
$= (4 \times 4)25$	$= 16(5 \times 5)$	$= (10 + 6)25$	$= 8 \times 50$
$= 4(4 \times 25)$	$= (16 \times 5)5$	$= (10 \times 25)$	$= 4 \times 100$
$= 4(100)$	$= 80 \times 5$	$\quad + (6 \times 25)$	$= 2 \times 200$
$= 400$	$= 400$	$= 250 + 150$	$= 400$
		$= 400$	

$n = 16 \times 25$	25	16	16
$= (16 \div 2)$	25	16	25⟌400
$\quad \times (25 \times 2)$	25	16	
$= 8 \times 50$	—	16	25
$= 400$	—	—	16⟌400
	—	—	
	+	—	
	400	+	
		400	

$n = 16 \times 25$
$= (2 \times 8)25$
$= 2(8 \times 25)$
$= 2 \times 200$
$= 400$

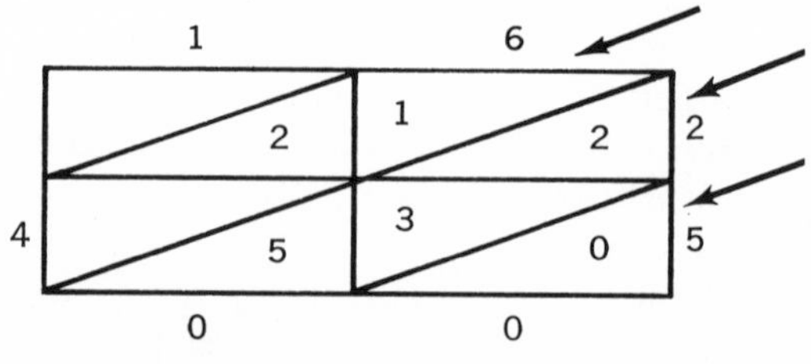

Figure 4.1

Close examination of the above will reveal pupil understanding of: (1) the commutative property of multiplication, (2) the associative property of multiplication, (3) the distributive property of multiplication, (4) the identity element, (5) inverse operations, (6) related operations, and (7) compensation.

Pupil understanding of the fact that numbers may be named in many different ways, i.e., 16 renamed as (4×4) and $(10 + 6)$, is also apparent. Such assignments give pupils an opportunity to provide evidence of their understanding and creative thought as well as to develop or further substantiate that mathematics is a man-made system and that man is in control of it and can use the system in whatever way he wishes to achieve his ends as long as he follows the rules of the game. To be creative, one becomes involved in thinking and doing in ways that are new or unique to him. Freedom to explore encourages creativity in thought and action and replaces the rigidity and conformity which all too often are characteristic of mathematics instruction.

Note then that the goal of creative thought is not something left merely to chance or simply a matter of providing opportunity for it to take place. We must channel our instructional efforts to this end if we wish attainment of this goal. Harry Emerson Fosdick said it best:

> No horse gets anywhere until he is harnessed. No steam or gas ever drives anything until it is confined. No Niagara is ever turned into light and power until it is focused, dedicated, and disciplined.[5]

It is important for all of us to realize that a fundamental understanding of the structure of mathematics is not an end in itself; rather, it is the relationship of this understanding to creative and divergent thought that provides its real value and meaning as an objective.

That the process goals, particularly those relating to inquiry and creativity, are being valued more and more today is an encouraging, not to be denied fact. That they may be considered even more important than the content-goals was implied years ago when Albert Einstein dared suggest that imagination was more important than information. The process goals then relate to the matter of helping children learn how to learn. Such goals further the development of such traits as originality, boldness, and flexibility. In the past, many of our schools, consciously or unconsciously, seemed to value conformity, timidity and rigidity. The focus was all too often on the "right answer" with little concern for the manner in which the answer was obtained.

The outstanding mathematics program of the present and the future will be one which has its strengths in creative and analytical abilities and

[5] Jacob M. Braude, *The Speakers Desk Book of Quips, Quotes, and Anecdotes* (Englewood Cliffs, N.J.: Prentice-Hall, Inc., 1963), p. 104.

fundamental understandings rather than mere assimilation and computation of indiscriminate facts and figures. Jerome Bruner, in his *Notes on a Theory of Instruction*, puts it well:[6]

> A body of knowledge . . . is the result of much intellectual activity. To instruct someone in those disciplines is not a matter of getting him to commit results to mind. Rather, it is to teach him to participate in the process that makes possible the establishment of knowledge. We teach a subject not to produce little living libraries on that subject, but rather to get a student to think mathematically for himself, to consider matters as a historian does, to take part in the process of knowledge getting. Knowledge is a process, not a product.

A fourth major goal recognizes the importance of *attitude*. Wherever goal-oriented instruction centers upon creativity and inquiry, children will also gain much in terms of personal enjoyment of learning. We should be as much concerned with helping children develop and maintain a zeal for learning as we are for them to acquire a specific quantity of learning. Not only is the knowledge we possess important, but also how we *feel* about the knowledge which has been acquired. Much of learning is an emotional experience. Knowledge itself can be used for good or evil, or perhaps not used at all. Attitude, as much as anything else, determines the direction that any one individual will go. We oftentimes wonder how many people actually realize how very close the relationship is between the formulating of sound positive student attitudes and the learning experiences which children encounter.

Changing goals affect the nature of instruction As goals change so also must methods of instruction; otherwise, great inconsistency and ultimately conflict will be evident among purposes, instruction, and eventually, evaluation. Too many people view the modern mathematics program as little more than a change in content—emphasis on the big ideas (structure), greater emphasis on geometry, the introduction of other numeration systems and different number bases, or simply a matter of pushing content into lower grade levels. They do not recognize that it is the very *basis* of instructional goals which has changed, or perhaps only partial recognition is made and accepted, with the result that the learning experiences are focused narrowly, and unfortunately, on computational skills and mathematical structure. The other imminent danger is that the people responsible for formulating learning experiences for children will fully recognize and even philosophically accept the changes in goal-emphasis, but for one reason or another fail to relate and reflect this knowledge in instructional practice.

[6] Jerome S. Bruner, "Notes on a Theory of Instruction," *Toward a Theory of Instruction* (Cambridge, Mass.: The Belknap Press of Harvard University Press, 1966), p. 72. Reprinted by permission of the publisher.

IN SUMMARY

As changes have been made in curriculum and in instruction, concern for specifying clear-cut purposes or objectives has not been typically prominent. Recent instructional innovations and curricular reorganization have reflected continuing concern for the techniques of teaching: use of inquiry, discovery, and problem-solving approaches, and the grade placement of content. Emphasis upon the mechanical aspects of instruction, such as homogeneous grouping and multiage grouping, has served to divert debate into procedural matters. And yet, one must recognize that the most crucial and most sharply defined differences among those who seek to influence instruction are to be found in their concept of the purposes and goals of the mathematics program in the elementary school. It will be as these differences are resolved and objectives are defined that we will see marked educational improvement, and it is to this end that we must put our efforts.

SUGGESTED READINGS

1. *Goals for School Mathematics*. Boston: Houghton Mifflin Company, 1963. This little booklet is the report of the Cambridge Conference on School Mathematics. A succinct and concise set of guidelines for future programs is described.
2. Kearney, Nolin C., editor, *Elementary School Objectives* (A report prepared for the Mid Century Committee on Outcomes in Elementary Education). New York: Russell Sage Foundation, 1953. This report was assembled for the purpose of describing for educators, test makers, and interested citizens the measurable goals of instruction in our elementary schools.
3. Mager, Robert E., *Preparing Instructional Objectives*. Palo Alto, California: Fearon Publishers, 1962. An excellent little paperback dealing with specific procedures on how to prepare instructional objectives in behavioral, or performance, terms.
4. Parker, J. Cecil and Louis J. Rubin, *Process as Content: Curriculum Design and the Application of Knowledge*. Chicago: Rand McNally and Company, 1966. An analysis of strategy as it applies to both the process and content goals of instruction. Available in paperback.

5 COMMON ELEMENTS OF METHOD

Paul C. Burns

BEFORE YOU READ   The identification of the sequential nature of
learning obligates the elementary school mathematics teacher to seek
variety in approaches to instruction.   The teacher must translate the
implications of contemporary theories of learning into a functional
instructional setting for children appropriate to this sequential nature of
concept development.   Professor Burns focuses on elements of methodology
which tend to coalesce the common tenets of learning theory found in the
previous contributions—most notably those discussed by Professor
Maertens and postulated by Professor Dienes—and translates them into an
operational framework for the teacher.   Substantive examples are used to
suggest how the teacher might function in regard to (1.) the sequencing
of instructional procedures as they relate to concept development, (2.)
selection of meaningful learning activities which focus on environmental
association, and (3.) the appropriate utilization of language.   In essence,
a multiple approach is advocated within which it is possible for the teacher
to maintain the unique integrity of individual learners.

   After reading this article the teacher should be able to describe
five basic premises for sound instruction, compare their characteristics to
selected major features of contemporary programs, and list the concomitant implications for teaching method.

From 1900 to 1935 the main emphasis in the teaching of elementary school
mathematics was on speed and accuracy.   Teachers resorted to drill and
more drill as a teaching technique.   After 1935 emphasis shifted to concern
for meaning and understanding.   With publication of the 1935 yearbook of
the National Council of Teachers of Mathematics, particularly the chapter
written by Brownell,[1] the terms "meaning" and "meaningful teaching"

[1] William A. Brownell, "Psychological Considerations in the Learning and the Teaching of
Arithmetic." *Tenth Yearbook*, National Council of Teachers of Mathematics, (N.Y.:
Teachers College, Columbia University, 1935), pp. 1–31.

Reprinted by permission of Paul C. Burns and the Association for Childhood Education
International, 3615 Wisconsin Avenue, N.W., Washington, D.C. Copyright © 1965 by the
Association. Reprinted from Membership Service Bulletin 16-A, *New Directions in Mathe-
matics*. Paul C. Burns is Professor of Education at the University of Tennessee.

began to appear frequently in the literature and discussions relating to arithmetic instruction. The concept of "meaningful arithmetic" was widely accepted—though perhaps not incorporated as widely—and there was general agreement that meaningful learning would result in better skills and increased stimulation to further mathematics learning. The *why* was considered as important as the *how*. It was hoped that pupils would learn the "why" of regrouping ("carrying" and "borrowing"); of "setting over" one place to the left when multiplying 12×26; of "counting off" two places in the product when multiplying 2.3×12.5; of "inverting the divisor and multiplying" when dividing 6 by 1/2. Pupils needed to know the rationale behind mathematical operations.

The emphasis has now shifted to a concern for new content to promote better understanding. Programs include new topics and extensions of topics that were not in earlier programs. Greater precision of language in relation to content is deemed important for increased understanding.

The new mathematics demands a precise vocabulary that gives it a rich, characteristic flavor. Many older definitions have been replaced by ones with greater accuracy and clarity. New symbolism and notations have been introduced to foster understanding. More mathematics and a more rigorous development of it have been accepted nationally for the elementary school mathematics program.

This does not mean that there should be blind incorporation of topics. Reorientation in elementary mathematics is more than just doing something "new" or absorption of different content. Unfortunately some published materials and some proponents of new content seem to have built the impression that if a mathematical topic is introduced early enough and presented in the most abstract manner something good automatically happens.

The goal in grades K-6 is still to teach the basic operations and concepts of arithmetic. New topics, precise terminology and modern approaches should be utilized, not because they are "new" but because they can strengthen basic topics and increase understanding and interest in mathematics. Understanding mathematical ideas such as sets, properties, geometry and other modern content should all contribute to this end. For example, the identity elements of multiplication and division should be utilized in learning about "different names for the same number," as $1/2 = 2/4$ since $2/2 \ (1) \times 1/2 = 2/4$ and $3/6 = 1/2$ since $3/6 \div 3/3 \ (1) = 1/2 \ldots$

It is necessary to integrate carefully the new topics and extensions of topics with content that has stood the test of time. It is also important to present contemporary content through teaching methods which make the content understandable. Unfortunately, sound content can be taught in a mechanical fashion. Excellent content is not enough; it must be accompanied by sound methodology.

SOME BASIC PREMISES FOR SOUND PROGRAMS

Concepts build gradually   *First* of all, to assure thorough learning, mathematics concepts must be built up gradually; the full import of an idea is rarely comprehended in one or two lessons, especially when the idea is a complex abstraction. Achievement of thorough understanding of an idea requires careful development. One does not start "full-blown" with a mature, sophisticated idea and then quickly move on; time is needed for its development through a variety of intuitive and informal representations of the skill or concept. For example, the use of the idea that $7 + 3$ and $3 + 7$ name the same number would precede the analysis of this property of numbers. Slower, more careful development is often the key to more rapid progress later. For this reason, only gradually is the use of a standard "algorism" reached—after considerable use of immature algorisms (non-standard algorisms). One example from subtraction will illustrate this point.

a. $43 = 4$ tens $+ 3$ ones $= 3$ tens $+ 13$ ones

$-18 = (1$ ten $+ 8$ ones$) = (1$ ten $+ 8$ ones$)$

2 tens $+ 5$ ones $= 25$

b. $\dfrac{43 = 40 + 3}{-18 \quad 10 + 8} = \dfrac{30 + 13}{10 + 8}$

$20 + 5 = 25$

c. $\begin{array}{r} \overset{3}{\cancel{4}}\overset{13}{\cancel{3}} \\ -18 \\ \hline 25 \end{array}$

d. $\begin{array}{r} 43 \\ -18 \\ \hline 25 \end{array}$

The reason for not starting with the standard algorism is that it leaves out much of the meaning—and meaning must be emphasized in contrast to manipulation. It is important to form a sound base so that pupils will more readily and more completely assimilate the content of more complex mathematics. Weaknesses that must be constantly under repair, due to too early and too rapid coverage, constitute wasteful practice.

The idea before the label   *Second*, mathematical ideas should be developed to the point of real understanding prior to attaching technical terminology, definitions and symbols to them. Understanding and use of a concept are far more important than the labels, names and signs. Premature emphasis upon terminology and symbols can lead to memorization rather than understanding. To emphasize ultimate refinements before the child has matured enough to appreciate them is a pedagogical mistake.

As a child's knowledge, experience and understanding grow, he will be able to follow more precise words and definitions; but even then these must be based on his own experiences and understanding. For example, pupils can have early experiences in associating numbers by tens; that is,

"Bob thought $8 + 4 = 12$. Then he checked by thinking $8 + 2 = 10$. $10 + 2 = 12$. Use his way to check your answer to $8 + 9$." This, of course, makes use of the associative property of addition; that is, $8 + 4 = 8 + (2 + 2) = (8 + 2) + 2 = 10 + 2 = 12$, but the technical symbols and terms would be left for later development . . . .

Experiences dealing with addition used to check subtraction can lead to the idea of the linkage between addition and subtraction. But bare words (*e.g.*, "inverse") won't do it, no matter how frequently repeated to the child. Too, the "different names for the same number" idea paves the way for use of expanded notation. The child as a learner must be remembered. The result of neglecting a child's point of view and his thinking may be a confused individual who avoids mathematics.

Learning through environmental association   *Third*, there is much greater assurance that an idea will be grasped when the work of pupils has an association with environmental situations. Natural, lifelike situations are more meaningful to the pupil at early stages than items unnatural to the environmental situation. This is why a circle on the playground is often used to convey the meaning of *inside, outside, on,* or a rhythm instrument is used to represent the idea of a *triangle*. Once the idea and the life situation are connected, there must be a strong program of building skills and of guided experiences in selecting mathematics to fit life situations (problem solving). *Too much emphasis upon numerals and other mathematical symbols in isolation dangerously postpones the development of skill in reading the verbal matter characteristic of mathematics materials.* In brief, teachers should stress the usefulness of mathematics and teach it so that it can be used when needed. In the development of the operations this is partially achieved through reference to their use both inside and outside school.

Continual reinforcement of concepts   *Fourth*, new material must be governed by concepts and experiences the pupil has acquired and retained. A program of mathematics requires that ideas and skills essential to each succeeding step in learning are thoroughly taught and maintained so that they will be available when an extension of a concept is begun. Frequent reinforcement of an idea is required if it is to be available when needed. This reinforcement calls for frequent use of ideas and skills in developing other concepts, in clarifying mathematical aspects and in making application more effective. Repetitive presentations should be varied, of course, through the use of various approaches . . . . But pupils still need time for refurbishing and maintaining concepts and skills. Practice alone, however, cannot be relied upon to develop meaning.

Considering individual needs   *Fifth*, teachers recognize that all pupils must be served in the elementary school mathematics program in ways that best fit individual needs. To meet individual differences, a variety of extensions of operations is provided for pupils who quickly achieve an understanding or skill and are ready to explore a topic in greater depth. For pupils who are slower in learning the basic essentials, topics are more deliberately paced. Nonscientists and non-future mathematicians also need arithmetic, and teaching must be adapted to the variations among individuals.

Furthermore, teachers recognize that arithmetic is only one part of the total enterprise of elementary education. Elementary education has many objectives, not just one. A great increase in time allotted to arithmetic means less time for other important subjects, such as reading and social studies. Since, generally speaking, more time cannot and should not be allotted to arithmetic instruction, arithmetic must be taught more efficiently.

Ways to improve mathematics teaching   *Finally*, teachers recognize many facets integral to an excellent elementary school mathematics program. This suggests there are many ways to improve the program besides attention to content. To strengthen the over-all program, attention should be given to:

> specific study procedures
> better ways of reviewing and summarizing learnings
> more effective approaches to orally presented quantitative ideas
> problem solving
> reintroduction of topics presented in earlier grades
> ways to differentiate instruction
> use of additional materials for instruction

MAJOR CONTRIBUTIONS OF NEW MATHEMATICS TO METHOD

Of course, the new mathematics at the elementary school level has contributed to new content such as sets and geometry, but it has also provided emphasis upon method.

Number line   The new directions in elementary-school mathematics utilize some old but formerly little-used procedures. One of these is the *number line*. Although this now widely accepted teaching aid had been used in algebra in connection with positive and negative numbers and had been presented in books on arithmetic prior to 1950, it was little used in classrooms until after it was advanced by new mathematics. The number line represents the sequence of numbers, helps pupils to compare quantities and illustrates the meanings of the basic operations.

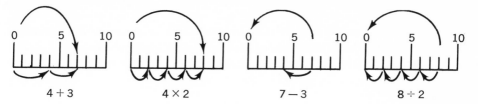

$4 + 3$ 4×2 $7 - 3$ $8 \div 2$

Figure 5.1

This illustrates how the number line helps to clarify the idea that subtraction undoes addition, that division undoes multiplication. Multiplication is repeated addition of equal sets; division is repeated subtraction of equal sets. Operations with fractions and decimals, as well as with whole numbers, can be illustrated on the number line. Concepts of negative integers are also reinforced through use of the number line.

Properties   Earlier books devoted some space to the *commutative, associative, and distributive properties of the operations.* Few persons, however, paid any attention in arithmetic to the properties of the operations until the new mathematics of the late 1950's appeared. Formerly no attempt was made to use properties at a time when the operation dealt with relatively simple numbers. The distributive property in multiplication can be used to illustrate the point. Under the older plan no attention was given to the distributive property until two-digit multipliers were introduced, and then the procedures did not really focus attention upon the properties. Under the new, the distributive property would be introduced in a situation in which pupils needed to use one-digit factors. The following is a teaching situation to illustrate:

> A teacher said, "Bill wasn't sure that his product for 7×3 was correct. He wrote $2 \times 3 = 6$ and $5 \times 3 = 15$, and then added 6 and 15!" Then, to direct study, the teacher asked, "Can you figure out what Bill did? What advantage do you see in his way of verifying the product 21? Can you use Bill's procedure to see if $8 \times 5 = 40$?"

Here it is possible to see the distributive aspect more easily than when the principle is postponed until two-digit factors are used, as in 14×28.

Different names for same number   Still another valuable instructional factor of the new mathematics is the recognition that a *number may have several names* .... Pupils are taught that 5 may be expressed as $2 + 3$, $1 + 4$, 1/3 of 15, or $60 \div 12$. All these expressions are names for the standard number 5. This provides the groundwork for pupils to think of numbers in different ways for different purposes. In subtracting 6 from 172, they must think of 172 as 1 hundred, 6 tens, and 12 ones in order to subtract 6 ones from 12 ones. In subtracting 90 from 172, they think of 172 as 17 tens and 2 ones in order to subtract 9 tens from 17 tens. Or let us take an example from the rationale of computation with fractions. In order to add 1/2 and 1/3 there is a need to arrive at fractions with like denominators. Other names for these fractions can be found. It can be seen that 1/2 and 3/6 are names for the same fraction, and 1/3 and 2/6 are names for the same fraction. By using 3/6 for 1/2 and 2/6 for 1/3, the principle may then be applied:

```
0       1/2        1
L_____|_____J

0    1/3  2/3       1
L_____|____|_____J

0   2/6 3/6         1
L__|__|__|__|__|__|_J
```

$$\begin{array}{r}
1 \text{ half} = 3 \text{ sixths} \\
+ 1 \text{ third} = 2 \text{ sixths} \\
\hline
5 \text{ sixths}
\end{array}$$ or $1/2 + 1/3 = 3/6 + 2/6 = 5/6$

Figure 5.2

$$\begin{array}{r}
1 \text{ half} = 3 \text{ sixths} \\
+ 1 \text{ third} = 2 \text{ sixths} \\
\hline
5 \text{ sixths}
\end{array}$$ or $1/2 + 1/3 = 3/6 + 2/6 = 5/6$

Mathematical sentences   The use of *number sentences and variables* as a help in modifying procedures of teaching mathematics has been promoted by the new mathematics. They aid in formulating clear statements of mathematical relations. The use of number sentences and variables, forerunner of work with algebra, not only makes for a good introduction to the important area of mathematics but also provides a practical and superior learning procedure . . . .

Multiple approaches and discovery   Perhaps the chief contribution of the new mathematics in the area of teaching procedures is the emphasis upon *discovery* and *multiple approaches* as means to *understanding*. While, as already noted, the importance of these ideas had been advocated, the procedures had not been generally utilized until the new mathematics movement appeared.

"FIND OUT FOR YOURSELF"

To develop meaning through discovery and multiple approaches, modern programs advocate a problem solving or "find out for yourself" approach to learning arithmetical operations. The emphasis is upon many solutions to problems, the demonstration of the correctness of answers and critical examination of arithmetical operations by pupils.

To illustrate, the following problem could be used in the initial presentation of multiplication of whole numbers: "Bill put 6 pencils in each of 4 pencil boxes. How many pencils did he put away?" The children would be asked to find the answer and show that the answer was correct. They might respond by making marks and counting, adding, using dot arrays or number line representation. Pupils would be given time to figure out and to evaluate the procedures which had been presented. They would be asked to explore the workings of the procedures and their merits. The difference between addition and multiplication operations would be determined with direction upon the identification of the number question. Four 6's equal how many? (four 6's = ?; $4 \times 6 = \square$). In the exploratory study, various forms of multiplication language would be used, such as "How many are four 6's? Four 6's equal what number?" and "When 6 is taken 4 times, what is the total?" In the study (analysis) of what is done, the operation would be identified. Further questions would be posed: "How is multiplication superior to addition? To counting? What do we do when we multiply two numbers? What would be a good way to verify answers to a multiplication question?"

Questions of this type provide a *setting* for genuine discovery. They give direction to pupil efforts and are a strong motivating factor to self-initiated exploration. It is not enough to supply primarily numerical and symbolic material that constitutes only the mathematical skeleton. The idea of discovery, or perhaps more properly rediscovery, is effective when the discovery is guided carefully to provide reasonable assurance that accurate conclusions can be reached without endless delay and discouragement.

ALTERNATE SOLUTIONS

Using several solutions to a quantitative situation is an integral part of the preceding method. This idea places emphasis upon pupil activity, leading to development of new facts and processes. Pupils who have had experience with various ways of finding answers when faced initially with the question, "How many are four 6's," may use such procedures as multiplication (that is, just thinking 24 is the equivalent of 4 sixes), adding, counting, number line representations, use of drawings. Some pupils might make use of distributive property of multiplication over addition (that is, two 6's = 12 and two more 6's = 12; then $12 + 12 = 24$). This would provide an excellent foundational experience for further development of this important property of multiplication.

Pupil's own experiences and knowledge, rather than teacher or textbook explanation, becomes the basis for understanding as we move from the "telling method" to "figure out the new from the old." In the "figure it out for yourself" approach, pupils are encouraged to ask themselves, "What idea, principle and skills have I learned from arithmetic that will be useful to me in this new situation?" This is entirely different from being given a set of exercises and told what to do and how to do it. A child who has been taught with a discovery approach, if asked to find 15×38 without having multiplied by two-digit factors might say, "I can do it. It may take me a long time but I would just add 38 fifteen times." Another pupil might say, "I can do it easier. I'd add 38 and 38 and 38 and get 114 and then I would add 114 five times." Understanding of a procedure is seldom acquired by just being told about the procedure.

The use of multiple solutions is not limited to initial teaching of operations. Alternate solutions can be utilized as ways of checking, for example:

$$
\begin{array}{c}
\boxed{\begin{array}{r}
17 \\
\hline
5)\overline{85} \\
50 \\
\hline
35 \\
35 \\
\hline
\end{array}}
\end{array}
$$

a.
$$
\begin{array}{r}
17 \\
\times 5 \\
\hline
85
\end{array}
$$

b.
$$
\begin{array}{r}
8 \\
\times 5 \\
\hline
40
\end{array}
$$

$$
\begin{array}{r}
9 \\
\times 5 \\
\hline
45 \\
+40 \\
\hline
85
\end{array}
$$

c.
$$
\begin{array}{r}
8 \\
+9 = 17 \\
\hline
5)\overline{85} \\
-45 \\
\hline
40 \\
-40 \\
\hline
\end{array}
$$

d. $85 = 40 + 40 + 5$

$$\frac{8}{5)\overline{40}} + \frac{8}{5)\overline{40}} + \frac{1}{5)\overline{5}}$$

$$85 \div 5 = 8 + 8 + 1 = 17$$

1 ten   7 ones

e. $5)\overline{85}$

$$
\begin{array}{r}
50 + 10 \\
\hline
35 \\
35 + 7 \\
\hline
17
\end{array}
$$

f. $5)\overline{8 \text{ tens } 5 \text{ ones}} = 5)\overline{5 \text{ tens } 35 \text{ ones}}$

g. $85 \div 5 = (50 + 35) \div 5 = (50 \div 5) + (35 \div 5) = 10 + 7 = 17$

Such verifying not only makes for understanding of facts and operations but builds a pupil's confidence in his arithmetical ability. Frequently pupils are told: "Find the answer. Then check by using different ways of finding it." Or they are asked, "Three solutions were offered today by pupils. Who found the simplest way?" or "What is the best way of checking the answer?" Varied ways of checking answers provide an excellent vehicle for the development of important properties about the operations (as can be noted by study of the division checks cited above) through discussion of the question, "Can you figure out what was done?"

Alternate solutions may be used during a mastery study period to show understanding of an operation, for example:

"Suggest other pairs of numbers equal to numbers, as $7 = 4 + 3$."

"Think of all pairs of numbers which could replace the frames to make each a true statement as, $\square + \triangle = 10$."

"Illustrate two different ways to find the sum of 13 and 9."

"Use subtraction, dot drawing, and number line to find the answer to $28 \div 7$."

Another use of multiple procedures is in thought-type questions. For example:

"What are three good ways to check a subtraction such as $547 - 128 = 319$?"

"How many different ways can be used to show that $7 \times 3 = 3 \times 7$?"

"What are three 'long ways' of multiplying 21×46?"

"What are some ways to show that quotients are correct?" Use $91 \div 7$ to demonstrate your suggestions."

The use of such thought-provoking questions not only results in better understanding of a topic but provides a good way to summarize and review that which has been studied.

Finally, in upper grades representation of the basic operations through different types of situations promotes understanding. An illustration of a fresh approach that provides opportunity for relearning and extension would be a situation such as this:

"What did Bill think when he did his subtraction this way?"

$$
\begin{array}{cc}
41 & 44 \\
& \rightarrow \\
-17 & -20 \\
\hline
& 24
\end{array}
$$

The important property of subtraction utilized here may be generalized as $a - b = (a + c) - (b + c)$.

SUMMARY OF SUGGESTED PROCEDURES

While the suggested procedures are not efficacious for all learning, they are in the minds of most good teachers associated with superior learning procedures. They are practical implications of modern theories of learning emphasizing discovery and understanding ahead of operational skills and stimulating interest in the subject of elementary school mathematics. While there are some inherent weaknesses in such procedures (*i.e.*, not all can be discovered by the pupil, nor will all pupils make the discovery), such procedures provide direction and are a strong motivating factor for pupil efforts. In this setting pupils are encouraged to investigate in the best sense of the word. There is truly a spirit of inquiry when situations create a need for a better solution and for new knowledge and when this need is felt by the pupil. As often as possible, contemporary mathematics should be taught in such a way that:

1. Children are helped to realize a need for learning something new. This can be promoted by giving pupils verbal problem situations which challenge them to figure out the best solution rather than requiring them to hear an explanation of each step and then to imitate the model.

2. Children are challenged to think and given time to think. This opportunity can be provided through procedures which develop independence, confidence and self-initiative. Concrete and semi-concrete materials may be used as needed by pupils.

3. Various procedures are encouraged through use of methods the pupil already knows. Here the arithmetic the pupil knows serves as the basis for new learning. This approach provides the basis for testing solutions, evaluation and discussion. The children do the showing and telling—not the teacher. Ways of checking and verifying answers also provide wide opportunity for multiple procedures.

4. Important relationships and concepts are discovered by the child. He draws his own conclusions and generalizations after experiences which equip him to do so. Questions, activities and discussion can provide the setting for discovery of important facts and relationships. The textbook can provide a check on his generalizations and conclusions. At all times, teacher guidance is provided in helping pupils note relationships and to generalize to the best of their ability.

Perhaps the new methodology is best expressed by Jones[2] with his two axioms:

Axiom 1. The best learning is that in which the learned facts, concepts, and processes are meaningful to and understood by the learner.

Axiom 2. Understanding and meaningfulness are rarely if ever "all or none" insights in either the sense of being achieved instantaneously or in the sense of embracing the whole of a concept and its implications at one time. Langford[3] offers these suggestions to mathematics teachers:

"The effective teacher of mathematics encourages creativity by helping pupils discover the basic idea, laws, or principles of mathematics; he aims for understanding ahead of skills of operation; and he seeks to give students a stimulation that comes from accepting and realizing worthwhile goals."

In brief, good pedagogy is required at all levels of instruction in mathematics. Methods are "good" to the extent that they achieve desirable goals. If the goals of today's program in elementary mathematics are to develop better pupil attitudes, more understanding, better thinking and greater independence, then to use methods which would fall short of the mark would be to deprive the child of his birthright.

Readers interested in further study of methodology are encouraged to read such publications as the following:

Brueckner, L. J., and Grossnickle, F. E. *Discovering Meanings in Elementary School Mathematics*, 4th ed., New York: Holt, Rinehart & Winston, 1963.

[2] Philip S. Jones, "The Growth of Mathematical Ideas Grades K-12," *Twenty-fourth Yearbook*, National Council of Teachers of Mathematics, 1959, Chapter 1, p. 1.

[3] Francis G. Langford, Jr., "The Growth of Mathematical Ideas Grade K-12," *Twenty-fourth Yearbook*, National Council of Teachers of Mathematics, 1959, Chapter 10.

Corle, Clyde G. *Teaching Mathematics in Elementary School.* New York: Ronald Press, 1964.

Spitzer, Herbert F. *The Teaching of Arithmetic*, 3d ed., Boston: Houghton Mifflin Co., 1961.

Swenson, Esther, *Teaching Arithmetic to Children.* New York: Macmillan Co., 1964.

6 FLOW CHARTING THE COMPONENTS OF TEACHING STRATEGY

William R. Arnold

BEFORE YOU READ   Every teacher has at some time read or been
told that it is his responsibility to provide meaningful learning activities,
use a variety of methods, and meet unique pupil needs. Too often, what
is meant by the clichés "meaningful learning activity," "variety of
methods," and "meeting unique pupil needs" is not delineated. Teachers
who are expected to learn such clichés without understanding them decry
professional courses. What is worse, teachers may not realize that teacher
behavior in the classroom may be inadequate simply because specifics of
the teaching task have not been spelled out.

Against this background it seems reasonable to assume that each
time teachers meet with pupils and attempt to help them to learn,
decisions are made. These decisions may often involve minimal thought
regarding the environment in which learning will occur, what the pupils
are supposed to learn, how they learn, and what the teacher can do to
prompt the learning. When teachers have a system for making decisions
in advance which result in unique strategies for a lesson, the resultant
teaching is likely to be successful. The system must possess features that
enable a teacher to make lesson plans in a manner consistent with modern
learning theory, delineate clearly what is to be taught, and engage
children in an active manner.

The next article focuses on a functional model teachers can use for
planning daily lessons. Since the time available for planning varies,
strategies can be more or less complex. Upon completion of the article
the teacher should be able to describe the categories of moves available,
diagram the general schematic for flow charting a lesson plan, and use the
schematic as a model for developing useful lessons from mathematical
ideas in the subsequent sections.

In attempting to improve the teaching of mathematics, educators have
developed numerous approaches. Consequently, a large number of materials,
textbooks, and teaching procedures have been made available. The new

---

This article is a revision of an original manuscript, accepted for publication in *School Science
and Mathematics*. Professor Arnold teaches at Colorado State College.

developments are exciting; many of them are helpful. To some extent, as new approaches have been developed and research has been done to determine their relative effectiveness, little information has been made available to teachers with regard to how they can or should alter their specific classroom behavior as the need arises.

Regardless of the approach used, a teacher makes a sequence of moves which determine what pupils do during a mathematics lesson. The nature of instruction provided and the tasks assigned basically determined what the teacher wants the pupils to learn. The environment in which learning occurs can facilitate or hinder learning. Collectively, learning; teacher moves; environment; and examples, exercises, or problems are the basic aspects of a teaching strategy about which a teacher must make decisions before a lesson is presented. When the instructor considers, quite specifically, a series of questions—what the pupils should learn; where the lesson will occur; what materials will be used; what moves will be executed; what examples, patterns, or exercises, if any, will be used—he is able to develop a unique teaching strategy for each lesson.

The approach reflected by a strategy will vary as the teaching situation changes. In all cases a strategy that is developed in this manner emphasizes a teacher's unique competencies. The purpose of this article is to discuss a functional model for developing teaching strategies. The lesson plans which reflect teaching strategies are written in flow-chart form, simple enough to be developed in the amount of time normally available for planning and still provide adequate cues to instruction.

When a teacher enters a classroom there are six types of moves he can utilize. Five of these should directly enable children to learn. At least the intent in making them is to enable children to learn. The sixth move deals with classroom management. While this is not noted on the flow chart, it is assumed the teacher will manage children in a humane and sensible manner, one that will not make them feel less adequate as human beings. To facilitate learning the teacher can make an exposition move, an illustration move, a demonstration move, a discussion move, or an exploration move. By varying the utilization of moves and the sequencing of moves the teacher can systematically and creatively attempt to facilitate learning. A brief description of the moves is provided below. There is no implicit significance in the order in which they are discussed.

EXPOSITION MOVES

The teacher is making an exposition move when he is explaining an idea or a procedure. A lecture is the classic example of exposition. That is, the teacher is giving information verbally. The assumption in using an exposition move is that the child can learn by listening and subsequently reinforcing what he hears. This type of move has been soundly criticized in educational literature. Yet the notion that people do not learn by listening is ridiculous. What needs to be understood is that exposition moves should not be used all the time or over long periods of time with young children.

ILLUSTRATION MOVES

The teacher is making an illustration move when he is showing the children a physical model, a drawing, a picture, a filmstrip, or motion picture. There may be some nominal accompanying talk but the emphasis is on the visual presentation of an idea or procedure. The assumption in using an illustration move is that the child can learn by looking and subsequently reinforcing what he has seen.

DEMONSTRATION MOVES

The teacher or a pupil is making a demonstration move when he is actively explaining and showing a procedure in a related manner. The assumption in using a demonstration move is that the child can learn by concomitantly listening and looking, and subsequently reinforcing by imitation the technique that has been demonstrated.

DISCUSSION MOVES

The teacher is making a discussion move when he is asking questions and encouraging students to ask questions. That is, there is verbal interaction of an inquiry-response type between the teacher and the children. This type of move is known to be effective for motivating topics, review, discovery, and clarification of ideas.

EXPLORATION MOVES

The teacher is making an exploration move when he gives directions which outline a task children are to undertake. Exploration moves either terminate direct teacher control of a learning situation and set children to work independently, or cause children sequentially to complete tasks in accordance with the teacher's instructions. The tasks may be as simple as reinforcing an idea by completing a worksheet, or as complex as solving a difficult problem or conducting some research. This type of task is designed to extend the pupils' ability to function. In another sense an exploration move may be designed to collect samples of a child's work in order to diagnose where to begin or how to continue a given topic, or to determine the extent to which certain objectives have been achieved. Exploration moves are very complex; it is absolutely necessary to use them because they determine and shape what a child is actually permitted to learn. Since what a child actually learns is determined by himself, the extent to which exploration moves are imaginative, creative, and suited to the intended learning shapes the extent of what the pupil learns and the extent to which this coincides with what the teacher had in mind.

CLASS MANAGEMENT MOVES

The teacher is making a class-management move when he is using commands or gestures to manage pupil behavior. These involve noninstructional actions such as going to recess, taking lunch count, determining time and place of instruction, and disciplining a child. The nature of class-management moves that are utilized determines the extent to which a child is free to do things.

In developing a flow-chart lesson plan learning is stated in terms which suggest behaviors the child should subsequently demonstrate to indicate that the desired learning occurred. This is important because it suggests sequences of moves to the teacher which are likely to succeed and helps determine the examples or patterns to be utilized. Further, it increases the probability that what the teacher wants the pupils to learn and what they actually learn will coincide. For example, a teacher might want to present a lesson on the distributive property. The phrase, "using distributive property to do written computations involving one and two digit factors," suggests what the lesson should accomplish and the level for which it is appropriate. As another example the statement, "the child should understand indirect measurement," does not suggest a specific focus for a lesson. The statement, "the child is able to use proportions to measure heights indirectly," provides a better focus for a lesson. An objective for a lesson, then, is a specific statement of what the child should be able to do.

During the planning of a lesson care should be given to the selection of examples, exercises, or problems which will be used to promote learning. To illustrate, suppose a group of pupils is to learn how to do written multiplications involving two-digit factors. The examples used for demonstration purposes and the exercises subsequently used for reinforcement should accommodate the range in ability of the pupils and still facilitate learning. Some examples which could be utilized in this lesson are:

(1.) $N = 13 \times 21 = (10 + 3)(20 + 1) = (10 \cdot 20 + 10 \cdot 1)$
$+ (3 \cdot 20 + 3 \cdot 1) = 200 + 10 + 60 + 3 = 200 + 70 + 3 = 273$

$$
\begin{array}{llll}
(2.) & \begin{array}{r} 56 \\ \times\ 64 \\ \hline \end{array} \sim \begin{array}{r}(50+6) \\ (60+4) \\ \hline \end{array} \sim \begin{array}{r} 3000 \\ 360 \\ 200 \\ 24 \\ \hline 3584 \end{array} &
(3.) \begin{array}{r} 16 \\ \times\ 12 \\ \hline 12 \\ 20 \\ 60 \\ 100 \\ \hline 192 \end{array} &
(4.) \begin{array}{r} 97 \\ \times\ 85 \\ \hline 485 \\ 776 \\ \hline 8245 \end{array}
\end{array}
$$

There are noticeable differences between these examples. Each one illustrates a procedure for multiplying two numbers. Consequently, the particular examples used by the teacher would depend on how the lesson was motivated. Practice exercises should be provided that are at least as easy as the third example and as difficult as the fourth example. One way to provide for individual differences is to let each pupil in the group complete some, but not all, of the assigned exercises.

The same principles can be applied to problems that are assigned. That is, the teacher should assign problems that can promote desired learning. He should include easy and difficult problems in the assignment and should let each pupil elect to solve some, but not all, of the assigned problems. Quite often the difference between a dull or an exciting lesson depends on the examples, exercises, and problems utilized.

There is increased demand for the teacher to consider environments other than the classroom for learning mathematics. Children are going to resource centers, computers, and laboratories. The teacher should attempt to select an environment which will facilitate learning. Since teaching situations vary immensely, this should be done by attempting to make appropriate use of all available resources. For example, the teaching of conventional procedures for computation can be accomplished in the classroom, while finding a solution to a problem might require the children to go outside to take measurements. Increasingly, teaching machines can perform expository functions, thereby freeing the teacher for discussion and exploration moves. There are numerous materials and textbooks available and their use should be determined by existing needs.

There is no magic place to begin a flow-chart lesson plan. A teacher might decide to vary his routine by going to a mathematics laboratory. He might then consider the equipment available, think of an idea the equipment can be used to promote, and outline a sequence of moves to make or pose a problem for solution. At other times a flow-chart lesson might begin when a teacher consolidates the ideas of several related pages of a textbook, considers the examples to be used, and selects moves to be made in the classroom. The essence of flow-charting lessons is that the teacher builds daily teaching strategies which enable him to vary the routine and are suited to intended learning. Several lessons devoted to rote learning and drill can be made relevant by moving to a related laboratory experience. Other lessons dealing with problem solving can be used to point out the need for learning some more routine procedures.

To begin flow-charting lessons the teacher should select an idea in mathematics with which he is familiar and write it down in terms of what the child should do. Then he should think of several possible sequences of moves and write down one that seems to have success potential. During this time the teacher should account for the examples, exercises or problems, and materials to be used. Good initial results are achieved if the lesson is simple and occurs in the classroom. As the teacher gains proficiency, more complex lessons can be planned and taught. With a little practice and study most pre-service and in-service teachers can become strategists who systematically vary their teaching style, expose children to all of the mathematics curriculum allocated to them, and make the instruction appropriate to learning.

Flow Chart Lesson Plan (Generalized form)

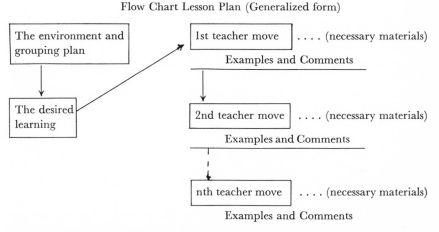

Figure 6.1 Flow-chart lesson plan, generalized form. *Note:* In a complete plan there may be several desired things to learn. These would be listed on the left with arrows leading to appropriate moves or with new moves noted.

The flow-chart lesson plans which follow were developed and successfully taught by pre-service and in-service teachers. They reflect some desirable differences in style. The intent in presenting them is to let the reader see how aspects of a teaching strategy are composed to form a unique plan for teaching.

The essence of Flow-Chart Lesson Plan No. 1 is that the teacher uses a pattern illustrated on the board so that the children discover negative integers. He decides that letting the children explore the pattern and then discuss possibilities would best accomplish his objectives. Perhaps some of the pupils' comments will include: "It can't be done"; "Minus one"; "One less"; and so on. If any feasible answer is given, the teacher writes down -1. The discussion is pursued to get at the subtractions $5 - 7$, $5 - 8$ . . . and the solutions $^-2$, $^-3$ . . . . If the discussion is successful, the teacher will explain the numbers $^-1$, $^-2$, $^-3$ . . . have the names "negative one," "negative two," "negative three," and so on, because it is unlikely the child can discover these conventional names. The implication in the lesson is that discussing patterns which have been explored can be a powerful aid to discovery. This lesson was taught successfully to a group of first-grade children late in the school year.

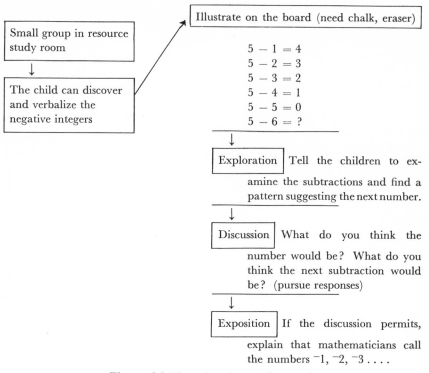

Figure 6.2 Flow-chart lesson plan no. 1

Not every idea in mathematics is subject to discovery. For example, the algorithms which facilitate computation are, for the most part, conventionalized procedures to be learned. The Flow-Chart Lesson Plan No. 2 deals with an intermediate algorithm for multiplication.

The primary intent of this lesson is to give the child a tool which will facilitate computation. Therefore, the teacher proceeds in a straightforward manner. Since part of the lesson deals with practice and providing individual help, the assignment given to the children plays a major role.

The focus of Flow-Chart Lesson Plan No. 3 is on a problem. The teacher wants the children to use knowledge and skills previously learned with as little help as possible. He is attempting to minimize the number of moves he makes, and maximize the role of the child as director of his own actions. This is a type of lesson which should be developed often in order to maintain interest and to make the mathematics program meaningful.

Through the use of flow-chart lesson plans the teacher can bring a degree of precision to planning which permits him to develop sequences of related lessons where he is at times active, at times passive, occasionally uses a textbook, sometimes uses the mathematics laboratory, and in general is meeting pupil needs.

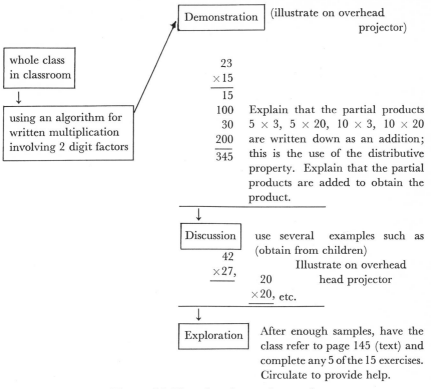

Figure 6.3 Flow-chart lesson plan no. 2

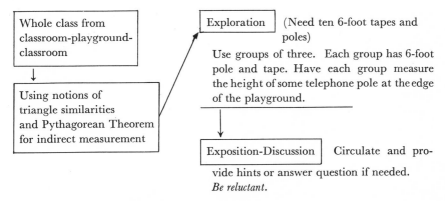

Figure 6.4 Flow-chart lesson plan no. 3

The pre-service and in-service teacher should be able to work out the task of teaching a mathematics lesson, develop a flow-chart lesson plan written in a form suggested by the general model, and subsequently use the plan to teach the lesson. When the lesson has been taught, the teacher can and should assess the effectiveness of the particular teaching strategy, and either proceed to develop new lessons or enlarge on the lesson already taught.

SECTION II

Basic Mathematical
Language: Constructing
Ideas Symbolically

"The Mathematicians are a sort of Frenchmen; when you talk to them, they immediately translate it into their own language, and right away it is something utterly different."

—Goethe

Introduction

63

INTRODUCTION

A young child will compare himself with his mother and remark that he is smaller. Within this statement there is the genesis of an idea in mathematics that is rediscovered by each generation of children. The idea is called an order relation. For example, in the comparison above the child faces the complex task of considering his size as an amount which may be represented by a symbol X. Next he must consider his mother's size, an amount represented by a symbol Y. Ultimately he can represent the relationship in the abstract form, $X < Y$. By doing this the child learns the language of mathematics. It is something he will do throughout his formal mathematics education. Clearly, if the child is to accomplish this learning task he will need help from teachers.

Unmistakably, mathematics is a language. In one sense it is a set of symbols, each representing an abstract idea. That is, a person can learn to rely on mathematical symbols instead of words in his thinking. The person who uses the language of mathematics to write a statement is recording his thinking just as surely as the person who uses French or English to write a sentence. For example, examine the following statement:

$$\forall \times \Sigma R, \exists! \ ^-X\Sigma R\Xi X + \ ^-X = \ ^-X + X = 0$$

Translated into English the sentence reads: "For every number in the set of real numbers, there exists a unique inverse such that their sum is zero, regardless of the order in which the two numbers are added." This example of using the language of mathematics clearly represents an economy of effort and a saving of space. More important, symbols, when considered in context, have precise meanings. This is one reason why mathematics is thought of as an exact science. Unfortunately, this may also be the cause of some of the difficulty one encounters in learning mathematics.

When assisting the child to learn the language of mathematics the teacher has at least three important tasks. First, he must know and be able to use the language. One good way to do this is to learn as the children learn, so that the teacher can begin to think of himself as a student of the language of mathematics. Second, the teacher must skillfully select the referents to be used by children when attaching meaning to symbols. For example, some suitable referents for the symbol "3" might be or "three fingers." Third, the teacher must insure that symbols are learned for some greater purpose. As an example, one does not learn the notation for a triangle is *ABC* without later using the notation in some meaningful exploration of triangles. Neglect of the latter aspect of learning the language of mathematics can result in a meaningless emphasis on language.

The professional teacher, in attempting to learn the language of mathematics, should ferret out and develop activities which enable the child to learn the language of mathematics through active utilization. This means that activities which enable the child to gather and process data are likely to be more appropriate than activities which force the child to provide specific responses. For example, children are often expected to complete exercises such as $5 + 3 = \square$. It may be beneficial to have children do this. But it is equally beneficial to engage pupils in activities which let them determine what the 5 and 3 represent, to write the equation $5 + 3 = \square$, to solve it, and to test the validity of the solution.

This Section contains articles which discuss the need for precision in learning mathematical terminology from logical, psychological, and lexical viewpoints. It should enable the teacher to understand more clearly the role of language in teaching mathematics.

7 SEMANTICS AND MATHEMATICS

M. Wiles Keller

BEFORE YOU READ   Elementary school pupils are regularly asked to complete arithmetic assignments. To do this they write symbols such as 5, =, %, and (3, 6). Presumably what the pupils write is meaningful, but often this is not the case. Some of the difficulty may be caused by pupil carelessness or indifference. Part of the difficulty may be caused by teachers who are inadvertently using symbols incorrectly to express mathematical ideas. For example, teachers could easily write an incorrect statement on the blackboard like $3 = \{a, b, c\} = \{\Delta, \Delta, \Delta\}$ when the correct statement would have been $n\{a, b, c\} = 3$. That is, "3" is the cardinal number of the set containing the elements a, b, c. Meaning is not enhanced when both the teacher and pupils do not understand precisely what is meant by the symbols they are using.

To some extent finding a solution to the problem of meaning in mathematics depends on the selection of appropriate referents for symbols, and subsequently establishing relationships between symbols and the context in which they are used. It is important to note that there must first be exploration of an idea before a child is likely to be able to associate the idea with a symbol or word in a meaningful way. The extent to which one should demonstrate a functional ability to use symbols at the expense of understanding them is debatable.

The next article by Professor Keller deals with the degree to which the language of mathematics can, and should, be made clear to children. By considering the problems associated with helping the child to understand terminology, the teacher should gain perspective in regard to the difficulties encountered in using language to make mathematical ideas meaningful. As a result of reading this article the teacher should be able to describe the role of vocabulary in teaching mathematics and to list at least three examples which illustrate the difficulties a learner encounters in relating language and mathematics meaningfully.

A revision of a talk given to the Mathematics Section of the Indiana State Teachers Association in Indianapolis in October of 1966; and reprinted in *School Science and Mathematics*, vol. 68, no. 2 (February 1968), pp. 103–113. Professor Keller is at Purdue University in Lafayette, Indiana.

It is not unusual to hear during discussions of the proposed curriculum revisions for the elementary and secondary schools the statement made that semantics is one of the problems. As a consequence semantics and mathematics appears to be an appropriate topic to consider. Before proceeding with such a discussion our first step should be to give a precise meaning to our subject. Let us consider first the word, mathematics. There have been many attempts to define what mathematics is. No definition that I know is completely satisfactory. However, let us assume that we know what is meant by mathematics.

Let us then turn to the word, semantics. There are, of course, several definitions given in the dictionary. The two principal ones I found were:

1. The science of meanings, as contrasted with phonetics, the science of sounds: the historical and psychological study and the classification of changes in the significance of words or forms, viewed as normal and vital factors in linguistic development.

    Had this definition stopped at the colon I might have been able to use it for this discussion. The amplifying phrases left no doubt that I was not prepared to use this definition in relation to mathematics.

2. The science dealing with relations between symbols and what they refer to and with human behavior in reaction to symbols, including unconscious attitudes, influences of social institutions and linguistic assumptions, and having as an objective the systemization of the language of science and the unification of knowledge.

    This definition is not appropriate either. It was at this point I decided that it would better serve my purpose to leave the problems implied by these definitions for others to pursue, and to introduce a new title—

What are you saying? What are you doing?

The very nature of language encourages, in a sense, misinterpretation and misunderstanding. You all are, I am confident, most familiar with this problem. You can sometimes read something carefully and then reread it and still be uncertain as to exactly what the writer had in mind. You can go to a lecture with a friend and when the lecture is over, you will find that you and your friend did not get the same interpretation from the lecturer's remarks.

As a matter of fact the twist in meaning and interpretation is the basis for some of our humor. Let me illustrate.

A lady was stopped for speeding. The first step, as some of you may know from first-hand experience, is a request from the officer for your driver's license. The lady's license was a restricted one stating that she was required to wear glasses when driving.

The officer not seeing any glasses asked where her glasses were.

She replied—But officer I have contacts.

To which the officer replied—I don't care who your friends are I'm giving you a ticket.

Or the man who enquired in a shoe store if they had any loafers. To which the floorman answered—Yes we have quite a number. I'll see if I can get one to wait on you.

Again—wife excitedly—Doctor do hurry! My husband is at death's door. To which the cooperative doctor replied—Don't worry we'll pull him through.

The problem of words has become a major issue in mathematics with the introduction of the so-called new or modern mathematics. As a matter of fact so much emphasis has been placed on words and the distinction between words at times that the real reason for the emphasis—better understanding—has all too often been lost in the shuffle of words.

At this point I should like to underline that good teachers that I have known throughout my learning experience and teaching career have always been concerned with the problem of understanding. This objective—and a worthy one—is not something that came in with the new mathematics nor does it necessarily follow, if you use a modern text, that your students will understand. This observation no doubt is redundant in talking to this group. But here is a real danger. As a matter of fact it can happen all too easily— that one set of memory exercises is merely substituted for another with the glib replies lulling you into the belief that the students now understand when actually the responses are as rote as the rule—To divide fractions: invert the divisor and multiply. Actually the rule had some virtue in that it gave the correct answer when properly applied even though the student did not understand the reason for rule, because correct answers are important if our planes are to fly, bridges not fall, etc. There is little virtue in merely understanding mathematics if it cannot be used to obtain correct answers as most of your students will use it as a tool; not as mathematics for mathematics sake.

Let me illustrate this thesis.

Last spring a graduate student, in engineering, needed to evaluate a double integral. The integral was of such a nature that it was not immediately evident how one could perform the integrations without resorting to approximation methods which he wished to avoid if possible. A little experimentation indicated that the integrand likely would simplify to a form that could be integrated if certain substitutions were made.

Substitution in a single definite integral is quite simple, but, as you know, this is not true for a multiple integral. Jacobians are involved along with other problems. Interestingly enough this student knew with precision the theorem he needed to use and I think he might have been able to prove it—at least he seemed to understand the theorem. However, he did not know how to apply the theorem to the solution of the specific problem.

This example illustrates a real danger—developing students who can prove interesting theorems, can even identify where the theorem applies but cannot use it to solve a problem.

What are you doing? What are you saying? Am I saying that proofs are not important? Of course not. If a student is to have an appreciation of mathematics it is important for him to know what constitutes a proof and some experience in constructing a proof. However, in the long run, constructing proofs is a job for the professional mathematician. It is often difficult and tricky business and can, at times, try the patience and skill of the most competent of mathematicians.

No, what I am saying is that being able to construct and/or understand a proof is not enough because most of the students taking mathematics will be consumers not creators of mathematics. I say, they must also be able to solve problems. When a student can solve a problem using a theorem then I say he really understands the theorem. Naturally I must qualify this statement because there are theorems such as existence theorems which must be excluded. Thus, the establishment of the existence of a differential equation may give one no clue as to how one might obtain the solution.

With the current emphasis on structure—what are you doing? What are you saying to be certain your students really understand and are not just responding to a pattern? Let me illustrate this with an experience I had this past year as a Visiting Scientist.

In one of the discussions that I used I talked about moving three pieces of furniture—a radio, television, and sofa—about in a room. The purpose was to develop with the students a model of a simple but non-trivial mathematical system and to determine its characteristics by experimentation.

Dispensing with details we found we needed to define symbols. Thus

$$\begin{bmatrix} R & S & T \\ T & R & S \end{bmatrix}$$

meant to place the table where the radio was, etc. From this we investigated the number of possible arrangements (these, of course, form a set) and the need to designate each by a single symbol for simplicity. From this we went to the idea of doing one arrangement followed by a second arrangement. When we had done this we found it was another one of the possible arrangements and thus we came up with the idea of closure.

At this point it was agreed it would be convenient to have a symbolic way to express this procedure. With strong leadership we agreed to write

$$A + B = C \text{ where } C \text{ is a member of the set.}$$

It was natural to enquire what

$$B + A = ?$$

You can guess what many said—They said it was equal to C. When I asked why it was equal to C they said because of the commutative property even though I had been careful to state that, although we were using a "plus" sign, they should understand that it was certainly not addition in the ordinary sense.

Now the words, commutative property, are a real nice set of words and this immediate response probably is a result of our recent excursion into modern mathematics although I cannot be certain.

What is the problem? I say the students who made this response just do not understand but they have certainly memorized some nice words and can probably spell them. It is my belief that since their experience has been limited to the properties of numbers, they generalize that all systems are commutative with respect to addition. Although many of our newer texts are mathematically better, or should I say more correct, it does not follow that this will provide the students with a better understanding and appreciation of mathematics unless we, as teachers, do something about it. This is difficult because from your student's experience where is the problem with

$$(a + b)c \text{ and } c(a + b)?$$

Can you make this meaningful to your students?

What are you saying? What are you doing?

I am a bit concerned about this emphasis on structure in some proposals and books before the student has had sufficient experience to be ready to understand and to appreciate structure. These are unifying concepts and to me you have something to unify first. Please note I said emphasis on structure—it is not structure but the emphasis I am concerned about. As a matter of fact in recent months others are expressing similar ideas.

The following quote is from the September 1966 issue of "Manpower Comments."

"A symposium on mathematics at Rutgers University at the end of August apparently concluded that the new mathematics is not completely effective. Some teachers are poorly trained in its use: the use of abstraction is excessive; the courses include unnecessary terminology. On the other hand, the mathematical community is proud of the progress made in introducing modern mathematical ideas into pre-college courses, and in helping students understand the why as well as the how of mathematical operations. They feel that future changes will and should be in the same direction, though probably at a slower pace than the past ten years."

As an aside I should like to observe that this word understanding as it relates to mathematics is an interesting word. Consider the field postulate.

For every element "a" of the set, except for the additive identity element, there exists an element "a^{-1}" of the set such that $a \cdot a^{-1} =$ the identity element for multiplication.

Consider next the rule—To divide fractions invert the divisor and multiply.

I presume, if we apply the field axiom correctly, this represents understanding while, if we follow the rule for division of fractions correctly, this represents rote learning. The line is fine.

What are you saying? What are you doing?

Another comment. In a book review on "The Prelude to Analysis" by Rosenbloom and Schuster, G.R. Rising, Mathematics Director for the Minnesota National Laboratory and a member of the staff of the Minnemath Center writes:

"One serious criticism of the stress on structure in modern mathematics is that formalism often leads to a strong emphasis on the spoon feeding or say after me school of teaching. Students barely comprehending the formal abstractions memorize not only proofs but even problem-solving procedures. Instead of freeing them from thousands of memorized algorithms, structure too often merely substitutes other equally trivial terminology . . . . This misplaced emphasis produces students in a very rigid mold, unable to attack original problems which they cannot fit into their few fixed patterns."

This criticism has the same ring as that leveled at the pre-modern mathematics era. This only serves to point out to me that the important ingredient in getting the students to understand mathematics is the teacher not the curriculum. For many years I have had a philosphy or a thesis which I am convinced is true. It is

Give me a teacher who understands the fundamental ideas of mathematics, and who is enthusiastic about the subject and I care not what the text or the curriculum is and I will show you a class that is learning mathematics—good mathematics.

Without the initial conditions—a good text or curriculum will not produce a class that is learning mathematics. True, I hope, under these adverse conditions a good text is better than a poor one but how much better is difficult to assess.

These comments only serve to emphasize that unless you can get your students to see the unifying and generalizing aspects of structure, structure can be as rote and meaningless to him as any rule.

There are many problems, as each of you know, associated with getting the student to understand the concepts of mathematics. Unfortunately there is no simple, effective panacea—not even the best of the current modern texts—in spite of those who would have you believe they have received the word and that, if you will just follow them, they will lead you into the promised land. A land where almost all students will understand mathematics and thrill to its structural beauty.

Once again I must emphasize that, in the large, I do not disagree with the basic philosophy which undergirds the changes being made in the mathematics curriculum. Today I am discussing some of our problems—

problems that are inherent in the learning process and that are inherent to mathematics.

Words and symbols in mathematics do present a problem in that some uses do tend to confuse the student.

One problem I will call a double use of words and symbols. Let me illustrate with a few examples

> Programming
> linear programming
> orthogonal trajectories
> orthogonal functions

a and the negative of a or the additive inverse of a, often denoted by ^-a

Use of same symbol to denote subtraction and the ultimate in that

$$a + (^-a) = a - a = 0$$

You can think of others. There are many of them. Can't you see how confusing this is to one trying to learn mathematics?

A second problem is a result of word choice that does not conform to common use. For example

> rational number or polynomial
> irrational number
> transcendental number
> complex number
> radical
> imaginary number

to list a few.

The third problem with words arises in our efforts to be precise. Precision or correct use of words in mathematics is a laudable objective to which I subscribe enthusiastically. However, one must be careful because it is possible to overdo or to overemphasize. This can lead to confusion rather than better understanding.

The best known example of this type of problem is the common and thoroughly overworked distinction between number and numeral.

Some handle it simply by saying—numerals are not the same thing as numbers. Numerals are names for numbers. Others get more involved. Thus,

Quotation marks are used to indicate that a symbol is being referred to, while a symbol without quotation marks refers to the object named by that symbol.

Example:

The dial of a watch has 12 on it. Now dial of a watch refers to the object named by those symbols so there are no quotes but 12 should be in quotes since it refers to the symbol not the number!

Or

25 is a number, but "25" is a numeral. Since the first 25 refers to the object named no quotes are needed, while the second 25 refers to a symbol and therefore should be in quotes.

One early experimental program spent some thirty pages working on the problem of distinguishing between number and numeral. The concept certainly has its subtle side. However, after reading the first several pages in this text I feel confident that the students had, at least, a vague understanding of the distinction being made. I also feel fairly confident that, if the student pursued the discussion twenty more pages, he was less certain because with this amount of emphasis the student was being convinced that there was more to this number and numeral distinction than he had originally thought and so he started to look for something more elusive and hence more uncertain as to whether he really understood the difference.

No student will think that the word "cat" is a cat. And on second thought he recognizes that V1, 12/2, etc. are indeed not the number but merely symbols to designate a number.

How far to pursue such things is indeed a problem—because if the student continues into advanced mathematics, he will learn very quickly that the accepted procedure is to ignore the distinction between a symbol and that which it represents. Since this tradition has undoubtedly led to the confusion of many students at certain times some discussion on this point is desirable.

What are you saying? What are you doing? It does get awkward even in relatively simple situations. Thus, consider—

The variable in $X + 7 = 12$ may be replaced by some numeral for a natural number.

Perhaps the ultimate in ultimates is the following statement which it is alleged—I hope not—was used by an instructor teaching a course in the new mathematics.

You will find on the bulletin board a reproduction of the representation that appears on your paper of the numeral which represents the number which is your grade in the course.

The representation problem gets a bit sophisticated in cases such as

$$1.000 \ldots$$

$$0.9999 \ldots$$

where both numerals represent the number one.

Another word which causes trouble is set. Have you looked at texts to learn how different authors handle this sticky wicket? It is an interesting and difficult situation. Most writers will say that we must start somewhere so that set will be taken as undefined. From what goes on in many books after this initial statement suggests that the word will not be defined but that which the word represents will be characterized and described in some detail—just what do you mean by a definition? The final or finishing touch is when the author says that when information is given which permits you to decide if an element is a member of the set, then the set is well-defined.

Words and our efforts to use them so that we will have better understanding will likely always be a problem.

I quote another example from an elementary text, "$-2x + 3y = 6$ is an open statement. The set of all two-component vectors that make the open statement true is defined as the truth set for the open statement."

One cannot argue about the mathematics but I, at least, would question if this approach will give a student a better understanding of what is meant by a solution of this equation. Incidentally your students had best have an opportunity to think of the ordered tuples which form the truth set as solutions because it is inevitable that they will encounter this language if they continue in mathematics or enter fields which use mathematics.

This is one of the basic problems. Much of the literature in mathematics that has been written and that is now being written doesn't make many of these distinctions or does not make them in the same way.

Thus a recent college text, which is being used extensively, uses basically the Dirichlet (1837) definition of a function. This definition states:

If for each value of a variable x, there is determined a value or set of values of another variable y, then y is called a function of x for those values of x. Here you can have multiple value functions.

This illustrates one of our basic semantic problems in mathematics. That is, we do not find agreement.

Another illustration.

Some authors proceed in this manner

In the sentence $x + 7 = 12$ the letter x does not represent any specific number. Others would say that x represents a specific number or set of numbers which makes the sentence true or a true statement.

This causes us to mention or note that some authors thus say that $x + 7 = 12$ is a sentence. However, once you introduce a numeral to replace x say 2 then the result $2 + 7 = 12$ is a statement.

If the replacement for x makes the sentence a true statement then that x-replacement is a solution.

In some texts precision and rigor are so emphasized in dealing with structure that it becomes quite formidable and could well be quite meaningless to students as a consequence of their fairly limited mathematical experience. Let me essentially quote from a recent text.

In addition to the eleven axioms of our real number field, there are three axioms of equality and a well definedness axiom for addition and multiplication. With these 15 assumptions, we can prove all the basic theorems concerning addition, multiplication, subtraction, division, the cancellation properties, and the important properties of 1 and 0.

Certain aspects of this statement are interesting. We could spend some time pulling this gem apart. I encourage you to think about it. But to the point I wish to make. The author then lists the 11 field axioms. These are followed by

$$a = a, \text{ reflexivity}$$

If $a = b$ then $b = a$, symmetry

If $a = b$ and $b = c$ then $a = c$, transitivity

If $a = b$ and $c = d$ then

$a + c = b + d$ and $ac = bd$, well definedness

You, of course, recognize that the first three of these postulates define an equivalence relation. The idea of an equivalence relation is fairly fancy for secondary school students, particularly, if their only experience with a binary relation is that of equality. If that is the limit of the student's experience then I would think that a reasonable, thinking student would wonder what all the shooting is about—and I would say rightfully so. If these statements are to be meaningful, you as his teacher will need to spend considerable time on this concept. You will need to illustrate the meaning of an equivalence relation with a binary relation other than equality.

As a matter of fact, with the equivalence properties of equality and the uniqueness property for addition for integers it is not difficult to prove the well defined relation. All this can be confusing.

At every step each of us tries to teach "good" mathematics. But this is not enough. It should not only be correct but it should also be meaningful and significant to the student in terms of a student's understanding and sophistication. One should not bother him with the obvious.

When I was teaching in high school the first theorem in the text we were using was to prove that vertical angles are equal. For those students, after several attempts in successive years, it was fairly evident to me that proving this theorem did not make any contribution to the student's understanding of the nature of a proof. At that point in time, for those students, with their limited mathematical experience, it was a waste of time because to them I was insisting that they prove the obvious.

Another semantic problem we have is the introduction of new words and symbols in our efforts to improve understanding. I know you can recall several of this kind.

Some more new ones have recently been reported. The report says that teachers tell them that their students (low achievers) cannot seem to remember the words numerator and denominator. Having presumably faced words like commutative, associative, distributive, multiplicative, etc., it was a bit of a shock for me to learn this. Anyway, in order to study the properties of fractions this group has introduced stretching and shrinking machines. They say that these machines are from the world of fantasy but that the machines soon become quite real to the students (fantasy becomes reality!) who find them extremely helpful in doing exercises which are usually guessing games.

These experimenters use these machines with sticks. Thus, a 3-inch stick goes through a 2-machine and comes out a 6-inch stick. This leads to many ingenious things such as a hook-up of several machines. Thus, if we had a hook-up of a 3-machine and a 4-machine a 2-inch stick would go through the hook-up and come out a 24-inch stick. I do not know what would happen if you put in an apple rather than a stick. Perhaps you would get apple-sauce.

Hook-ups such as this, it is observed, are essentially compositions so the notation

$$(3 \cdot 4) \text{ 2-inch stick} \rightarrow \text{24-inch stick}$$

is introduced.

It is noted that by determining machines to be used in a hook-up to get a certain job done, the student has been factoring and these kinds of exercises develop the notion of factoring before the word, factoring, is introduced. Thus, the student, before he sees the word, factoring, learns that factoring is a "fancy way" of describing a familiar (easy) concept—so they say.

As you have guessed, a 6-inch stick goes through a 2-shrinking machine and comes out a 3-inch stick. A symbol is introduced to designate a shrinking machine. So $\bar{2}$ names a machine that shrinks a stick to one-half of its original size. Of course the students discover that a 3-machine and a $\bar{3}$-machine are inverses because the $\bar{3}$-machine undoes what the 3-machine does.

Finally the students are let in on the fact that $a \cdot b$ is simply a "fraction in disguise."

By not following this material through in detail perhaps I am unfair to these experimenters. If so, I apologize.

There are many things involved in this material which you should think about and discuss with your colleagues. Numerators are now stretching machines and denominators are shrinking machines. This is a mnemonic device, it appears to me, that could well improve technique ability in certain operations with fractions. However, it is not clear to me that this procedure will improve the student's understanding of the nature of a fraction as a number. As a matter of fact it could confuse him for it produces an arithmetic for sticks but not apples. At any rate it is truly a problem in semantics.

A recent article relative to an engineering problem stated—

"By not knowing to an ever increasing number of decimal places, great feelings of confidence are generated."

Let me change this statement to

By changing an ever increasing number of words and introducing more gadgets great feelings of confidence are generated:

a) Confidence that it is better mathematics

b) Confidence that these changes will produce understanding.

Change is necessary because it is indicative of our desire to improve the curriculum in mathematics and also it is an indication of our dissatisfaction with the results we have achieved in the past.

Change we must but let us do it critically—both from a mathematical and pedagogical point of view—only then is it good.

There is much to be done. Progress is our most important problem!

8 DEFINITIONS WITHOUT EXCEPTIONS

Charles H. D'Augustine

BEFORE YOU READ   No one would deny that definitions are important in mathematics. The extent to which definitions should be mathematically precise, while remaining pedagogically sound, is less clearly understood. The following article by Professor d'Augustine explores these aspects of mathematical definition by considering the basis for two approaches to the definitions of multiplication. The article demonstrates the importance of consistency in the language of mathematics and the need for teachers to utilize referents which will not have to be discarded or relearned later.

After reading the article the teacher should be able to compare the relative merits of the "cross-product" and "array" definitions of multiplication and describe the weaknesses of "modifying definitions."

Sometimes there exists a conflict between what is mathematically possible and what is pedagogically sound. Mathematicians, in an attempt to justify the inclusion of definitions which continually need modification for the exceptions, use as an argument that it is common practice to start with a basic definition and modify it as the universal set is "enlarged." For example, let the universal set be the set of counting numbers, then $x^n = x_1 x_2 x_3 \ldots x_n$. When the universal set is "enlarged" to the set of whole numbers, then we define $x^0 = 1$ for all x except $x = 0$ (0^0 is left undefined).

Let us examine an instance of this type of "modification for the exceptions" which is found in some elementary school mathematics texts. It is common technique to define the multiplication of two whole numbers in terms of repeated addition. Thus, $3 \times 4 = 4 + 4 + 4 = 12$. Since there does not exist addition without two addends, and repeated addition without at least three addends, in cases where the multiplier is either 0 or 1 or 2 the exceptions are handled by addendum definitions, i.e. $1 \times N = N$, $0 \times N = 0$, and $2 \times N = N + N$.

The author feels that it is better pedagogy to start with a basic definition which provides for the "fewest" possible exceptions as a universe is "enlarged."

Reprinted from *The Mathematics Teacher*, vol. 58, no. 1 (March 1965), pp. 221–222. Professor d'Augustine is at the College of Education at Florida Technical University in Orlando, Florida.

As a case in point, let's examine some definitions for the product of two whole numbers other than the repeated addition definition.

The array definition defines NX as the total number of elements in N rows, each of which contains X elements. (For a mathematical basis for this definition, we need only consider this definition as a coordinate approach to determining the number of ordered pairs in the cross product of a set A [for which $n(A) = N$] and a set B [for which the $n(B) = X$].) This definition to some extent requires modification for the cases where $N = 0$.

The cross product definition is the most sound pedagogically, if we define a definition as being the most sound pedagogically when it requires the "fewest" number of modifications as the inverse is "enlarged."

Let us consider the types of problems which require modification when the basic definition is multiplication; i.e., the $1 \cdot X$ and the $0 \cdot X$ cases. It is easily seen that the number of ordered pairs in A cross B is X for cases where $n(A) = 1$ and $n(B) = X$, since the element of A will be the first element of each of the ordered pairs and there will be one ordered pair for each element of B, thus $n(A$ cross $B) = X$.

Where $n(A) = 0$, it is easily seen that A cross $B = \emptyset$ and, thus, $n(A$ cross $B) = n(\phi) = 0$.

The following concrete examples will serve to illustrate finding a product when the product has been defined in terms of the number of ordered pairs in A cross B. Suppose we wished to illustrate to children why $2 \times 3 = 6$. Consider the following example:

We have two kinds of bread (white and rye) and three kinds of meat (pork, beef, lamb). How many different kinds of sandwiches could we make if we must use one kind of bread and one kind of meat to make each sandwich?

It would be possible to make the following six types of sandwiches:

rye-pork	white-pork
rye-beef	white-beef
rye-lamb	white-lamb

Suppose we had zero kinds of bread and three kinds of meat. How many kinds of sandwiches could we make? It is easy to see that we could make zero sandwiches.

Let us consider a second reason why "modifying definitions," if not necessary, may prove pedagogically unsound.

Let us examine the repeated-addition definition of multiplication. If we define multiplication in terms of repeated addition, are we failing to have the child identify multiplication as a distinct binary operation? When the child "discovers" the commutative and associative properties of multiplication, has he really discovered anything? Do the modifications actually hinder discovery?

A third and possibly the most significant reason that "modifying definitions" may be unsound is that course-to-course continuity may be destroyed by "modifying definitions."

As a case in point, let us examine the effect of attempting to modify the "repeated addition" definition in order to build a definition of the operation of multiplication on the set of fractional numbers. The tendency is to retain the definition for NX, where N is any whole number and X is any fractional number, and to modify it for all other cases. For those who recognize the inadequate nature of the "repeated addition" definition for fractional numbers, there has been a tendency to say, "Now forget everything you learned about operations on whole numbers, children. We are going to study fractional numbers, which have a whole new set of rules."

While the author objects to the utilization of "modifying definitions" as the basic definitions for introducing concepts, he recognizes that these "modifying definitions" serve a useful function in the development of algorithms. For example, the operation of division is defined best (mathematically and pedagogically) in terms of its being the inverse of multiplication. However, when one is interested in developing an efficient division algorithm, for the set of whole numbers, then one employs a *repeated* subtraction "interpretation" of division, even though the interpretation needs modification for the cases $N \div 0$ and $N \div N$. One resorts to the basic definition to justify why N divided by zero is impossible and why N divided by N is one.

In summary, the author feels that, pedagogically, a definition is best when it requires minimum modification as the universal set is "enlarged." Definitions should be of such a nature as to provide for a continuity of learning from grade to grade, rather than a series of disjoint learning experiences.

If the spirit of "modern" mathematics is to provide a "consistent" mathematics, which has a "unifying" style and which serves to clarify mathematical thought, then let us give special attention to those definitions which by their very nature may be consistent only through modification and represent a "disunifying" style.

9 A NONTRIVIAL ISSUE OF SYMBOLISM IN MULTIPLICATION

J. Fred Weaver

BEFORE YOU READ   The symbols $+$, $-$, $\times$, and $\div$ ought to have precise and consistent meanings in mathematics.   Sometimes this is not the case.   Since these symbols represent basic operations they are a crucial part of the language of mathematics.   This article by Professor Weaver discusses two ways to interpret multiplication.   Although the article does not require an extensive introduction, it should be subjected to careful scrutiny by the teacher because multiplication occupies a central role in elementary mathematics programs.   Particular attention should be given to the ways the symbol "$\times$" can be interpreted with regard to the use of equivalent disjoint sets and arrays as a referent for multiplication exercises.   Specifically, the teacher should be able to describe the function of the symbol "$\times$" by noting the advantages of referring to $n \times m$ as n "multiplied by" m rather than n "times" m.

Consistency is not necessarily a virtue in all things, and inconsistency in some things does not necessarily imply lack of virtue.   But in the case of a deductive mathematical system, for instance, consistency is more than a virtue; it is a necessity.   And inconsistency is more than lack of virtue; it is an intolerable condition.

There are other instances in mathematics, however, where inconsistency is not as damning and we are at least willing to tolerate it.   For example, we can learn to live with alternative definitions of *trapezoid*,[1] providing we understand the logical consequences of each and are aware of which definition is intended within a given context.

But we should pause and reflect upon some of these tolerated inconsistencies within the framework of mathematical learning among young children at the elementary school level.   It is not unlikely that certain inconsistencies inhibit pupils' mathematical understanding.   A case in point well may be the way in which we commonly interpret the symbol for the

---

[1] Under one definition a trapezoid is characterized as a quadrilateral with *at least* one pair of parallel sides, under another definition it is characterized as a quadrilateral with *exactly* one pair of parallel sides.   In the first case, *parallelogram* is a proper subclass of *trapezoid;* in the second case, parallelogram and trapezoid are disjoint classes.

Reprinted from *School Science and Mathematics*, vol. 68, no. 7 (October 1968), pp. 629, 630, 639–642.   Professor Weaver is at the University of Wisconsin, Madison, Wisconsin.

operation of multiplication [×], in contrast with the way in which we interpret the operational symbols for addition [+], subtraction [−], and division [÷].

AN INTERPRETATION OF +, −, ÷

Let us first consider the following illustrations:

$$12 + 4 = 16 \qquad [12 \ plus \ 4 \ \text{is equal to } 16] \qquad (9.1)$$

$$12 - 4 = 8 \qquad [12 \ minus \ 4 \ \text{is equal to } 8] \qquad (9.2)$$

$$12 \div 4 = 3 \qquad [12 \ divided \ by \ 4 \ \text{is equal to } 3] \qquad (9.3)$$

Virtually without exception, mathematics programs for elementary-school children reflect a similar interpretation for each of these three instances: the first number, 12, is treated as the *operand* [the number operated on] and the second number, 4, is treated as the *operator* [which "acts" on the first number in accord with the operation specified (+ or − or ÷)]. The terms *operand* and *operator* are not used with elementary-school pupils, to be sure; but the *ideas* named by these technical terms clearly are in evidence.

INTERPRETATIONS OF ×

Now let us consider this illustration:

$$12 \times 4 = 48 \qquad (9.4)$$

If we read "12 × 4" as "12 *multiplied by* 4," we are consistent with the preceding interpretation for addition, subtraction, and division: the first number, 12, is treated as the operand and the second number, 4, is treated as the operator [in this instance in accord with the operation of multiplication].

But suppose we follow a much more common practice at the elementary-school level and read "12 × 4" as "12 *times* 4." Then we are treating the first number, 12, as the *operator* and we are treating the second number, 4, as the operand.

These two interpretations clearly do *not* mean the same thing. For example, some persons suggest that we associate the multiplication of counting numbers with the union of equivalent disjoint sets. If this is the case, "12 *multiplied by* 4" is associated with equivalent sets of 12 things, and the product of 12 and 4 is the number of elements in the union of 4 such sets. On the other hand, "12 *times* 4" is associated with equivalent sets of 4 things, and the product of 12 and 4 is the number of elements in the union of 12 such sets. [In either instance, of course, the equivalent sets are disjoint.]

Material on multiplication in most professional books, articles, etc. for elementary-school teachers usually includes no mention of this ambiguous interpretation of the operational symbol, $\times$. A notable exception, however, is found in Fehr and Phillips' opening discussion of "Multiplication of Cardinal Numbers" in which the following point of view is expressed:

> "It might be well if the 'times' language were never introduced, since it makes the symbols for a multiplication the only ones children have to 'read backward.' Some of the new textbooks are not using it for this reason. However, it does have certain advantages, and it is widely used. When teachers use the language 'times' and 'multiplied by,' they should know which numeral refers to the operator and which to the operand and express the operation accordingly in any work they do with a class. Since multiplication is commutative, it is not a serious matter if a child gets an occasional example 'turned around.' "[2]

LOOKING FURTHER

But let us look a bit further. In particular, let us look to certain mathematical sentences which relate the operations of multiplication and division. We shall do this, however, by first considering some mathematical sentences which relate the operations of addition and subtraction. The following properties are true for every real number a and every real number b:[3]

$$(a + b) - b = a \qquad [\text{e.g.}, (12 + 4) - 4 = 12] \tag{9.5}$$

$$(a - b) + b = a \qquad [\text{e.g.}, (12 - 4) + 4 = 12] \tag{9.6}$$

$$a - b = a + {}^-b \qquad [\text{e.g.}, 12 - 4 = 12 + {}^-4] \tag{9.7}$$

In each of these cases it makes sense mathematically to treat a [or 12] as the operand and to treat b [or 4] as the operator at the outset. The remaining part of each sentence is consistent with this initial interpretation of operand and operator.

Now let us turn to the counterparts of properties (5), (6), and (7)

---

[2] Howard F. Fehr and Jo McKeeby Phillips, *Teaching Modern Mathematics in the Elementary School*. (Addison-Wesley, 1967). pp. 101–102.

[3] These properties also are valid for some but not all distinguished subsets of the real numbers. For instance, they continue to be valid if a and b are rational numbers, or if a and b are integers. But suppose that a and b are whole numbers $[W = \{0, 1, 2, 3, 4, 5, 6, \ldots\}]$. Sentence (5) remains valid for every $a \in W$ and every $b \in W$. Sentence (6), however, is meaningful and valid only when $a \geq b$. And sentence (7) is meaningless, since the concept of an additive inverse does not even apply within the set of whole numbers [i.e., for $b \in W$, ${}^-b \notin W$]. Notice also that sentence (6) is a logical consequence of the mathematical definition of subtraction in terms of addition: $a - b = c$ is true if and only if there exists a number c such that $c + b = a$. Also, sentence (5) is a logical consequence of the implication: if $a + b = c$, then $c - b = a$.

for the operations of multiplication and division, where a is any real number and b is a real number such that $b \neq 0$:[4]

$$(a \times b) \div b = a \qquad [\text{e.g.,} \ (12 \times 4) \div 4 = 12] \qquad (9.8)$$

$$(a \div b) \times b = a \qquad [\text{e.g.,} \ (12 \div 4) \times 4 = 12] \qquad (9.9)$$

$$a \div b = a \times \frac{1}{b} \qquad \left[\text{e.g.,} \ 12 \div 4 = 12 \times \frac{1}{4}\right] \qquad (9.10)$$

The sense of each of these properties casts b [or 4], and not a, in the role of an *operator*, with the consequent interpretation of "$\times$" as "multiplied by" rather than "times."

Notice that if we read the left-hand side of sentence (8) as "(*a times b*) *divided by b*," then the intended sense of this "doing-undoing" property is *not* maintained. Similarly, the intended sense of (9) and (10) is *not* maintained if "$\times$" is read as "times" [and "$\div$" is read as "divided by."][5]

If we insist upon reading "$\times$" as "*times*" and still wish to maintain the intended sense of the property exemplified by sentence (8), *without involving the additional property of commutativity of multiplication*, we have two alternatives. If b is to be an operator, then we should write

$$(b \times a) \div b = a \qquad [\text{e.g.,} \ (4 \times 12) \div 4 = 12] \qquad (9.11)$$

On the other hand, if a is to be an operator, then we should write

$$(a \times b) \div a = b \qquad [\text{e.g.,} \ (12 \times 4) \div 12 = 4], \qquad (9.12)$$

in which case we must apply the restriction that $a \neq 0$ rather than $b \neq 0$.

It should not be necessary to illustrate specifically the fact that we encounter similar problems with sentences (9) and (10) if we read "$\times$" as "*times*" and wish to maintain the intended sense of the property involved in each case.

ARRAYS

In an earlier journal article I advocated a basic characterization of the multiplication operation in terms of arrays.[6] In that article I was

---

[4] Observations analogous to those in footnote 2 apply here but are not stated explicitly. The reader may wish to do so for himself, however.

[5] At some mathematical levels we prefer to symbolize "*a divided by b*" as $\frac{a}{b}$ or as a/b rather than as $a \div b$. In each of these instances the operator is b, so that $a \div b = \frac{a}{b} = a/b$. These symbols,—particularly the last one,—should not be confused with the symbol $a \mid b$, which we may read as "*a divides b*" [i.e., a is a factor of b]. In the case of $a \mid b$, the operator is a rather than b.

[6] J. Fred Weaver, "Multiplication Within the Set of Counting Numbers." *School Science and Mathematics*, 67: 252–70; March 1967.

concerned principally with some other issues and, to avoid beclouding them, more or less followed the common practice of treating *a* as the *operator* in expressions of the form *a* × *b* [read as "*a times*" *b*].   Now, however, I wish to emphasize the desirability of treating *b* as the operator in connection with an array characterization of multiplication.

    We commonly name an array with 5 rows and 7 columns, for instance, as a 5-*by*-7 array [Figure 9.1]. This 5-by-7 array, and every 5-by-7 array has 5 × 7 or 35 elements.

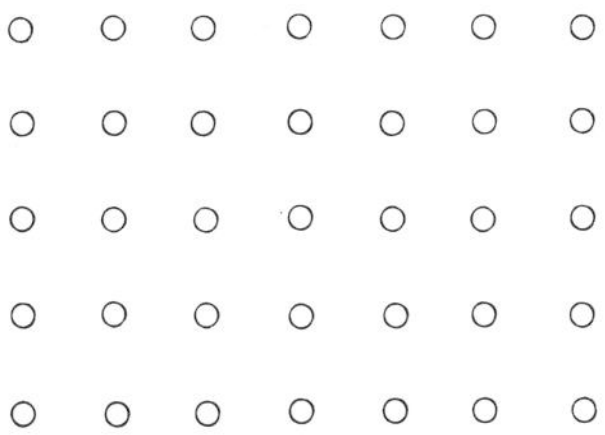

○   ○   ○   ○   ○   ○   ○

○   ○   ○   ○   ○   ○   ○

○   ○   ○   ○   ○   ○   ○

○   ○   ○   ○   ○   ○   ○

○   ○   ○   ○   ○   ○   ○

Figure 9.1 A 5-by-7 array

More generally, an array with *a* rows and *b* columns is termed an *a-by-b* array, and has *a* × *b* elements [where *a* and *b* are counting numbers.][7]

    When we speak of a 5-*by*-7 array, for instance, it seems sensible and consistent to think of 5 × 7 as "5 *multiplied by* 7." In general, when we speak of an *a-by-b* array, it seems sensible and consistent to interpret *a* × *b* as "*a multiplied by b*."

    Notice also that when a 5-by-7 array, for instance, is viewed as a union of disjoint equivalent sets, it is preferable to think of the array as being generated in the form of Figure 9.2 rather than in the form of Figure 9.3 if we are to interpret "5 × 7" as "5 *multiplied by* 7."

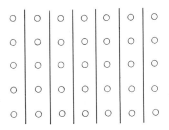

Figure 9.2

[7] As indicated in the preceding article, the array interpretation of *a* × *b* for counting numbers may be extended to whole numbers, to cover those instances in which *a* = 0 or *b* = 0, and *a* × *b* = 0.

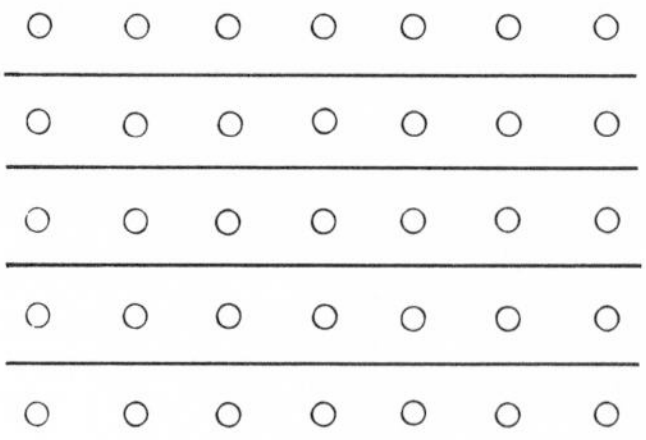

Figure 9.3

The sense of Figure 9.3 would lead to interpreting "5 × 7" as "5 *times* 7" rather than as "5 multiplied by 7," if we are thinking of the array as being generated in relation to the union of disjoint equivalent sets.

IN CONCLUSION

It is true that the symbol for multiplication [×] may be interpreted ambiguously without affecting the product of two real numbers. Since multiplication is commutative [when applied to real numbers], "5 *times* 7" and "5 *multiplied by* 7," for instance, indicate the same product, 35. In general, for every real number a and every real number b, "a times b" and "a multiplied by b" designate the same real number.

At certain stages of mathematical learning this ambiguity undoubtedly is of trivial consequence. But this is *not* a trivial matter for children's mathematical learning at the elementary-school level. If we tolerate an ambiguous interpretation of "12 × 4," for instance; if we are willing to accept either "12 × 4" or "4 × 12" as expressing the sense of a particular problem, etc.; and if we are just as free with "12 + 4" and "4 + 12,"—then we are inviting confusion on the part of children between expressions such as "12 − 4" and "4 − 12," and between "12 ÷ 4" and "4 ÷ 12."

Let us attempt to build for elementary-school pupils an unambiguous interpretation of the symbol, ×, for multiplication. And in the interests of advantages likely to be gained by consistency of interpretation in relation to the symbols for addition [+], subtraction [−], and division [÷], let us consider seriously the interpretation of "×" as "*multiplied by*" rather than as "times." This non-trivial issue at the elementary-school level deserves more than token attention in terms of empirical exploration and investigation.

A POSTSCRIPT

The manuscript for this article was prepared and submitted before I read in the November 1967 issue of *School Science and Mathematics* Professor Rappaport's reaction to my previous discussion of "Multiplication Within the Set of

Counting Numbers,"[8] in which he contends that I emphasized "logic at the expense of psychology."[9] This reaction has given me no cause to modify either the suggestion I advance in this present article or the position I advocated in my previous discussion.

I am intrigued by the fact that my emphasis upon "logical" [mathematical] considerations which Rappaport interprets to be at the "expense of psychology" can be viewed, instead, to have *support* from "psychology." For instance: In a recent discussion of meaningful verbal learning, Ausubel[10] states: "It is self-evident that before new ideas can be meaningfully learned, they must be adequately discriminable from similar established ideas in cognitive structure. If the learner cannot discriminate clearly, for example, between new idea A' and previously learned idea A, then A' enjoys relatively little status as a separately identifiable meaning in its own right, even at the very onset of its incorporation into cognitive structure."[11]

Rappaport asks, "Is it not possible to develop mathematical principles in accordance with sound psychological principles?"[12] Certainly it is,—and I am very much interested in doing so. In view of the principle mentioned by Ausubel, I have both *psychological and mathematical* reasons to question Rappaport's contention that "Repeated addition serves as an excellent introduction to multiplication,"[13] and to favor an array interpretation independent of addition.

Finally, interested readers may wish to relate two articles from another journal to the issue in question:

Robert D. Bechtel and Lyle J. Dixon, "Multiplication—Repeated Addition?" *Arithmetic Teacher*, 14: 373–76, May 1967.

David Rappaport, "Multiplication—Logical or Pedagogical?" *Arithmetic Teacher*, 15: 158–60; February 1968.

[8] David Rappaport, "Logic, Psychology and the New Mathematics." *School Science and Mathematics*, 67: 681–85; November 1967.
[9] *Ibid.*, p. 684.
[10] David P. Ausubel, "Facilitating Meaningful Verbal Learning in the Classroom." *Arithmetic Teacher*, 15: 126–32, February 1968.
[11] *Ibid.*, pp. 131–32.
[12] Rappaport, *ibid.*, pp. 681–82.
[13] *Ibid.*, p. 684.

10 COUNTING IS NOT BASIC

H. Van Engen

BEFORE YOU READ   Although this is not an article which deals with
mathematical language directly, certainly the various ways to interpret
counting are closely related to the language of mathematics.   There is rote
counting, which amounts to saying number words—such as one, two,
three; or *uno, dos, tres*—in their correct order.   There is also rational
counting, which is essentially a matching process used to determine the
cardinality of a set.   In another sense counting, instead of being an
associating operation similar to addition, is an outgrowth of a child's
attempt to determine the cardinal number of a finite set which contains
discrete elements and to determine the manner in which they are ordered.
Thus, counting is subtly complex, because it is intrinsically related to
fundamental ideas such as one-to-one correspondence, Piaget's notion of
conservation, and equivalent and nonequivalent sets.   Counting,
then, as an idea tends to generate and order the natural numbers—1, 2, 3,
4, . . . — which are, in essence, the same thing as the cardinal numbers.
Considered conjunctively, these become an important part of the language
of mathematics.

   After reading the article the teacher should be able to state one
reason why counting is an outgrowth of an investigation of related ideas
more than it is an operation, and give a description of the meaning of the
term "cardinal number" by using the notions of one-to-one correspondence and equivalent sets.

There is a persistent myth that counting is the basic "operation" of arithmetic. This idea can be found in the arithmetic methods books and, in the
recent past, over nationwide television programs about educating the
preschool child. It is high time that this idea be laid away among the dodo
birds. Nothing less than such a drastic burial will enable the universities,
colleges and schools to develop a sound arithmetic program for the preschool
child.

Figure 10.1

Reprinted from *School Science and Mathematics*, vol. 68, no. 8 (November 1968), pp. 720–722.
Professor Van Engen is at the University of Wisconsin, Madison, Wisconsin.

There are, in fact, a number of ideas that are more basic than counting. One of these is one-to-one correspondence. Even before a child can recognize a set as having five elements, he can make a judgement that the two sets in Figure 10.1 are equinumerous, that is, there are as many squares as circles. Undoubtedly, he does this visually, by setting up a 1-1 correspondence between the squares and the circles. He learns to express the equinumerousness idea by saying, "There are as many squares (circles) as circles (squares)." Experience will teach him that if the objects appear in a scattered arrangement, as shown in Figure 10.2, he can arrange them as in Figure 10.1, to determine that the elements of the two sets can be put into 1-1 correspondence. Incidentally, it is a fundamental theorem about sets that enables one to state that if the correspondence is 1-1 the correspondence is 1-1 regardless of how the correspondence is set up.

Figure 10.2

The child also learns that if he tries to set up a 1-1 correspondence between the two sets of objects shown in Figure 10.3, he will fail. He has one square that cannot be uniquely matched with a circle. He learns to say that, "There are more squares than circles" or "There are fewer circles than squares."

Figure 10.3

Another idea which is essential if the child is to feel at home with arithmetic has been labeled by Piaget as the conservation of numerousness or conservation of number. Basically, conservation means that if we have objects in some arrangement as in Figure 10.4A, then when the objects are rearranged as in Figure 10.4B, the number of objects has not changed. In other words, the number of objects does not change (is invariant) under a transformation or "shifting around" of the objects. Surprising as it may seem, many kindergarten and first grade children do not know this.

Figure 10.4

Children must also learn that certain sounds are associated with each set. For example, 'five" is associated with the fingers on one hand. Then the child associates this same sound with any set that can be placed in 1-1 correspondence with the fingers of the hand. In this way, he learns that "five" is associated with any set that is equivalent to the set of fingers on one hand. He learns to ignore size, shape, color, and many other physical characteristics of the objects, and center his attention on the 1-1 correspondence (intentionally or otherwise) between two sets of objects. Similarly, the child associates sets with the sounds "one," "two," "three," etc. Ideally, children should learn to order sets in terms of "more than" and "less than" before he learns to say the number words in sequence. In fact, counting should be approached through this activity.

If one selects a set of two or more objects, it is possible to form two other sets that are "one more than" and "one less than" the given set. In this way one arrives at a visual ordering of sets as illustrated in Figure 10.5.

		X	XX	XX	XXX	
X	XX	XX	XX	XXX	XXX	etc.
One	Two	Three	Four	Five	Six	

Figure 10.5

Ideally, the number names are then learned in sequence and children learn that it is possible, and convenient, to discard the sets and just use the sounds (numbers) "one," "two," "three," etc. to arrive at the cardinal number associated with a set of objects (the cardinality of the set).

In the previous paragraph, the word "sound" has been used as almost synonymous with "cardinal number" during initial learning experiences. A good case can be made for this position. As described in the article the sound "five" becomes associated with a set of objects and all sets equivalent to this model set (the fingers on one hand, for instance). Experience demonstrates that these sounds can be combined in systematic ways and even have properties that are of interest. Of course, the sounds are called numbers and the numbers have properties. For example, some numbers are odd and others even. Operations are introduced first as the union of two sets with which the sounds are associated. For example, $3 + 2$ introduces the new word "plus" and the new idea that $3 + 2$ is associated with the union of a set of cardinality three and a set of cardinality two. This, of course, introduces the meaning of addition.

One could continue pointing out how the "sounds" become numbers, but this would detract from the principal point of the paper. Ideally, counting is an outgrowth of the ideas of a feeling for the relations of "more than," "less than" and "equal to." These ideas and their many ramifications should be in the kindergarten program of schools. They do not involve counting. They are basic to counting.

Nothing will be more detrimental to the development of a sound program for kindergarten arithmetic than the myth that arithmetic starts with counting. Even worse, in one program receiving national attention the arithmetic of the preschool child starts with $1 + 0 = 1$. Those interested in making arithmetic easy and meaningful should protest. Zero is a difficult concept—more difficult than the cardinal numbers greater than zero.

The recent flood of money from the Federal Government has stimulated activities in the school curriculum. This is good. However, projects on which tax money is being spent should be mathematically well conceived. Any other standard can well lead to disaster.

11 MATH HAS ITS PHRASES AND SENTENCES TOO

Lola May

BEFORE YOU READ   The ability to express problem relationships as equivalent mathematical statements is important to verbal problem solving. The symbolism of such mathematical statements can be learned apart from any external reason for such knowledge. For example, one could expect children to learn that "3" and "8" are symbols which represent amounts; $=$ and $<$ are symbols which represent relationships between amounts; and $+$ and $\times$ are symbols which cause amounts to be composed. Computations which represent the manipulations of symbols are more complex. Yet computations, too, can be learned, apart from any external reason for performing them. Further, computations can be done outside of a consideration of the properties on which they are based.

Still more complex are mathematical sentences, such as equations and inequalities. Again, a pupil can learn how to solve these apart from any external reason for doing so, by finding solutions to written exercises such as $27 + n = 38$. But when all of these aspects of mathematics are combined to solve problems the pupil becomes aware of and begins to appreciate the beauty and power of mathematics.

A natural consequence of this notion is that lessons should be presented in some manner which enables the child to learn the meaning of symbols, to perform computations, and to solve problems. Many lessons can focus on these aspects of learning at the same time. The article by Professor May discusses how this may be done by considering the nature of mathematical sentences. In the article the author discusses the use of symbols to construct equalities and inequalities, and considers some of the techniques used to find solutions to them.

When he has finished, the teacher should be able to define the term "variable"; state the meaning of the symbols $=$, $\neq$, $>$, and $<$; and develop an open number sentence, and subsequently determine whether it is true or false.

Numerals are the symbols we write to convey numbers. Numerals can be digits such as 4, 12, 123, and 1,079. A numeral may consist of a combination of symbols for numbers plus symbols for operations. In this case, numerals are usually called a phrase or an expression.

Reprinted from *Grade Teacher*, vol. 84, no. 4 (December 1966), pp. 81–83. Dr. May is the Mathematics Consultant for the Winnetka, Illinois, Public Schools.

The number phrase 3×4 is a numeral for the number 12. Simplifying a number phrase or expression means finding the simplest name for the number represented by the phrase or expression. In order to avoid confusion, the following convention for the order of operations is adopted: parentheses are simplified first; multiplication and division are done in the order in which they appear; and, finally, addition and subtraction are performed in the order in which they appear. The following expression would be simplified this way:

$$18 + (4 \times 5 - 3) - 3 \times 6 \div 2 = 18 + 17 - 9 = 26$$

It is important that all teachers in the elementary grades know the rules for simplifying phrases. As soon as students are faced with more than one operation in a phrase, they should learn the proper way to simplify the expression.

A mathematical sentence consists of number phrases and a symbol for a verb phrase. The following are examples of verb phrases:

$=$ means "is equal to"

$\neq$ means "is not equal to"

$>$ means "is greater than"

$\not>$ means "is not greater than"

$<$ means "is less than"

$\not<$ means "is not less than"

Pupils learn early in the primary grades how to write simple mathematical sentences. These sentences can either be true or false. Most of the time, teachers want true sentences. The following are examples of closed sentences:

$$7 + 3 = 10 \qquad \text{(true)}$$
$$8 + 3 \neq 10 \qquad \text{(true)}$$
$$7 + 4 = 10 \qquad \text{(false)}$$

The sentences are called closed sentences because all the parts are given and there is nothing to find. A mathematical sentence that involves a letter symbol or a frame that represents a variable is called an open sentence. The word variable is just another word for unknown and should not scare teachers or pupils.

In the open sentence $\square + 4 = 13$ the square represents a variable.

If the square is replaced by 6, the false sentence $6 + 4 = 13$ is obtained.

If the square is replaced by 9, the true sentence $9 + 4 = 13$ is obtained.

Often in the middle and upper grades, the letter N is used in place of a frame to stand for the variable. Later, in algebra, the x, y, and z are used for the variables.

For an open sentence, a set of numbers is given—or assumed to be given—that represents the permissible replacements for the variable. The subset of the domain that makes the sentence true is called the solution set or the truth set of the sentence. The domain is always the set of permissible replacements for the variable. All of these terms—domain, subset, solution set, and truth set—do not need to be used in the early elementary grades, but the concepts can be taught. The terms can be learned in the sixth, seventh, and eighth grades.

If the domain is {0, 1, 2, 3, 4, 5}

$$3N = 12$$
$$N = 4$$

then the solution set is {4}.
If the domain is {0, 1, 2, 3}

$$3N = 12$$

the solution set is {   }, the empty set.
If the domain is the set
of whole numbers {0, 1, 2, 3, . . .}

$$3N = 12$$
$$N = 4$$

the solution set is {4}.

In new mathematics, the term "finding the solution set" or "finding the truth set" means solving the mathematical sentence. Children learn very early that some sentences, as in the case of the second example above, have no solution.

The domain is assumed to be the set of whole numbers unless otherwise specified.

In the example below, the sentence has more than one solution that will make it true.

$N < 6$
$N = 0, 1, 2, 3, 4, 5$
The solution set is {0, 1, 2, 3, 4, 5}.

Equivalent open sentences or equivalent equations are sentences that have the same solution set:

$$X + 6 = 14$$
$$X = 14 - 6$$
$$X = 8$$

The solution set for each sentence is 8. The three sentences are equivalent sentences or equations. Children learn in first grade that sets having the same number of members are called equivalent sets. From this concept comes the concept that sentences having the same solution set are equivalent sentences. The equations above are not the same, but they do have the same solution so they are equivalent.

In the upper grades, compound number sentences start to appear, and the beginning of logic is started as well as the solution of sentences. A compound mathematical sentence contains a connective such as "and," "or," "not," etc.

$$2 < 6 \text{ and } 3 \times 4 = 12$$

The first simple sentence says that 2 is less than 6 and is true. The second simple sentence says that $3 \times 4 = 12$ and is true. Therefore, the compound sentence is true. When the connective "and" is used, the compound sentence is true if—and only if—each of the simple sentences is true.

$$5 > 1 \text{ and } 4 \times 5 = 15$$

The compound sentence above is false because the second simple sentence is false. The first simple sentence is true, but both must be true to make the compound sentence true. In the following compound sentence, the connective "or" is used:

$$2 < 6 \text{ or } 3 \times 5 = 10$$

The first simple sentence says that 2 is less than 6 and is true. The second simple sentence says that $3 \times 5 = 10$. This is false. But the compound sentence is true. When the connective "or" is used, the compound sentence is true if *either* of the simple sentences is true, or if both are true. In other words, the only time a compound sentence with the connective "or" is false is when both simple sentences are false.

Compound number sentences can be open sentences. When they are open, the solution set can be found.

$$N < 4 \text{ and } N + 4 = 7$$

The solution set of $N < 4$ is $N = \{0, 1, 2, 3\}$.

The solution set of $N + 4 = 7$ is $N = \{3\}$.

The solution set of the compound sentence

$$N < 4 \text{ and } N + 4 = 7 \text{ is } \{3\}.$$

The solution set for the "and" compound sentence is the *intersection* set of the two solution sets. This means the members or numbers they have in common. The only number the two solution sets have in common is 3. This can be shown by a Venn diagram like this:

$N < 4$ $N + 4 = 7$

The following is an example of a compound sentence with the connective "or." The compound sentence is open so the solution can be found.

$$N < 4 \text{ or } N + 4 = 9$$

The solution set of $N < 4$ is $N = \{0, 1, 2, 3\}$.

The solution set of $N + 4 = 9$ is $N = \{5\}$.

The solution set of the compound sentence

$$N < 4 \text{ or } N + 4 = 9 \text{ is } \{0, 1, 2, 3, 5\}.$$

The solution set for the "or" compound sentence is the *union* set of the two solution sets. This means all the numbers in both solution sets but without repeating any numbers.

In conclusion, it should be noted that set language and the operations of sets—union and intersection—are used in learning how to solve mathematical sentences. Set language makes the learning of mathematics more precise and should be used constantly in the elementary grades. Teachers who spend two weeks teaching a unit on sets and then drop the whole idea the rest of the year are wasting the children's time. If set language is taught, it should be used to make mathematics clearer.

In solving mathematical sentences, children in all grades get the needed practice in adding and subtracting. They are learning how to think about numbers and are doing drill work at the same time. Teachers should remember that inequalities—"greater than" and "less than"—are not any more difficult for children to grasp than equality. In fact, children think in terms of inequality long before they think in terms of equality. Teachers should not judge a child's difficulty by their own. Try it and see what success you will have.

1 2 GRAMMARMATHICALLY SPEAKING

King W. Jamison, Jr.

BEFORE YOU READ   The language of mathematics and the English language, to the extent they are learned by most people, are probably equivalent in their degree of abstractness.   For example, the degree of abstractness of the meaning of "3" and "cat" is as nearly similar as is the degree of abstractness of "function" and "democracy."   Yet children seem to understand the English language better; and they certainly use it more.   This article by Professor Jamison describes a unique method of translating sentences written in the English language into sentences written in the language of mathematics.   The article does not contain content that is likely to become an established part of the curriculum, yet it focuses on mathematics as a language in such a way as to give teachers a broader perspective in regard to notions such as number, relations, and equations.

By carefully reading the article the teacher should be able to appreciate and describe the complexity of relationships between English and mathematics.

AN ART, A SCIENCE

Much has been said which identifies mathematics as an art.   Few students, teachers of mathematics, and laymen would deny the esthetic value of mathematics, and tradition labels mathematics as an art.   As one example, the curriculum of the medieval university included mathematics among the seven liberal arts.   Mathematics has also been thought of as a science for a long time.   Now, aided by modern communications, even the most uninterested person associates mathematics with science and scientists.   It is therefore comparatively easy to accept the notion that mathematics is an art and that mathematics is a science.

ALSO A LANGUAGE

Without a close look, however, the full impact of the statement that *mathematics is a language* escapes most of us.   The truth of the matter is that mathematics *is* a language and many teachers are missing an opportunity to teach

Reprinted from *The Mathematics Teacher*, vol. 59, no. 7 (November 1966), pp. 640–644.
Professor Jamison is at Middle Tennessee State University, Murfreesboro, Tennessee.

it as such, or at least to show a strong correlation between a mathematical expression and an English sentence. The almost simultaneous exposure of students to sentence diagramming and elementary algebra is too happy a coincidence to let pass without capitalizing upon it.

PARTS OF SPEECH

The following question therefore arises: What has sentence diagramming to do with algebra problems? The answer in simple terms is that sentence diagramming helps identify parts of speech in an English sentence—nouns, verbs, adjectives—and can help in translating the English of an algebra problem into the symbols (parts of speech) of a mathematical sentence. Translating predicates, of course, the teaching of a mathematical vocabulary. Following is a list of more common mathematical nouns, verbs, and adjectives or, if the reader prefers, Class 1 symbols, Class 2L symbols, and Class 3 symbols.[1]

Nouns (Class 1 Symbols)

Mathematics	English
x	number
x_1, x_2, x_3, etc.	numbers
x_1	
x_2	quotient, ratio (note that the prepositional phrase of *numbers* is not necessary)
$x_1 - x_2$	difference
$x_1 + x_2$	sum
$(x_1) (x_2)$	product

Verbs (Class 2L Symbols)

Mathematics	English
$>$	is greater than
$=$	is, are, equals, equal
$<$	is less than

---

[1] The latter classification is one used by modern textbooks on grammar. See *Structural Essentials of English*, cited in the references at the end of the article, and Don M. Wolfe and Laurada K. Osborn, *A Teacher's Manual*, "Enjoying English Series" (Chicago: L. W. Singer Co., 1964).

Adjectives or Modifiers (Class 3 Symbols)

Mathematics	*English*
$(\ )^2$	squared, the square of, whose square
$(\ )^3$	cubed, the cube of, whose cube
$(\ )^{1/2}$	square root of, whose square root
$(\ )^{1/3}$	cube root of, whose cube root
$2(\ )$	doubled, twice, two times
$\frac{1}{2}(\ ), \frac{(\ )}{2}$	one-half of, $\frac{1}{2}$ times
$\frac{1}{3}(\ ), \frac{(\ )}{3}$	one-third of, $\frac{1}{3}$ times

TRANSLATIONS

With this elementary vocabulary we can now translate a few English mathematical statements into *symbol sentences*. First let us analyze the translation of a simple sentence in a modern language: *Su casa es hermosa* becomes *Your house is beautiful.* One can sometimes substitute an English symbol for a Spanish symbol meaning the same thing: *Your* for *Su*, *house* for *casa*, *is* for *es*, and *beautiful* for *hermosa.* This is an oversimplification, of course, but true in many cases. It is helpful to observe that the same thing is done when a translation is made from a simple English sentence to a corresponding mathematical statement, or symbol sentence.

Following are a few simple mathematical statements in English which will be translated into mathematics. They are chosen to require a varied selection from the mathematics vocabulary.

Example I

If zero is the difference between five and a number's ratio to two, find the number.

Example II

If the sum of a number's half and its double is fifteen, find the number.

Example III

Find two numbers whose product is six and whose sum is five.

Example IV

The sum of a number and three is greater than five. Find the number.

Example V

The product of six and a number is less than nine. Find the number.

DIAGRAMMING

By using these examples a connection between sentence diagramming, language translation, and algebraic processes can be shown. The first of the above English-mathematical sentences is diagrammed as follows:

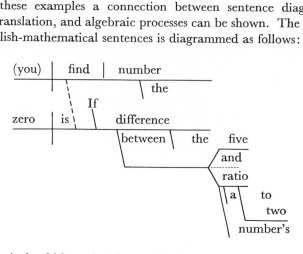

Here it should be pointed out that English imperatives, such as *show that* or *find*, are not translated into mathematics. They are implied by the symbol sentence. The word *if* is not translated, either. The word *if* is merely a cue for the mathematician to assume something. In the above instance, therefore, one needs to concern oneself with only that part of the diagram which mentions number and its modifiers: that is, the clause containing the verb *is*. By consulting the mathematics vocabulary, the part of the diagram which contains the clause becomes:

When the prepositional phrase is used to limit the parenthesis of the mathematical word, ( ) — ( ), the diagram further simplifies to:

The mathematical sentence emerges when the scaffold of the diagram is removed. The symbol sentence is:

$$0 = 5 - \frac{x}{2}.$$

Complying with the implied imperative, *find x*, the student can apply the algebraic operations with which he has already been made familiar. He finds that *x* is 10.

Following is an explanation of the remaining examples:

Example II.   If the sum of a number's half and its double is fifteen, find the number.

Step 1: Diagramming

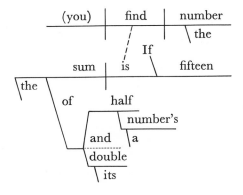

Step 2: Elimination of the imperative

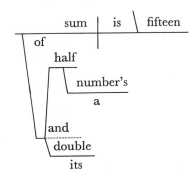

Step 3: Translation

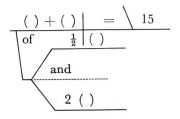

Step 4: Use of modifiers to limit nouns

$$\underline{\tfrac{1}{2}(x) + 2(x) = 15}$$.

Step 5: Removal of diagram scaffold

$$\tfrac{1}{2}(x) + 2(x) = 15.$$

Step 6: Solution of algebraic processes

$$x = 6.$$

English Translation: "The number is six."

Example III.   Find two numbers whose product is six and sum is five.

Step 1: Diagramming

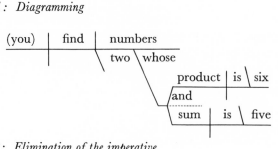

Step 2: Elimination of the imperative

Step 3: Translation

Step 4: Use of modifiers to limit nouns
(In this particular example, there are no modifiers of the nouns, *sum*
and *product*. Therefore Step 4 is not called for.)

Step 5: Removal of diagram scaffold

$$(x_1)(x_2) = 6.$$
$$(x_1) + (x_2) = 5.$$

Step 6: Solution of algebraic processes

$$x_1 = 2 \text{ or } 3.$$
$$x_2 = 3 \text{ or } 2.$$

English Translation: "The numbers are two and three."

Example IV.   The sum of a number and three is greater than five. Find the number.

Step 1: Diagramming

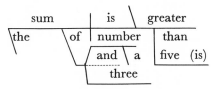

Step 2: Elimination of the imperative
(The diagram can remain unchanged since the imperative was stated separately.)

Step 3: Translation

$$(\ ) + (\ ) \ |> \backslash \ 5 \, .$$

Step 4: Use of modifiers to limit nouns

$$(x) + (3) > 5 \, .$$

Step 5: Removal of diagram scaffold

$$(x) + 3 > 5.$$

Step 6: Solution by algebraic processes

$$x > 2.$$

English Translation: "The number is any number greater than two."

Example V.   The product of six and a number is less than nine. Find the number.

Step 1: Diagramming

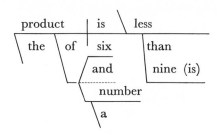

Step 2: Elimination of the imperative
(Same as Example IV.)

Step 3: Translation

$$\overline{( )\ ( ) \mid < \backslash\ 9}$$

Step 4: Use of modifiers to limit nouns

$$\overline{(6)\ (x) \mid < \backslash\ 9}$$

Step 5: Removal of the diagram scaffold

$$6(x) < 9.$$

Step 6: Solution by algebraic processes

$$x < \tfrac{3}{2}.$$

English Translation: "The number is any number less than three halves."

A FUNCTIONAL APPROACH

When one understands the functions of the words, phrases, and clauses in the word problems, it is not absolutely necessary to diagram the sentence in exactly the above manner. The traditional approach to diagramming could give way to a type of diagramming advocated by some writers of modern textbooks on grammar. This latter type is part of a movement to blend traditional grammar with recent linguistic studies. At present it is not widely practiced, but relative to this discussion it bears looking into.

Illustrating a modern, structural approach, the same examples presented previously are solved again:

Example I.   If zero is the difference between five and a number's ratio to two, find the number.

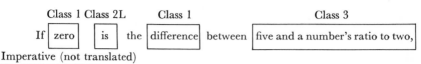

Class 1 Class 2L   Class 1   Class 3

If | zero | | is | the | difference | between | five and a number's ratio to two, |

Imperative (not translated)

| find the number. |

Basic Structure: $0 = (\ ) - (\ )$.

Modified Structure: $0 = (5) - \left(\dfrac{x}{2}\right)$.

Solution: $10 = x$.

English Translation: "Ten is the number."

Example II.   If the sum of a number's half and its double is fifteen, find the number.

Class 1   Class 3   Class 2L   Class 3

If the | sum | of a | number's half and its double | | is | | fifteen, |

Imperative (not translated)

| find the number. |

Basic Structure: $(\ ) + (\ ) = 15$.

Modified Structure: $\frac{1}{2}(x) + 2(x) = 15$.

Solution: $x = 6$.

English Translation: "The number is six."

Example III.   Find two numbers whose product is six and sum is five.

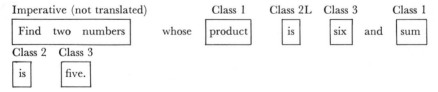

Imperative (not translated)   Class 1   Class 2L   Class 3   Class 1

| Find   two   numbers | whose | product | | is | | six | and | sum |

Class 2   Class 3

| is | | five. |

In this problem, as in the preceding two problems, the subordinate clause contains, for the mathematician, far from subordinate information. In this example, the subordinate clause, then, receives major attention. The translation of the clause is

Basic $(\ )\quad(\ ) = 6$.   Solution: $x_1 = 2$ or 3.

Structure: $(\ ) + (\ ) = 5$. $x_2 = 3$ or 2.

Modified $(x_1)\quad(x_2) = 6$.   English Translation: "The numbers are two

Structure: $(x_1) + (x_2) = 5$.   and three."

Example IV.   The sum of a number and three is greater than five.

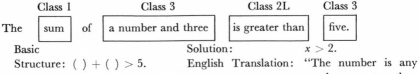

Basic
Structure: $(\ ) + (\ ) > 5.$

Modified
Structure: $(x) + (3) > 5.$

Solution: $x > 2.$

English Translation: "The number is any number greater than two."

Example V.   The product of six and a number is less than nine.

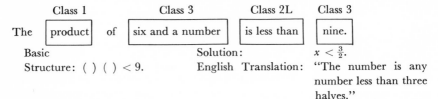

Basic
Structure: $(\ )(\ ) < 9.$

Modified
Structure: $(6)(x) < 9.$

Solution: $x < \frac{3}{2}.$

English Translation: "The number is any number less than three halves."

SUMMARY

On the surface one might get the impression that the above discussion is no more than another mathematics teaching method and can benefit only elementary algebra teachers. Granted, it is a method aimed primarily at aiding the mathematics teacher. However, there are other interesting byproducts related to unity in the public school curriculum and better communications between disciplines. The proponents of language study in the elementary grades, for instance, might through this method see more clearly the validity of their appeal. At the same time the English teacher and the mathematics teacher might find themselves working together more often. Furthermore, the English student might appreciate, to a greater degree, the utility and importance of his discipline and the mathematics student is apt to have a healthier respect for his English assignments.

REFERENCES

Books

Banks, J. Houston. *Elements of Mathematics* (2nd ed.). Boston: Allyn & Bacon, 1961. Chap. i.

Roberts, Paul. *Understanding English.* New York: Harper & Row, 1958.

—————. *Understanding Grammar.* New York: Harper & Row, 1954.

Sauer, Edwin H. *English in the Secondary School.* New York: Holt, Rinehart & Winston, 1961.

SMSG. *Introduction to Secondary School Mathematics* (student text, rev. ed.). New Haven: Yale University Press, 1963, Vol. II, Part II, chap. xviii.
Whiehall, Harold. *Structural Essentials of English.* New York: Harcourt, Brace & World, 1956.
Wolfe, Don M., and Lewis, Josie. *Enjoying English 9* (teacher's ed.). Chicago: L. W. Singer Co., 1964.
Wolfe, Don. M.; Nelson, Ruth; and Osborn, Laurada K. *Enjoying English 11* (teacher's ed.) Chicago: L. W. Singer Co. 1964.

Periodicals

Gleason, H. A., Jr. "What Grammar," *Harvard Educational Review, XXXIV* (Spring 1964), 267–81.
Marckwardt, Albert H. "Linguistics Issue: An Introduction," *College English, XXVI* (January 1965), 249–54.
Miller, Frances. "Structural Plotting for Understanding," *The English Journal, LI* (December 1962), 632–39.
Steinberg, Erwin R. "Needed Research in the Teaching of Secondary School English," *The English Journal, LI* (December 1962), 617–20.
Strickland, Ruth G. "The Contribution of Structural Linguistics to the Teaching of Reading, Writing, and Grammar in the Elementary School," *Bulletin of the School of Education, Indiana University, XL* (January 1964).

SECTION III

Relationships and Properties: Developing an Understanding of Structure

*"Angling may be said to be so like the mathematics,
that it can never be full learnt."*

Izaak Walton, *Compleat Angler*, "Epistle to Reader"

Introduction

109

INTRODUCTION

There is probably no more appropriate way for pupils to develop an understanding of the structure of mathematics than by exploring patterns used to discover mathematical properties and relationships. Much has been said about the need for pupils to discover concepts. What pupils *can* discover has been less clearly identified; and the amount of information children need to be given and the time required to enable them to make a discovery has not been clearly determined. This implies at least two things. First, in order to make a discovery the child must purposefully explore something, or he must systematically acquire some information. Second, the child must incorporate his new knowledge with previously learned knowledge and skills in order to generate a new idea.

There are some ideas which children are not likely to discover either because the idea grew out of mechanical rather than logical considerations or because it is too advanced for a child at a particular time in his development. For example, it is unlikely that children would or could discover routine notations, such as set-builder notation or the conventional manner for drawing a coordinate plane. These ideas are a part of the language of mathematics and can be taught fairly quickly by using an expository-illustrative approach or by using a demonstrative approach.

In elementary school mathematics programs much time is given to the whole number system, which is the set of whole numbers $W =$ 0, 1, 2, . . . together with the operations of addition $(+)$ and multiplication $(\times)$. For this system the following properties are true:

(1.) *Closure property.* Whenever any two whole numbers are added or multiplied, the resulting sum or product is also a whole number.

(2.) *Addition and multiplication are commutative operations.* That is, the order in which two whole numbers are added or multiplied does not affect the sum or product.

(3.) *Addition and multiplication are associative operations.* That is, any number of whole numbers may be added or multiplied in accordance with any method of grouping the numbers without affecting the sum or product.

(4.) *Multiplication is distributive with respect to addition.* That is, whenever a, b, c, and d are whole numbers and $d = b + c$, then $a \cdot d = a (b + c) = a \cdot b + a \cdot c$.

(5.) *There are unique identity elements for addition and multiplication.* That is, for any whole number n, $n + 0 = 0 + n = n$ and $n \cdot 1 = 1 \cdot n = n$.

The properties listed above can and should be discovered by elementary school children. They are examples of discoverable ideas because it is easy to develop a pattern from which they can be generalized. The justification for emphasizing, at least intuitively, the properties mentioned is that most of the procedures for doing computational exercises are based on the properties of the whole number system. Other properties, such as the trichotomy axiom (whenever $a < b$ and $b < c$, then $a < c$), may also be discovered by children. In general, any idea in mathematics that is an axiom, a postulate, a theorem, and law, or a property of some system can be discovered by children.

Most teachers can demonstrate acceptable competence in their knowledge of mathematical properties. It is in the area of guiding children to discover mathematical relationships and properties that many teachers need to develop additional competence. There are probably several reasons why teachers who philosophically accept the notion of discovering relationships do not utilize appropriate discovery techniques. A likely reason is the lack of specific guidelines delineating how teachers can develop lessons intended to facilitate discovery. The development of discovery-oriented, active-learning, teaching sequences requires a thoughtful and knowledgeable consideration of:

(1.) the environment in which the pupils will work;
(2.) the materials and media to be used;
(3.) the patterns or problems pupils are to explore or solve; and
(4.) the nature of the discussion or exploration moves to be used.

These guidelines, when utilized with those axioms and relationships which may be discovered efficiently, constitute the basis wherein active learning may be used to help children find out about properties and relationships.

The selections in this Section provide mathematical reinforcement of basic notions for teachers, while suggesting certain specific contexts within which the ideas may be introduced to children.

I3 YOU CAN'T PLAY THE MATH GAME IF YOU DON'T KNOW THE RULES

Lola May

BEFORE YOU READ   A number system consists of a set of numbers and one or more operations in which certain properties are true for the system. The system most used by elementary school pupils is called the whole number system. It incorporates a set of numbers—$W = (0, 1, 2, 3, \ldots)$— and two operations called addition $(+)$ and multiplication $(\times)$.

The properties of the whole number system and their uses are discussed in the following article by Professor May. Two examples are included involving fractions instead of whole numbers, for all of the properties of the whole number system are properties of the rational number system.

As a result of reading this article the teacher should be able to define the commutative property of addition and of multiplication, the associative property of addition and multiplication, and the distributive property of multiplication over addition. He should also be able to name the identity elements for addition and multiplication and recognize the use of these properties in computational exercises.

Every game has its special rules. This is true of the game called mathematics. Here, the rules are sometimes called the structural properties of mathematics. In this article, we shall see how these properties help children to understand the real meaning of mathematics.

In the first grade, one of the primary goals is the learning of the addition and subtraction facts through the number 10. One of the goals of second grade is to complete the 100 basic addition and subtraction facts. A child starts out by joining two sets of objects and making a third set. A set of three members is joined to a set of two members and the result is a set of five members. Also, a set of two members is joined to a set of three members and the result is a set of five.

The child is discovering that you can interchange the beginning sets and the joined set will be the same. The teacher writes the symbols for this activity as: $2 + 3 = 5$ or $3 + 2 = 5$. The 3 and the 2 in the equation are called addends and the 5 is the sum.

Reprinted from *Grade Teacher*, vol. 83, no. 3 (November 1965), pp. 69–70. Dr. May is the Mathematics Consultant for the Winnetka, Illinois, Public Schools.

From the first grade on, children learn you can interchange the addends and the sum remains the same. This is known as the *commutative property of addition.*

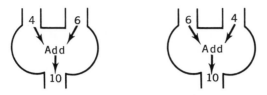

Figure 13.1

In the adding machines represented in the pictures above, it is apparent that addition is a binary operation, since you can add only two numbers at one time. When you add more than two numbers, you need more than one adding machine, like this:

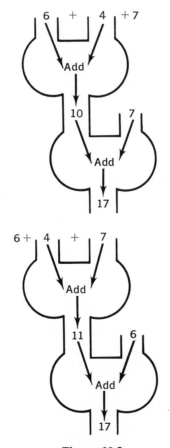

Figure 13.2

In adding $6 + 4 + 7$, you must decide which two numbers you are going to add first. Parentheses are used to indicate the numbers added first, like this:

$$(6 + 4) + 7 = 6 + (4 + 7)$$

On the left side, 4 is associated with 6; on the right side, 4 is associated with 7. This is known as the *associative property of addition*. Ask a class to add $98 + 47 + 2$ and the answer is 147 immediately. If you ask someone how he worked the problem, the answer is always that he added $98 + 2$ and then added 47. What makes it possible for the student to change the problem?

$98 + 47 + 2$	Original problem	$(98 + 2) + 47$	Associative property of addition
$98 + 2 + 47$	Commutative property of addition	$100 + 47$	Binary operation of addition

No one need go through all of these steps to do the problem. What is important is that children understand that shortcuts work because there are properties that allow you to take the shortcuts.

Most of us became aware of the associative property of addition when we learned column addition. The teacher told us to add the numbers 6, 5, and 3.

$$
\begin{array}{l}
14 \\
\hline
6 \\
+5 \quad (6 + 5) + 3 = (5 + 3) + 6 \\
3 \\
\hline
14
\end{array}
$$

Then the teacher said to add the column starting from the bottom and write the answer at the top.

When children start multiplication in the second or third grade, they discover that $2 \times 5 = 10$ and that $5 \times 2 = 10$. The 2 and 5 are called factors and the 10 is called a product. In multiplying numbers, you can interchange the factors and the product remains the same. This is known as the *commutative property of multiplication*. This property is true for whole numbers, fractional numbers, decimal numbers, irrational numbers, etc. If one is aware of the commutative property of addition and multiplication, it cuts the basic facts to be learned in half. If a child knows that $7 \times 8 = 56$, then he also knows $8 \times 7 = 56$.

Since you can only multiply two factors at one time, the operation of multiplication is also binary. When you multiply three factors, you need to decide which two factors will be multiplied first.

$$(5 \times 4) \times 6 = 5 \times (4 \times 6)$$

Parentheses are used to indicate which factors are multiplied first. On the left side, 4 is associated with 5; on the right side, 4 is associated with 6. This is known as the *associative property of multiplication*. For example, if you asked a class to multiply $25 \times 7 \times 4$, the answer would be given as 700. Then if you asked someone how he worked the problem, the answer would be that he multiplied 25×4 to get 100 and then multiplied 7×100 to get 700. What makes it possible for the student to change the problem?

$25 \times 7 \times 4$ Original problem	$(25 \times 4) \times 7$ Associative
$25 \times 4 \times 7$ Commutative	property of
property of	multiplication
multiplication	100×7 Binary operation
	of multiplication

Again, no one needs to go through all these steps to solve the problem. What is important is that the shortcut works because there are properties that allow you to take the shortcuts.

Zero and one are special numbers in our number system. In the first grade, children learn that, when you add zero to an addend, the sum is the same as the addend. Zero is known as the *identity element of addition*. When you multiply a factor by one (1), the product is the same as the factor. One is known as the *identity element of multiplication*.

5	3		
XXXXX	XXX	7×8	$= 56$
XXXXX	XXX	$7 \times (5 + 3)$	$= 56$
XXXXX	XXX		
7 XXXXX	XXX	7×5	$= 35$
XXXXX	XXX	7×3	$= 21$
XXXXX	XXX		
XXXXX	XXX	7×8	$= 56$

In the array above, there are 7 rows and 8 columns. This is a picture of the multiplication fact 7×8. The line renames the number 8 as $(5 + 3)$. On the left side of the line, there are 35 Xs because $7 \times 5 = 35$. On the right side of the line, there are 21 Xs because $7 \times 3 = 21$. One factor can be renamed in 2 parts and the other factor multiplied by each. The sum of the 2 results is the product of the original factors. This is the *distributive property of multiplication over addition*. Everyone good at mental arithmetic has used this technique without knowing it was a property. Most children know their multiplication facts through five. If they have difficulty, it is with 7×8, 7×9, 6×9, 8×9, 6×8. If you forget that $8 \times 9 = 72$, you can rename 9 as $(5 + 4)$ and multiply 8×5 and then multiply 8×4 and add the products.

$$8 \times (5 + 4)$$

The only way a teacher can explain compound multiplication is through the use of the distributive property.

$$
\begin{array}{r}
47 \\
\times\ 23 \\
\hline
141 \\
940 \\
\hline
1081
\end{array}
$$

$$47 \times \quad (20 + 3)$$
$$47 \times \ \ 3 = \ 141$$
$$47 \times 20 = \ 940$$
$$47 \times 23 = 1081$$

In multiplying 47 by 23, the three is multiplied by 47, then 20 is multiplied by 47. The use of the distributive property indicates that you name the factor 23 as $(20 + 3)$ before you multiply by 47.

Children today who are taught by the distributive property learn that they are multiplying not by 2 but by 20 and that, when you multiply by tens, the answer is in tens. Therefore, you write the product starting in the tens column. The same distributive property is used in multiplying whole numbers by fractional numbers, like this:

$$4 \times 6\tfrac{1}{2}$$
$$4 \times (6 + 1/2)$$

$$4 \times 6 \quad = 24$$
$$4 \times 1/2 \ = \ \ 2$$
$$4 \times 6\tfrac{1}{2} \ = 26$$

Zero and one have other properties besides the identity properties already mentioned. When you multiply a number by zero the product is zero. The number can be a whole number, fractional number, decimal number, irrational number, etc. This is known as the *property of zero*. Any number divided by itself, except for zero, is equal to one. This is known as the *property of one*.

Dividing by zero does not work in our number system. Division is an inverse operation of multiplication and can be explained only in terms of multiplication. For example, 8 divided by $4 = 2$ only if $2 \times 4 = 8$. If you have the problem 8 divided by 0, the question is: What is the answer? What number times zero equals 8? The property of zero says that any number times zero is zero. Therefore, there is not a number in our number system that can satisfy the condition.

The property of one is used in the intermediate grades to explain the simplification of fractional numbers. To simplify the fraction 4/6 means to give another name for the number where numbers used for the numerator and denominator are smaller:

$$\frac{4}{6} = \frac{2 \times 2}{2 \times 3} = 1 \times \frac{2}{3} = \frac{2}{3}$$

Two divided by two equals one, and one times two-thirds is two-thirds. What most adults call canceling is using the property of one.

Knowing the properties of our number system provides students of mathematics with the rules of the game. There is great security in knowing that you can tackle a problem you have never seen before because you have the tools at hand to help you solve it.

I4 EQUIVALENCE AND EQUALITY

Walter J. Sanders

BEFORE YOU READ Teachers and pupils are familiar with the term
"equals" and make much use of it. Less used, but often more appropriate,
is the term "equivalent." Some of the distinctions between these two
terms are described in this article by Professor Sanders. With fundamental
emphasis on the conditions which make two or more things equal or
equivalent, numerous exercises and problems are used to illustrate that it
is an application of mathematical properties, in many instances, that
determines whether two things are equal or equivalent.

    The nature of the transformations used as examples in this article
illustrates the versatility of the language of mathematics, which was a
concern in Section II. For example, the exercise $\begin{array}{r} 16 \\ \times\ 8 \\ \hline \end{array}$ may be expressed
as an equivalent exercise $\begin{array}{r} (10 + 6) \\ \times\ 8 \\ \hline \end{array}$. In the latter exercise the distributive
property is more clearly illustrated than it is in the former. In either
exercise a person would obtain the expression $80 + 48$, which is equal to
128.

    The terms equal and equivalent represent basic aspects of mathe-
matics, and it is important for teachers to understand appropriate distinctions in order to guide pupil development. Several illustrations from
the article can be used directly in flow charting a lesson or several lessons.

    As a result of reading this article the teacher should be able to
contrast the terms "equal" and "equivalent" and describe situations
appropriate to the application of each term.

Nancy was setting the table for the evening meal. When it was time to put
the silverware on the table her little sister Valerie asked to help. Nancy
said, "Get six teaspoons, six forks, and six knives from the silverware drawer
and place them around the table.

    1. Does it matter which six forks Valerie takes from the drawer?
    2. Does Valerie have to worry about which knife to place at a given
       place setting? Why?
    3. Eric came along later and switched spoons at two of the places. If no
       one saw him do this, do you think anyone will notice the switch?
       Would they notice if he switched a fork with a knife?

Reprinted from *The Arithmetic Teacher*, vol. 16, no. 4 (April 1969), pp. 317–322. Walter J.
Sanders is with the University of Illinois Committee on School Mathematics at Urbana,
Illinois.

4. When the silverware has been washed and dried it is put back into the silverware drawer. How does one decide into which of the partitioned sections each piece of silverware should be put (Fig. 14.1)?

Figure 14.1

EQUIVALENCE

When Valerie placed teaspoons, forks, and knives around the table it didn't matter which teaspoon was included in any given place setting; any one of the teaspoons is as suitable as any other for the use to be made of it. We say that, as far as ordinary usage is concerned, each teaspoon is *equivalent* to each of the other teaspoons. Similarly, any fork is equivalent to any other fork as far as its use for dinner is concerned.

> Whenever it makes no difference which of two objects is chosen to do a given job we say that the objects are *equivalent* with respect to that job.

Mrs. Smith asked Faye to hand out one sheet of red paper and one sheet of blue paper to each child in her art class.

1. Does it make any difference which red sheet is given to Eric?
2. Are all of the red sheets equivalent for the art lesson?
3. Lisa and Paul each received two sheets of paper, but by mistake both of Lisa's were red and Paul's were both blue. Are Lisa's two sheets equivalent to Paul's? Are either Lisa's or Paul's two sheets equivalent to those of the rest of the class?
4. Lisa gave Paul one of her red sheets in exchange for one of his blue sheets. Does it matter which sheets they exchanged? Why?

Often what one does when confronted with an arithmetic problem is try to find a different problem which he knows will have the same answer and is easier to complete. For example,

$$(25 + 37) + 75$$

has the same answer as

$$(25 + 75) + 37.$$

The second problem is much easier to complete, so one would work it rather than the first problem. We say that the two problems are equivalent (with respect to their answers).

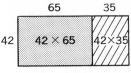

Figure 14.2

The diagram in Figure 14.2 can be used to see that $(42 \times 65) + (42 \times 35)$ and $42 \times (65 + 35)$ are equivalent problems. The area of the 42-by-65 rectangle is 42×65, and the area of the 42-by-35 rectangle is 42×35. The area of the large rectangle is the sum of these two areas: $(42 \times 65) + (42 \times 35)$. But the dimensions of the large rectangle are 42 by $(65 + 35)$, so the total area is also given by $42 \times (65 + 35)$.

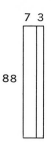

Figure 14.3

1. Are $(88 \times 7) + (88 \times 3)$ and $88 \times (7 + 3)$ equivalent problems? (Fig. 14.3.)
2. Are 6×75 and 7×75 equivalent problems?
3. $8 + 2$ and 2×5 are equivalent problems since they have the same answer. Give a problem which is equivalent to $53 \times 1 \times 17$.
4. Give a problem that is equivalent to $(77 \times 387) + (23 \times 387)$ but easier to compute (Fig. 14.4.)

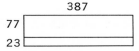

Figure 14.4

Ordinary multiplication of two numbers uses this same idea. The example below shows how the answer to the problem 32 × 7 is found working the equivalent problem (2 × 7) + (30 × 7).

$$
\begin{array}{r}
32 \\
\times 7 \\
\hline
14 \leftarrow\ \ 2 \times 7 \\
210 \leftarrow 30 \times 7 \\
\hline
224
\end{array}
$$

(Addition, subtraction, and division are treated similarly; the given problem is replaced by an equivalent problem that is easier to calculate.)

Figure 14.5

Eric's mother said he could have one cookie. The cookies were made from three different cookie-cutters as shown in the picture (Fig. 14.5). Do you think it matters to Eric which cookie he takes? Are some of the cookies equivalent, as far as Eric is concerned, but others not? Explain. Faye wasn't very hungry, but she didn't wish to refuse a cookie. Do you think that she will choose the same shape cookie as Eric?

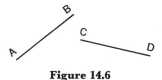

Figure 14.6

Figure 14.6 shows segment *AB* and segment *CD*.

1. How many segments are pictured?
2. The two segments pictured have the same length. Are they equivalent with respect to length?

3. Is segment *AB* different from segment *CD* in any way? If so, how?
4. The picture shows segment *BA*. Does this mean that there are three different segments in the picture?
5. Are segment *AB* and segment *CD* the very same segment?
6. Are segment *AB* and segment *BA* the very same segment?

EQUALITY

In the picture of the two segments above, segment *AB* and segment *BA* are the very same segment. That is, there are just two ways of naming the one segment. We say that

segment *AB* *equals* segment *BA*.

On the other hand, segment *AB* and segment *CD* are two different segments. They occupy different positions in space. Point *C* is an element of segment *CD* but not an element of segment *AB*. So,

segment *AB* is not equal to segment *CD*.

Of course, segments *AB* and *CD* have the same length, so it is correct to say that the length of segment *AB* equals the length of segment *CD*. But, to say that their *lengths* are equal is not to say that *they* are equal.

> A pair of things are *equal* if they do not differ in any way whatsoever. Thus, a statement of equality is a claim that only one thing is under consideration; two different things can never be equal.

The three figures in the picture (Fig. 14.7) all have the same height.

Figure 14.7

1. Is the *height* of the shaded figure equal to the *height* of the triangle?
2. Is the shaded *figure* equal to the *triangle*? (That is, are they the same figure?)
3. Is the shaded figure equal to the circular figure?
4. The second figure is equal to the _____ figure.
5. Since the height of the triangle equals the height of the square, the triangle and the square are _____ with respect to height.

SORTING PROBLEMS IN MATHEMATICS

Many of the fundamental ideas of mathematics center around classifying objects according to a particular property. Thus we learn in arithmetic to classify problems that have the same answer so that we may choose an easier problem than the one we are given to work. In algebra we classify equations according to their solution sets—two equations are equivalent if they have the same solution set. Then we learn ways of deciding which equations are equivalent so that we can choose easy equations to solve. For example, one rule for finding equivalent equations involves adding the same number to both members of an equation. If we are given

$$3 \times \square - 7 = 8$$

we can add 7 to both members to get

$$(3 \times \square - 7) + 7 = 8 + 7,$$

which simplifies to

$$3 \times \square = 15,$$

an equivalent equation that is easier to solve than the original equation. Thus we see that in arithmetic we use the idea of equivalent problems to simplify our work, and in algebra we use equivalent equations to simplify our work.

Some kinds of equivalence are used so often that they are given special names. In geometry when two figures have the same shape (that is, they are equivalent with respect to shape) they are said to be *similar*. Two figures that are similar and also the same size (equivalent with respect to both shape and size) are *congruent*. Lines that are equivalent with respect to direction are *parallel*.

A part of language study is finding out which sentences say the same thing, that is, sentences that are equivalent with respect to meaning. Such sentences are said to be logically equivalent.

EQUIVALENCE CLASSES

In sorting the silverware into the sections of the silverware drawer, all the knives go into one section, all the teaspoons into another, all the forks into a third, and all the tablespoons into a fourth. Thus all the items in one section are equivalent to the others in that section, but not equivalent to silverware in other sections. We call a sorting into piles of equivalent objects like this a *partitioning into equivalence classes*.

In the above example involving red and blue art paper, the red sheets were equivalent to each other and the blue sheets were equivalent to each other, so there were just two equivalence classes: the set of red sheets and the set of blue sheets.

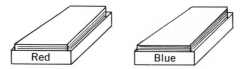

Figure 14.8 Equivalence classes of art paper

In sorting geometric figures by congruence, each triangle goes into the pile with the triangles that are congruent to it. Since there are lots of triangles that have different sizes and shapes there will be lots of different piles for triangles. And there will be lots of other piles for different sized circles, and others for different size squares, and so forth.

Figure 14.9 Equivalence classes for congruence

FRACTIONS

Fractions are equivalent if they name the same number. So

$$\frac{2}{4} \quad \text{and} \quad \frac{15}{30}$$

are equivalent, but

$$\frac{1}{3} \quad \text{and} \quad \frac{1}{7}$$

are not equivalent.

The usual way to find the sum

$$\frac{2}{3} + \frac{1}{4}$$

is to find fractions which are equivalent to the given fractions and which have the same denominator. One way to do this is to look at the equivalence classes for the fractions

$$\frac{2}{3} \text{ and } \frac{1}{4} :$$

Equivalence class for $\frac{2}{3}$	$\frac{2}{3}$	$\frac{4}{6}$	$\frac{6}{9}$	$\frac{8}{12}$	$\frac{10}{15}$	$\frac{12}{18}$	$\frac{14}{21}$	$\frac{16}{24}$	$\frac{18}{27}$	$\frac{20}{30}\ldots$
Equivalence class for $\frac{1}{4}$	$\frac{1}{4}$	$\frac{2}{8}$	$\frac{3}{12}$	$\frac{4}{16}$	$\frac{5}{20}$	$\frac{6}{24}$	$\frac{7}{28}$	$\frac{8}{32}$	$\frac{9}{36}$	$\frac{10}{40}$ $\frac{11}{44}\ldots$

Figure 14.10

We see that the problem

$$\frac{8}{12} + \frac{3}{12}$$

is equivalent to the given problem. Since

$$\frac{8}{12} + \frac{3}{12} = \frac{11}{12},$$

it follows that

$$\frac{2}{3} + \frac{1}{4} = \frac{11}{12}.$$

SUMMARY

Whenever it doesn't matter which of two things you use to do a certain job, the two things are equivalent for that job. This idea is used over and over again in mathematics. Thus, to simplify the work in arithmetic, one learns various ways to transform a given problem into an equivalent problem that is easier to work. In algebra the theory of equation solving rests on rules for transforming equations into equivalent equations that are easier to solve. In geometry much of the simplification of problems results from noting the equivalence of two triangles with respect to size or shape.

At other times one is interested in reporting that two different-appearing expressions really describe exactly the same thing. In such a case the proper word to use is "equals." One must be careful to pay attention to what it is that is being described, however. Thus, two different forks are equivalent for a certain use, but they are not equal. (They are not the same fork.) In the same way, two pencils may have the same color and markings but the pencils are not equal. They are two different pencils, and one may be sharpened without affecting the other. But it may be that the *color* of one pencil equals (is exactly the same as) the *color* of the other.

These two ideas—equivalence and equality—are fundamental in mathematics. Children can understand and appreciate these ideas through examples such as were suggested throughout this article.

The payoff for children who do understand equivalence and equality will be an increased understanding of the processes ordinarily undertaken in school mathematics.

I5 THE PROPERTIES OF MULTIPLICATION

BEFORE YOU READ   This article and the one immediately following by William J. Oosse should be read in conjunction, for both deal with similar types of properties. Yet they are very different. The first contains what might be called an intuitive consideration of the properties of multiplication. That is, the examples used to facilitate an understanding of the operation of multiplication suggest the existence of the properties. The article by Professor Oosse, on the other hand, contains what might be called a foundational consideration of the properties of an operation. That is, the properties of an operation are established by a logical consideration of the operation itself.

By comparing and analyzing the two articles one is helped to recall that a child learns and is able to understand mathematics in a more comprehensive manner through investigating concepts at successively increasing degrees of abstractions over time. In essence, concepts must be revisited many times in a variety of contexts before they can be understood in comprehensive fashion.

By reading both articles the teacher should be able to note differences with regard to the use of repeated addition and arrays as a basis for developing an understanding of the operation of multiplication, and illustrate the independence of the commutative and associative properties with several specific examples.

If an adult were asked to multiply 3 and 2, he would quickly think of 6 without bothering to think how he arrived at that number. Most adults know how to work simple multiplication problems too well to think about them. Most children, however, don't know anything about multiplication until they learn it at school. How does a teacher show children that 6, rather than some other number, is the product of 3 times 2? In other words, how would he teach them what multiplication means?

Perhaps the most familiar approach to understanding multiplication is through repeated *addition*. A child who can compute the sum of $2 + 2 + 2$ can then be shown the expression 3×2 as a more economical way of finding the sum of three 2's.

Reprinted from the *National Education Association Journal*, vol. 55, no. 4 (April 1966), pp. 23–25. This article is based on the color film, *Multiplication and Its Properties*, produced by the National Council of Teachers of Mathematics, an NEA department. The film is No. 5 in the series, *Films in Mathematics for Elementary School Teachers*, made possible by a grant from the National Science Foundation.

The advantage of multiplication over repeated addition becomes a great deal more obvious when the child encounters a problem like the following:

A boy buys 23 bags of marbles and each bag contains 12 marbles. How many marbles should he have?

Instead of adding up a column of twenty-three 12's the child will learn to find the result much more quickly by computing 23 × 12 using the usual or traditional multiplication computation procedure. But by the time a child learns to multiply a set of numbers or factors with two or more digits, such as 12 and 23, he may have already forgotten the relationship between addition and multiplication. Like most adults who "know how to multiply," he may not be able to tell you why 3 × 2 = 6, except that "it just does."

Instead of relying solely on the repeated-addition approach to multiplication, a teacher might have his pupils examine another approach to multiplication which will help them to develop a meaningful concept of it.

Especially useful in developing an understanding of multiplication is the *array*. An array is a rectangular arrangement in which each row has the same number of objects, and each column has the same number of objects.

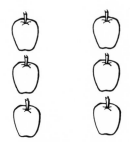

Figure 15.1

The above is a so-called 3 by 2 array, because it is customary to name the number of rows (horizontal) first. Any array can be interpreted in various ways. For example, the above array represents 2 + 2 + 2, or 3 × 2 objects, or 3 jumps of 2 intervals each on a number line.

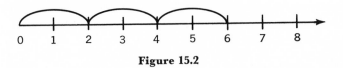

Figure 15.2

Because it can be applied so generally, the array is a useful device for developing a definition of the product of whole numbers. Using "*a*" to represent the number of rows in any array and "*b*" to represent the number of columns, one can say that for *any* whole numbers *a* and *b*, the number of elements in an *a* by *b* array is $a \times b$; that is, the product of any pair of whole numbers in an array can be expressed by the number of rows times the number of columns. Furthermore, in an *a* by *b* array, the numbers *a* and *b* are called *factors*.

For example, in the following specific array, what number does *a* represent? How about *b*?

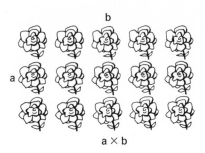

$a \times b$

Figure 15.3

How would one express the number of elements in this array?

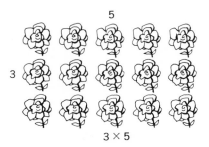

3×5

Figure 15.4

Although 3×5 is the product of its factors, 3 and 5, this product has other names. Its standard name, which a child could determine easily by counting the objects in the array, is 15. Thus, he learns that $3 \times 5 = 15$. He also learns that multiplication assigns one and only one product to the pair of numbers 3 and 5 though different numerals, such as 3×5 or 15, may be used to name the product.

An array can also be used to teach children certain properties of multiplication. In order to do this, however, it is necessary to review briefly some of the things they should have learned about addition.

Children learn that addition assigns a number called a *sum* to a pair of numbers called *addends*. Multiplication is somewhat similar in that it assigns a number called a *product* to a pair of numbers called *factors*.

Another thing children learn about addition is that it is commutative. This simply means that changing the order of two addends does not affect their sum. Thus, $2 + 4 = 4 + 2$. Does the same principle apply to multiplication? That is, does changing the order of two factors affect the product?

The answer, of course, is obvious to an adult, but to children who are learning the basic facts of multiplication for the first time it is not obvious that, let's say, 3×4 and 4×3 name the same number.

With the aid of an array on a feltboard, however, a teacher can easily demonstrate the commutativity of multiplication.

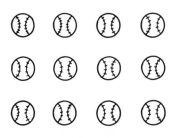

Figure 15.5

The above is a 3×4 array. To find its number of elements, one multiplies the number of rows, 3, times the number of columns, 4.

Tipping the array makes it look like this:

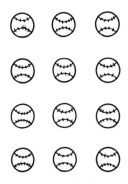

Figure 15.6

It is now a 4×3 array, and its number is 4×3. Because the number of elements remains the same, children can see that $3 \times 4 = 4 \times 3$. They now understand that changing the order of two factors does not affect the product.

Knowing that multiplication is commutative reduces the number of facts children have to memorize in learning to multiply. For example, if they know that 8×3 is 24, then they also know that 3×8 is 24; or that, in general, for any whole numbers a and b, $a \times b = b \times a$.

Another property shared by addition and multiplication is that, for practical purposes, both are *associative*. In doing addition, for instance, for any whole numbers a, b, and c,

$$(a + b) + c = a + (b + c).$$

Children who know that addition is associative may try to see whether the same property applies to multiplication. In the example below it does apply.

$$(4 \times 3) \times 2 = 4 \times (3 \times 2)$$
$$12 \times 2 = 4 \times 6$$
$$24 \quad = \quad 24$$

After working several such examples, children might conclude, at least tentatively, that multiplication *is* associative, that is, for any whole numbers a, b, and c, $(a \times b) \times c = a \times (b \times c)$.

Children use the associative property of multiplication when they first learn to compare products like 3×20. They may think of 3×20 as $3 \times (2 \times 10.)$ Because of the associative property, $3 \times (2 \times 10)$ is the same number as $(3 \times 2) \times 10$, or 6 tens . . . or 60.

Another property or characteristic of addition is its *identity element*—zero. That is, the sum of zero and any number is that number.

$$4 + 0 = 4$$

Does multiplication have an identity number? Is there a number such that whenever it is one of two factors, the product is identical with the other factor?

If challenged, children can readily produce an array which will answer this question. For example, below is a 4 by 1 array that has a product of 4×1 or 4 and a factor of 4.

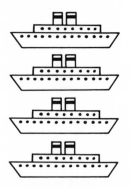

Figure 15.7

In any array with only one column, the number of elements in the column is the number of elements in the array. Also, in any array with only one row, the number of elements in the row is the number of elements in the array.

Figure 15.8

Therefore, if the number 1 is one of two factors, the other factor and the product will be identical. Another way of expressing this is, for any whole number a, $a \times 1 = 1 \times a = a$. And the identity element for multiplication is 1. No other number plays this role in multiplication.

It is essential that children learn that multiplication and addition have different identity elements; that for multiplication it is one, and for addition, it is zero.

Although zero is not the identity element in multiplication, it does play a special role in the process. Trying to illustrate this role with an array, however, may be somewhat difficult. Imagine a child's confusion in trying to picture a 5×0 array—an array with five rows and no objects in each row—or a 0 by 5 array—an array with no rows, yet five objects in each row. Actually, an array with no rows and no columns might be called an empty array, and the number of objects in an empty array is obviously zero.

Perhaps a more convincing way of showing that 0×5 and 5×0 are equal to zero is through the *cross product* approach.

The following diagram represents the cross product of two sets of items—a set of three kinds of pie: apple, blueberry, and cherry; and a set of two kinds of ice cream: strawberry and vanilla.

Figure 15.9

The dots represent the possible combinations of pie and ice cream (apple-strawberry, apple-vanilla, blueberry-strawberry, etc.). The number of all the possible combinations of pie and ice cream is called the cross product of the two sets, in this case, 6. The cross product, then, is a set of combinations.

The following example illustrates how this approach can be used to show that 0×5 and 5×0 are equal to zero:

Several boy and girl couples are needed to do a dance in the class play. The diagram below represents the set of boys and the set of girls who volunteered to try out for the dance parts.

Figure 15.10

There are 5 girls, but alas, and perhaps typically, 0 boys. How many possible couples are there for the dance? When one of the sets is empty, there are no couples, and the cross product is also empty. One can say logically that if the number of elements in one of two sets is zero, the number of pairs in their cross product is also zero.

The special role of zero in multiplication can be expressed by the statement that for any whole number a, $a \times 0 = 0 \times a = 0$. Putting it more simply: Any number times zero or zero times any number equal zero.

Although the array is a highly effective approach to an understanding of multiplication, it can be even more helpful to children when used in combination with a variety of other approaches. Some of these other approaches, such as repeated addition, the number line, and cross product have been touched upon in this article.

The newer programs in elementary school mathematics provide a wealth of material for developing a meaningful concept of multiplication. The teacher's own understanding of and enthusiasm for this new material can, in turn, stimulate interest, and even excitement, in his pupils.

16 PROPERTIES OF OPERATIONS: A MEANINGFUL STUDY

William J. Oosse

One of the problems faced by middle-school-aged children in the study of mathematics finds its root in the properties of binary operations when confronting various mathematical systems. By the time these children begin the study of the properties of each of the four basic operations, they have already done extensive work with the operation itself. That is, children have learned to add, subtract, multiply, and divide long before the properties of these operations are introduced formally. By the time formal study of the operations and their properties is begun, the students are often no longer able to distinguish the property under consideration from the operation itself. Thus it becomes quite difficult to explain to some children exactly what is meant by the words "closure, associative, commutative, identity, and inverse." Even though a teacher may succeed in fixing these concepts in the minds of his students, he must then face the problem of convincing each student, in a meaningful way, that every operation that is associative is not necessarily commutative, and vice versa. This is not an easy task, because the student is generally aware that addition and multiplication in the set of natural numbers have both properties, whereas subtraction and division in the same set have neither; in fact they do not even possess the closure property!

The purpose of this article is to exhibit several examples of operations as defined upon various sets, which illustrate that the commutative and associative properties are independent. It is our conviction that students will understand the independence of these properties if they can actually experience this independence. Therefore we strongly recommend that each student be allowed to experiment with the following examples, under guidance by the teacher, until he is able to appreciate, at least in an intuitive way, what is meant by a property (or lack of it) of an operation. The teacher could then follow this investigation with a discussion of why certain of the algorithms which the student has learned to use are successful. (Certainly, at this stage, a student should be convinced that the addition of a column of numbers in a "downward" direction or an "upward" direction yields the same result. However, after the study of these properties, he should be able to understand why it does!)

Reprinted from *The Arithmetic Teacher*, vol. 16, no. 4 (April 1969), pp. 271–275. William J. Oosse is Mathematics Consultant for Public Schools in Grand Rapids, Michigan.

In each of the following examples, the set is composed of tangible objects or familiar numbers in order to make the ideas that the student should discover seem more real to him. It is suggested that each student be allowed to progress through each example at his own pace; therefore, it will be necessary for the teacher to accumulate enough materials so that a natural progression can occur. It is very possible that each student would like to construct his own set of materials. We leave each teacher to his own creative thoughts concerning the supplying of materials.

1. COMMUTATIVE, BUT NOT ASSOCIATIVE

Example Ia. (*An abelian loop*).—The set upon which we will define an operation will consist of a sack of colored rods as suggested in Figure 16.1. The sack should contain several of each of the colored rods.

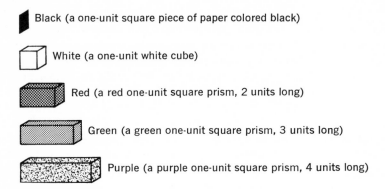

Black (a one-unit square piece of paper colored black)

White (a one-unit white cube)

Red (a red one-unit square prism, 2 units long)

Green (a green one-unit square prism, 3 units long)

Purple (a purple one-unit square prism, 4 units long)

Figure 16.1

Define an operation, denoted by $\otimes$, on the set of colored rods as follows: If x and y are elements of the set, $x \otimes y$ means, "stand the x rod on its square surface, then place the y rod on its square surface to the right of the x rod." The answer will then be the rod which when placed upon the shorter of the two rods makes the heights as nearly equal as possible. For example, green $\otimes$ red = white because if the red is placed to the right of the green, the white is required on the red to make the heights as nearly equal as possible.

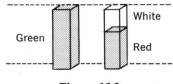

Figure 16.2

At this point, the students should be allowed to investigate many problems of this type and find the answers. After much experimentation, each student should build an appropriate operation table. (See Table 16.1.)

Table 16.1

⊗	*black*	*white*	*red*	*green*	*purple*
black	black	white	red	green	purple
white	white	black	white	red	green
red	red	white	black	white	red
green	green	red	white	black	white
purple	purple	green	red	white	black

After completing the table, the students should investigate to see which of the following properties are possessed by this operation.

1. Closure
2. Commutativity
3. Associativity
4. Identity element
5. Inverse for each element

We note that all but the associative property hold in this system, and can conclude that the commutative property does not imply the associative property.

A counter-example for associativity:

$$(red \otimes white) \otimes green \ ? \ red \otimes (white \otimes green)$$
$$white \otimes green \ ? \ red \otimes red$$
$$red \neq black,$$

therefore, not associative.

Example Ib.—Define an operation, denoted by #, on the set of rational numbers as follows: If x and y are elements of the set of rational numbers, $x \# y$ shall be the arithmetic mean of x and y. Property investigation is left to the reader.

Example Ic.—Define an operation, denoted by ⊗, on {0, 1, 3, 4} as follows: if x and y are elements of the set, then $x \otimes y$ shall be the absolute value of the difference between x and y, i.e., $|x - y|$. The reader should investigate the properties.

II. COMMUTATIVE AND ASSOCIATIVE

Example IIa. (*An abelian group*).—Suppose we had a rectangle with a mark in one corner, and a frame in which the rectangle could be placed. (See Fig. 16.3.)

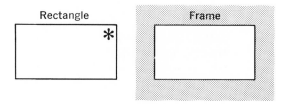

Figure 16.3

The student should be allowed to discover that there are four possible ways that the rectangle can be placed in the frame so that the edges coincide. Let the set of the four positions be the set for this example. If the frame is fixed, we will denote the four positions as follows:

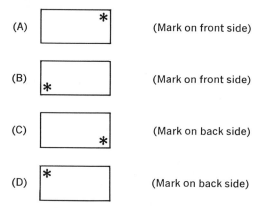

Figure 16.4

Now one of the positions is arbitrarily established as "starting position." We choose to establish position *A* as starting position in this example.

With each position there is a corresponding movement of the rectangle which will move the rectangle from the starting position to the named position.

(A) Pick up the rectangle and place it down as it was.
(B) Rotate the rectangle 180° about its center.
(C) Flip the rectangle 180° on its horizontal axis.
(D) Flip the rectangle 180° on its vertical axis.

Define the operation, denoted by $\oplus$, on the set $\{A, B, C, D\}$ as follows: If x and y are elements of the set, $x \oplus y$ means "place the rectangle in the starting position, then perform the movement corresponding to x, directly followed by the movement corresponding to y."

Again, the students should be allowed to experiment with various problems in the system, culminating with the development of an operation table for $\oplus$.

$\oplus$	A	B	C	D
A	A	B	C	D
B	B	A	D	C
C	C	D	A	B
D	D	C	B	A

Figure 16.5

The students are then ready to investigate to determine which properties are exhibited by this system.

1. Closure
2. Commutativity
3. Associativity
4. Identity element
5. Inverse for each element

It should be noted that all five of the properties hold in this system. The teacher could follow the study of this system with a comparison between the set of natural numbers under addition, and this system.

Example IIb.—Define an operation, denoted by $\#$ on $\{0, 1, 2, 3\}$ as follows: If x and y are elements of the set, then $x \# y$ is the remainder that results when dividing the sum of x and y by 4. (Note that this is addition modulo 4.) Investigation of properties is left to the reader.

III. ASSOCIATIVE, BUT NOT COMMUTATIVE

Example IIIa. (A group).—Suppose we had an equilateral triangle with a mark at one of its vertices, and a frame in which to place the triangle. (See Fig. 16.6.)

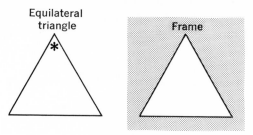

Figure 16.6

The student should be allowed to discover that there are six possible positions in which the triangle can be placed in the frame so that the edges coincide. Consider the set of the six positions as noted.

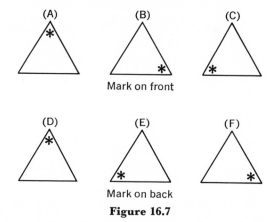

Figure 16.7

As in Example IIa, one of the positions should be designated as the starting position, say *A*. With each of the positions, we now define a corresponding motion that would move the triangle from the starting position to the named position.

(A) Pick up the triangle and place it down as it was.
(B) Rotate the triangle 120° clockwise about its center.
(C) Rotate the triangle 120° counterclockwise about its center.
(D) Flip the triangle 180° on its vertical axis.
(E) Flip the triangle 180° on its upper-left lower-right axis.
(F) Flip the triangle 180° on its upper-right lower-left axis.

Define the operation, denoted by $\bigcirc$, on the set $\{A, B, C, D, E, F\}$ as follows: If x and y are elements of the set, $x \bigcirc y$ means "place the triangle in starting position, then perform the motion corresponding to x, followed directly by the motion corresponding to y." The answer is the resulting position. For example, $B \bigcirc D = E$.

The students should experiment with various problems and then build an appropriate operation table. (See the following figure.)

$\bigodot$	A	B	C	D	E	F
A	A	B	C	D	E	F
B	B	C	A	E	F	D
C	C	A	B	F	D	E
D	D	F	E	A	C	B
E	E	D	F	B	A	C
F	F	E	D	C	B	A

Figure 16.8

Upon completion of the table, the student should determine which properties hold in this system.

1. Closure
2. Commutativity
3. Associativity
4. Identity element
5. Inverse for each element

It is to be noted that all but the commutative property hold for the operation as defined on $\{A, B, C, D, E, F\}$.

A counter-example for commutativity:

$$E \bigcirc B \ ? \ B \bigcirc E$$
$$D \neq F$$

therefore, not commutative. Thus we note that associativity does not imply commutativity.

Example IIIb.—Define an operation, denoted by $*$ on the set of natural numbers as follows: If x and y are elements of the set of natural numbers, then $x * y$ shall be the natural number obtained by placing x to the left of y. $(2 * 15 = 215)$. The reader should investigate the properties.

SUMMARY

It is felt that a student can be stimulated to look at other similar systems of his own invention by simply asking the question, "What properties would be exhibited by the motions of other regular geometric plane figures in a frame?" Students should also be encouraged to find a plane geometrical figure that would have only rotations and no flips in its set of legal moves. (That is, flips would be illegal because the flipped figure would not coincide with the frame.) Following a unit such as this, the student should have a better understanding of the properties of an operation, and could attach proper importance to these properties when dealing with familiar systems.

I 7 SETS: A UNIFYING FACTOR

Sister Ann Dominic Tassone

BEFORE YOU READ   To learn the structure of mathematics one must learn basic concepts and the properties. Sets are the foundation from which the concepts are developed and on which the properties are based. This is especially applicable to notions that can be learned by working with concrete materials. For example, work with sets can lead to the development of concepts such as cardinal number, operation, and relation. Work with sets can also lead to understanding that some relations have certain properties.

This article by Sister Ann Dominic Tassone discusses some of the ways in which sets are used to develop basic ideas. After reading it, the teacher should be able to describe a rationale for the use of sets in teaching number ideas, and define with appropriate illustrations the terms "condition" and "function."

The modern approach to mathematics stresses understanding. The changing curricula are so structured that the basic concepts are broadened and deepened as content is presented sequentially. Mathematics educators indicate that there are basic structures produced by the recurrence of fundamental ideas. A study of arithmetic, algebra, and geometry reveals common patterns which suggest a closer integration of these subdivisions. In various contemporary curricula, we note increased emphasis on several concepts which unify and effect this integration, namely, the concepts of a set, of a number system, of a mathematical condition, and of a relation.

The influence of sets as a unifying concept provides insight and an overall grasp of many underlying principles of the mathematics taught in the secondary school. The notion of a set enables us to provide more understanding and better learning of mathematics by establishing a meaningful treatment of some fundamental mathematical ideas. Everyone is familiar with a set of objects. Indeed, it is one of the simplest concepts. This simplicity makes it an ideal foundation for building mathematical concepts on both the elementary and the secondary school levels.

Reprinted from *Catholic School Journal, September, 1966-pp. 79–81* with permission of the publisher. This article is copyrighted. © *1966* by CCM Professional Magazines, Inc. All rights reserved. Sister Ann Dominic Tassone is at Avila College, Kansas City, Missouri.

NUMBER

Set is discussed as a key pre-number idea. By so doing we have the beginnings of a way by which we will be able to connect numbers to sets of physical objects. This connection is important because it enables arithmetic to be applied to the physical world. Through working with sets, we effectively teach numbers to children.

An important part of the idea of a set is that a set is completely specified when its members are specified. A set may be determined by naming its members (without regard to their order) or describing them by some property they have in common. If there is a one-to-one pairing of all members of one set with all the members of another set, we have a matching of the two sets and a one-to-one correspondence of their members. The sets are defined as equivalent sets and share a common property, cardinal number.

There are set operations, namely, union and intersection, which when used on two sets produce one new set. Such operations are called binary operations. Addition (the union of two disjoint sets) and multiplication are binary operations on numbers since they assign single numbers to pairs of numbers. Number and its properties are ideas associated with sets and properties of sets.

CONDITION

To communicate ideas in writing or speech we use sentences, usually declarative sentences. A declarative sentence expresses an idea about which a decision can be made as to whether the idea is true or false. Declarative sentences that express true or false ideas are called closed sentences. The ideas expressed by closed sentences are termed statements. Sentences that are not closed are open sentences. Whereas closed sentences express statements, open sentences express *conditions* that when satisfied produce true statements.

We choose to define an equation as a true statement that is expressed by a sentence containing the symbol for "equals." The condition $x + 8 = 17$ is not an equation, since it is not a statement that is true. However, we see that the condition $x + 8 = 17$ is expressed by an open sentence that has the symbol for "equals." When we refer to such a condition as an equation, we really mean that it is a condition for an equation. It implies that our intention is to obtain an equation from the condition after we make replacements. The replacements are selected from a designated set of numbers. Those numbers which make the sentence true constitute the solution set.

A more detailed study of solution sets of conditions in two variables follows. Consider two sets A and B that have elements a and b respectively. The set $[a, b]$ is identical with the set $[b, a]$ since the order in which the elements of a set are listed does not affect the fact that a given object belongs to the set. However, there are occasions when the order in which two

elements are given is important, and to cover such situations, it is necessary
to introduce the concept of an ordered pair of elements.

If a is an element of set A and b is an element of set B, we say the
symbol (a, b) represents an ordered pair of elements whose first entry is a and
whose second entry is b. Two ordered pairs (a, b) and (c, d) are regarded as
equal if, and only if, $a = c$ and $b = d$. Therefore, the pairs $(5, 9)$, $(9, 5)$, and
$(5, 5)$ are all distinct ordered pairs.

With this notion, it is possible to define another set operation. If A
and B are sets, the set of all ordered pairs whose first entry is an element
of A and whose second entry is an element of B is called the Cartesian
Product $A \times B$ of A and B.

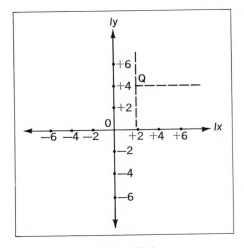

Figure 17.1

In a fashion similar to that in which real numbers can be represented
on a line, the elements of $R \times R$ (where R is the set of all real numbers) can
be represented on a plane. Let lx and ly be mutually perpendicular real
number lines in a plane and the point of intersection of lx and ly have the
coordinate 0 in each system. We can identify any point in the plane with a
unique pair of numbers. The first number of the pair is the x-distance found
on the lx line and the second is the y-distance found on the ly line. Let Q
be any point in the plane that contains the lines lx and ly, and consider the
lines through Q parallel to lx and ly. The line through Q parallel to ly will
meet lx at a point corresponding to some number x, which in the diagram
is 2. The number x, or 2 in this case, is the first coordinate of Q. Similarly,
a line through Q parallel to lx will meet ly at a point corresponding to a
number y called the second coordinate of Q. In the diagram 4 is the y-
distance, or the second coordinate of the ordered pair. The ordered pair

(2, 4) represents a point in the plane. In this manner, each point in the plane is assigned a unique ordered pair of numbers, and conversely. $R \times R$ and the points of the plane containing lx and ly are called the Cartesian coordinate system determined by lx and ly.

RELATION

Conditions like $y \div x$, $x \leq y$, $y = 2x$, and $y = 5x + 3$ are true of two things at a time, or more exactly, of ordered pairs of things. Once we specify the set of elements to be considered, then the cross product of this set furnishes all ordered pairs of elements which are then the elements to be tested by the condition. The conditions given above express a certain relationship between x and y. The mathematical meaning of the relationship so expressed is taken to be the set of ordered pairs which satisfy the condition. Thus it can be said that a relation in a set R is a set of ordered pairs from $R \times R$. The domain of a relation is the set of all first members of the pairs which make up the relation. The range of a relation is the set of all second members of the pairs which make up the relation.

FUNCTION

Relations that are considered may differ from others in at least one respect. In some relations the first element of each ordered pair in the relation is paired with only one second element. In other words, for each element of the domain there corresponds one and only one element of the range. This type of relation is known as a function. Thus a function is a set of ordered pairs, no two of which have the same first component or coordinate.

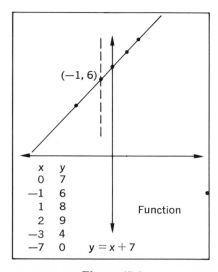

Figure 17.2

In the relation $y = x + 7$, we may say that "y is a function of x," since to every x selected, there corresponds one and only one y. This relation states that each y has the value $x + 7$, and therefore the ordered pair is expressible in the form $(x, x + 7)$. Some of the ordered pairs resulting from this relation are $(0, 7)$, $(^-1, 6)$, $(1, 8)$, $(2, 9)$, $(^-3, 4)$, and $(^-7, 0)$. For each pair (x, y) there is one and only one y associated with the x.

On the other hand in the relation $x = y^2$, we cannot say that "y is a function of x," since to any x there corresponds two possible y's: $(0, 0)$, $(1, ^-1)$, $(1, 1)$, $(4, 2)$, $(4, ^-2)$, etc.

If we examine the graphs of relations, we can determine if they are functions by applying this test: A is a function if A is a relation and if each vertical line intersects the graph of A in at most one point.

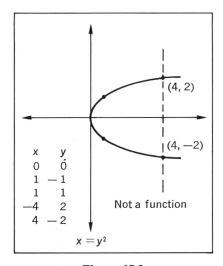

Figure 17.3

The significance of the definition is obvious. If a vertical line intersects the graph of a relation more than once, there would have to be at least two points of the graph of the relation in this vertical line. In order for this to be true, the points in question must have the same first coordinate. Apparently A is not a function. For example (see Figure 17.3).

Since a function is a special type of relation, the terms "domain" and "range" are used and interpreted for functions, just as they are interpreted for relations.

SPECIAL CASE

It can be shown that binary operations are special cases of the function concept. We recall that binary operations act on two elements to produce single elements, e.g., forming the intersection and union of sets and the addition and multiplication of numbers. Binary operations, such as addition and multiplication, may be defined as sets of ordered pairs where the first element is itself a pair of numbers. For example: $5 + 2 = 7$ in the notation of an ordered pair is represented as $[(5, 2), 7]$ where $(5, 2)$ is the first entry and 7 is the second entry. Working with the integers we see that it is possible to consider functions in which the domain of the function is a set of $I \times I$ and the range is I.

Ample material has been presented to acquaint us with the sound basis that evolves from consideration of definitions and elementary topics of mathematics in this manner. We recognize as we trace the powerful notion of set which threads its way throughout the discussion that the mathematical structure spirals, and as its whorls increase in breadth, real mathematical understanding and progress are afforded us through such a structured presentation. The concept of set is one of the major avenues to arrive at the desirable goals of minimizing the separation of mathematics into disjoint subdivisions and of clarifying and improving the understanding of mathematics.

SECTION IV

Basic Operations: Utilizing Forms of Composition and Decomposition

" 'Reeling and writhing, of course, to begin with,' the mock turtle replied, 'and the different branches of Arithmetic—Ambition, Distraction, Uglification, and Derision.' "

Lewis Carroll, *Alice in Wonderland*

Introduction

INTRODUCTION

The basic operations of addition and multiplication, together with the defined operations of subtraction and division and their accompanying procedures for computation, receive more emphasis than other aspects of the elementary school mathematics program. It is axiomatic that the operations must be learned. However, pupils often learn their basic addition and multiplication facts only to be asked to solve an almost unlimited number of computational exercises. Pedagogical rationale for such assignments is that the work helps students master a procedure for arriving at a correct answer.

It was pointed out in Section I that the mental discipline theory was discarded in favor of theories which could better explain how people learn. Despite the need for meaningful drill, long, repetitive assignments of similar substantive content do not appreciably aid learning. Teachers today realize that the child who can correctly solve four exercises such as $N \times 8 < 613$, $N \times 3 < 292$, $N \times 6 < 356$, and $N \times 7 < 632$ is not likely to gain much by completing twenty additional similar exercises. The same may be said for those children who do not understand. If a child cannot correctly solve four similar exercises he will not likely gain by attempting others.

There are at least two things wrong with assigning repetitive exercises which are basically similar and asking children to seek solutions by employing a specified procedure. First, it is pedagogically unsound. The numbers used in the exercises are not directly associated to amounts with which the child has worked. They are simply things written on a page. Second, nothing is done to make it possible for the child to recognize the set of conditions which would lead to the development of the exercises. That is, the exercises do not seem to be related to anything existing in the child's frame of reference. These related criticisms suggest that computations which do not arise as an outgrowth of problem solving, or that are not directly related to problem solving, are of less value than those in which the child has a stake in developing the basis for which the computation is required. This is certainly consistent with the notion of providing active and purposeful learning.

With regard to computational exercises, it is interesting to note the algorithms that may be used. For example, consider the task of subtracting 27 from 43. Some procedures that could be used are:

$$
\begin{array}{llll}
 & work & & work \\
 & 43 \quad 46 & & 43 \quad (30 + 13) \\
(1.) & -27 \quad -30; & (2.) & -27 \quad -(20 + 7) \qquad ; \\
 & \overline{} \quad \overline{16} & & \overline{} \quad \overline{10 + 6} \;\; -16
\end{array}
$$

work

$$(3.) \quad \begin{array}{r} 43 \\ -27 \\ \hline ^-4 \\ 20 \\ \hline 16 \end{array} \qquad (4.) \quad \begin{array}{r} 43 \\ -27 \\ \hline \end{array} \quad \begin{array}{r} ^343 \\ -27 \\ \hline 16 \end{array}$$

All of the procedures produce the desired answer. In fact, there is probably no best way to do the given exercise. Certainly there appears to be no intrinsic superiority in the traditional procedures, which evolved from clerical needs.

Since most of the computation done in the elementary school involves rational numbers (whole numbers, fractions, or decimals) it is reasonable to suggest that the procedures used to do the exercises should be selected in accordance with how the numbers are being represented. There are many names for a number. Thus, depending on the instructional setting, the amount represented by 16 2/3 might be written as $10 + 6 + 2/3$, 16.66, or 50/3.

An earlier mention was made of the need for children to work with concrete materials and to learn mathematical properties. Suppose the child were asked to add the numbers 25, 5, 5, 10, 1, 1, and 1. The conventional way to do this might be:

$$\begin{array}{r} 25 \\ 5 \\ 5 \\ 10 \\ 1 \\ 1 \\ 1 \\ \hline 48 \end{array}$$

Now suppose the numbers represent a quarter, two nickels, a dime, and three pennies. One way of representing the total value of the coins that better reflects what a child might do is

$$\begin{aligned} (25 + 5) + 10 + 5 + (1 + 1 + 1) &= (30 + 10) + 5 + 3 \\ &= (40 + 5) + 3 \\ &= 45 + 3 \\ &= 48. \end{aligned}$$

This procedure is longer, but recall that children do not always seek the shortest and most efficient way of doing things.

This Section contains articles selected for their focus on one or more of the basic operations. They contain much of the substantive content teachers should know to guide children as they develop facility with computational procedures. In addition, the content will help teachers construct appropriate exercises for pupils to solve. Parenthetically, the articles incorporate the language of mathematics and discuss mathematical properties. This is consistent with the notion that mathematics transcends any unique set of discrete categories which may be established.

Individually, the articles in this Section bring to the teacher one or more of the notions mentioned above. Dr. May, for example, illustrates how a child could go about setting up an exercise in accordance with the way amounts are being represented. This leads directly to some properties of addition and subtraction. The articles by Professors Weaver and Smith focus on basic aspects of how the idea of an operation can be intuitively developed. Yet, in doing this, these authors identify quite clearly the connection between referents for and representation of a number. This suggests computational procedures which are based on the use of properties rather than tradition. In like manner the other readings focus upon equally rewarding ideas which will profit the teacher who maintains conscious awareness of the wide variety of ways used to represent numbers and subsequently to perform computations with operations.

18 VENN DIAGRAMS STRENGTHEN CHILDREN'S MATHEMATICAL UNDERSTANDING

Lewis B. Smith

BEFORE YOU READ   The basic operations of addition and multiplication of whole numbers initially make sense to the extent that they are related to sets of objects. The same is true for the defined operations of subtraction and division. That is, sets are the referents which lend credibility to the operations. At the same time pupils should be led to gain increased maturity in mathematics. This means teachers must utilize more abstract referents for ideas as children become able to learn from them, while maintaining the association between numbers and amounts. Venn diagrams are an excellent vehicle for presenting problems, as well as being an excellent semiabstract referent for sets. Both aspects of Venn diagrams are well developed in the subsequent article by Professor Smith.

After reading the article the teacher should be able to draw a Venn diagram and develop a high interest exercise which can be solved by using a Venn diagram. In addition, the reader should be able to use these diagrams to represent set union and intersection and, subsequently, apply the illustrations to subtraction and addition exercises.

Venn diagraming provides an exceptional method of understanding some arithmetic problems that cannot be easily interpreted by traditional mathematical processes. Venn diagrams contribute to a child's ability to see relationships and to interpret data. It helps him construct a model which gives him fuller perception and ability to analyze problem situations.

Fortunately we find that the Venn method of analyzing arithmetical situations is gradually becoming a working tool used confidently in the classroom. The efforts to help teachers grasp the full significance and meaning of this approach led to the illustrations and explanations reported in this article. These experiences did much to strengthen teachers' and pupils' understandings of Venn principles.

Venn diagrams were developed in 1880 by John Venn, an English

---

Reprinted from *The Arithmetic Teacher*, vol. 13, no. 2 (February 1966), pp. 92–99. Lewis B. Smith is affiliated with the Department of Curriculum and Instruction at the University of Wisconsin, Madison, Wisconsin.

mathematician. To employ his ideas, we let the inside of some closed plane figure, such as a circle, represent a set of objects. Another set of objects is represented by a second closed figure. The figures are drawn to illustrate the relationship of the two sets. They may be shown adjacent, overlapping, or with one contained in the other. These circles are labeled with capital letters. The drawing serves to clarify the relationship between members or groups in the problem, and also reveal the result that actions have upon them. Actions may include joining, separating, and noting identity or common membership in both groups.

Let us look at a sample problem involving Miss Jones, a fifth-grade teacher.

Miss Jones assigned five of her capable fifth-grade children as members of the safety patrol (set P). Four others of her class were members of the band (set B), as shown in Figure 18.1. We can note the information in this way: $n(P) = 5$; and $n(B) = 4$ (n meaning the number of elements in the set). When asked how many children were in the band and patrol, she thought of the union of these two sets $n(P \cup B)$, or $5 + 4$, and answered "9."

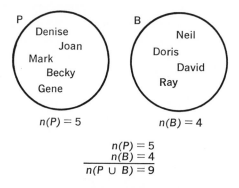

$$
\begin{array}{r}
n(P) = 5 \\
n(B) = 4 \\
\hline
n(P \cup B) = 9
\end{array}
$$

Figure 18.1

Later in the year we find that Doris and Ray became members of the patrol, and Joan and Becky became members of the band (Fig. 18.2). Miss Jones noted that she now had 7 children in the patrol and 6 in the band. When asked how many children were in the band and patrol, Miss Jones thought: $7 + 6$, and answered "13," but quickly doubted her conclusion.

Miss Jones realized that some children were in both sets. It was accurate for her to think "I have 7 members in the patrol and 6 members in the band for a total of 13 members in the two sets," but she knew she did not have that many children participating. On reviewing assignments she found that 4 children were in both activities. They were identical to themselves and could not be counted twice. This led to diagraming as in Figure 18.3, and the conclusion that $n(P \cup B)$ in Figure 18.2 was inaccurate.

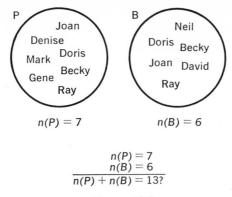

$$n(P) = 7$$
$$n(B) = 6$$
$$\overline{n(P) + n(B) = 13?}$$

Figure 18.2

Doris, Joan, Becky, and Ray were members of both groups but were the same children, no matter which group they were in. Each child could be enumerated only once in finding the total number of children involved. These four children were in the intersect region. They are shown in Figure 18.3 occupying a place as members of the patrol *and* as members of the band. The circles depicting the sets of children are intentionally overlapping. The identity of the objects or members common to both groups is thus distinguished. The number of P union B is nine: $n(P \cup B) = 9$. The intersect of P and B is four: $n(P \cap B) = 4$.

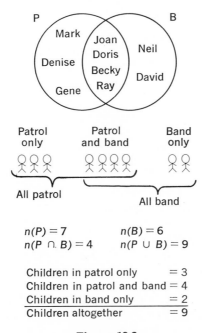

$$n(P) = 7 \qquad n(B) = 6$$
$$n(P \cap B) = 4 \qquad n(P \cup B) = 9$$

Children in patrol only	= 3
Children in patrol and band	= 4
Children in band only	= 2
Children altogether	= 9

Figure 18.3

Addition, in most texts for children, involves adding the number of elements in two disjoint sets to find the total number of elements in their union. Figure 18.4 shows this type of example, and the union is the total of all elements appearing in each of the original two sets. We can describe their union using notation like that in Figure 18.4.

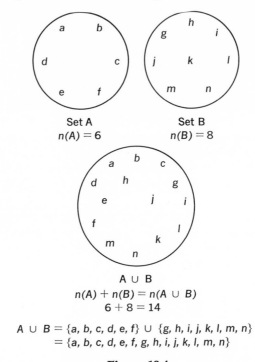

$$A \cup B$$
$$n(A) + n(B) = n(A \cup B)$$
$$6 + 8 = 14$$

$A \cup B = \{a, b, c, d, e, f\} \cup \{g, h, i, j, k, l, m, n\}$
$\quad\quad\quad = \{a, b, c, d, e, f, g, h, i, j, k, l, m, n\}$

Figure 18.4

Expanding this concept to find the total number of elements when each set contains some elements common to the other is shown in Figure 18.5. Note that elements e, f, and g are present in both original sets. The union of these sets accounts for their presence but once, since they are identical to themselves.

Thus, though we start with $n(A) = 7$ and $n(B) = 10$, their total is not 17 but 14, because 3 of the members of the two sets being united are identical.

We can also diagram the above information as shown in Figure 18.6.

After this preparation and introduction, the children were asked to shade the following drawings. (See Figures 18.7A and 18.7B.)

UNION

The union of sets A and B is the set of all elements belonging to A or B or both. It is written A ∪ B, and is illustrated by the shaded regions in Figure 18.7A.

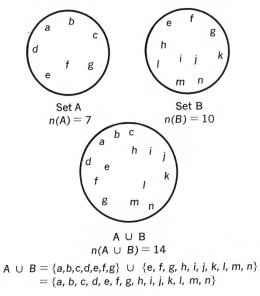

Set A
$n(A) = 7$

Set B
$n(B) = 10$

A ∪ B
$n(A \cup B) = 14$

A ∪ B = {a,b,c,d,e,f,g} ∪ {e, f, g, h, i, j, k, l, m, n}
       = {a, b, c, d, e, f, g, h, i, j, k, l, m, n}

Figure 18.5

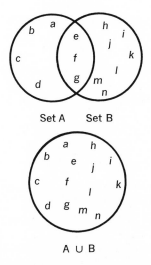

Set A   Set B

A ∪ B

Figure 18.6

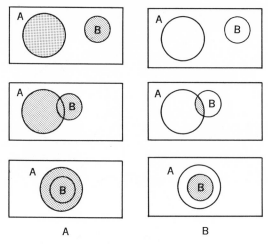

Figure 18.7

INTERSECTION

The intersection of sets A and B is the set of all elements belonging to both A and B. It is written A ∩ B, and is illustrated by the shaded regions in Figure 18.7B.

Now they were able to make these generalizations:

UNION

Always shade both set A and set B on union.

When sets A and B have no identical elements (nothing in common) you shade all of each set.

When sets A and B have some identical members you shade all of A not in the intersect, all of the intersect, and all of B not in the intersect.

When a large part of set A is identical to set B, shade just a little more than either A or B.

If all of set B is a part of set A, shade all of A.

INTERSECTION

When sets A and B do not have identical members there is no intersect and no shading of either A or B.

When sets A and B have some identical elements, shade only the overlap or intersection, where the members are identical.

When sets A and B have most of their elements in common (identical) shading the intersection means shading most of both A and B.

If all of set B is a part of A, shade all of B for intersect.

The class then shaded Venn diagrams such as those in Figure 18.8.

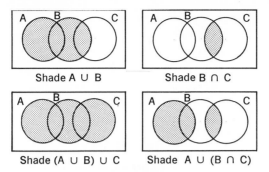

Shade A ∪ B   Shade B ∩ C

Shade (A ∪ B) ∪ C   Shade A ∪ (B ∩ C)

Figure 18.8

In the preceding examples, not every set had elements in common with two other sets. In the examples in Figure 18.9 every set has elements in common with the other two sets.

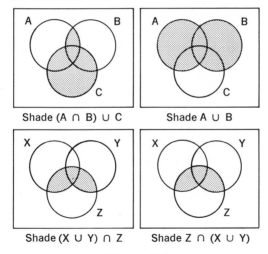

Shade (A ∩ B) ∪ C   Shade A ∪ B

Shade (X ∪ Y) ∩ Z   Shade Z ∩ (X ∪ Y)

Figure 18.9

Can the shaded areas in Figures 18.10 and 18.11 be described using union and intersect notation?

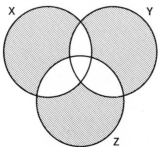

Figure 18.10

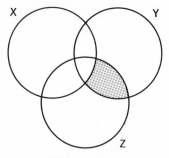

Figure 18.11

Some method of identifying subtraction with sets is helpful in describing these shaded areas. Consider the following notation for Figure 18.10:

$$[(X \cup Y) \cup Z] - [(X \cap Y) \cup (Y \cap Z) \cup (X \cap Z)]$$

Consider this notation for Figure 18.11:

$$(Y \cap Z) - [X \cap (Y \cap Z)]$$

Traditional subtraction is useful when all the members to be subtracted are members of the total group. $15 - 12 = 3$ implies that all 12 members (elements) have been taken from the original 15 elements. Many texts treat only subtractive situations of this kind. The application of Venn principles strengthens understanding of subtractive situations of another kind. Recall the circumstances of Figure 18.3, reproduced in brief form in Figure 18.12.

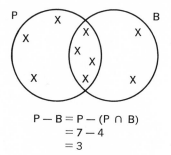

$$P - B = P - (P \cap B)$$
$$= 7 - 4$$
$$= 3$$

Figure 18.12

We have 7 members on the patrol and 6 members in the band. If the 6 who are in the band are out of the room for practice, can a patrol meeting be held? How many patrol members are left in the room?

The traditional $n(P) - n(B)$, or $7 - 6 = 1$, is not descriptive of this situation. With the help of Venn diagrams we can see that $P - B = 7 - 4$; the 4 is derived from those children who were members of both P and B $(P \cap B)$. The result is 3, which accurately portrays the situation. Only those members of the band who are on the patrol can be subtracted from the patrol group. Thus, 7 (patrol members) minus 4 (members of both patrol and band) leaves 3 (patrol members).

The following figures will help clarify subtraction involving disjoint and joint sets.

$A - B = A$ is illustrated in Figure 18.13. A and B (as they are drawn to show) have no elements in common. You cannot take from A what is not some part of it. Subtraction in this instance leaves A and B unchanged.

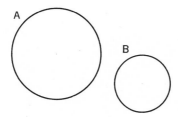

Figure 18.13

(This is the kind of subtraction seldom expressed. It is intuitively obvious— you cannot take a small number of giraffes from a large number of elephants.) $A - B$ in Figure 18.14 has the meaning which we usually associate with subtraction. All of B is identical with part of A, and $A - B$ denotes all of A, except that part of A which is also B. Thus $A - B$ is the shaded region.

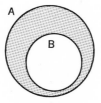

Figure 18.14

This is the form used in most subtraction problems appearing in children's textbooks.

A — B, when part of B is common to A, denotes what is left of A after the B in A has been subtracted. (See Figure 18.15.) Members of B not in A, as in Figures 18.15 and 18.16, do not become negative—they just are not expressed. Only that part of B which is in A may be subtracted from A. Thus, A — B is the shaded region.

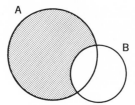

Figure 18.15

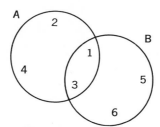

Figure 18.16

In Figure 18.16 the elements of sets A and B are 1, 2, 3, 4, 5, and 6. If A = {1, 2, 3, 4} and if B = {1, 3, 5, 6}, then

$$A - B = A - (A \cap B)$$
$$A - B = \{1, 2, 3, 4\} - \{1, 3\}$$
$$A - B = \{2, 4\} \ (\text{not } 2, 4, {}^-5, {}^-6).$$

The following problem is an example of the traditional use of the principles of Venn diagraming.

Problem

The children in Mr. Morgan's classroom were all in at least one activity. The activities were patrol (P), chorus (C), and the athletic team (T). Some children were in two activities and a few were in all three activities. Can you find the total number (n) of children in Mr. Morgan's classroom? (Fig. 18.17).

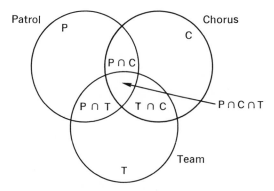

A total of 14 were in the patrol.
A total of 26 were in the chorus.
A total of 20 were on the team.
There were 8 in patrol and chorus.
There were 9 in patrol and team.
There were 12 in chorus and team.
There were 4 in chorus, team, & patrol.

Figure 18.17

The data given in Figure 18.17 is that amount generally included in this type of problem. The equations below with their addends provide helpful notation to complete the problem.

n = children in P ∩ C ∩ T = ——————
   + children in P ∩ C only = ——————
   + children in P ∩ T only = ——————
   + children in C ∩ T only = ——————
   + children in P only   = ——————
   + children in C only   = ——————
   + children in T only   = ——————

————————————————————————————

Total number of children (n) = ——————

A series of polygons were used to explore Venn principles with upper-grade children and also with the teachers. A music staff liner using three chalks was used to make squares resembling graph paper on the board. Chalks of different color were used to outline each polygon. The value of any given polygon was the area, expressed as the number of blocks enclosed by the polygon.

Venn diagrams do not always vary in size according to the number of elements in the circles. These polygon examples represent a departure from Venn principles because their size is directly related to the number of the elements (blocks) in the set. This departure, however, is fully in keeping with Venn principles and increases one's understanding of these principles.

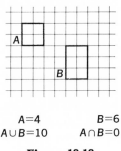

A=4　　　　B=6
A∪B=10　　A∩B=0

Figure 18.18

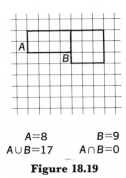

A=8　　　　B=9
A∪B=17　　A∩B=0

Figure 18.19

In the first examples, Figures 18.18 and 18.19, children were asked the value of A, the value of B, the value of their union, and the value of their intersection. All results were expressed as the numerical value of the number of blocks.

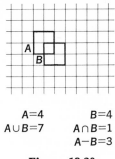

$$A=4 \qquad B=4$$
$$A\cup B=7 \qquad A\cap B=1$$
$$A-B=3$$

Figure 18.20

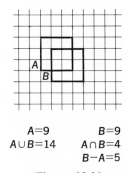

$$A=9 \qquad B=9$$
$$A\cup B=14 \qquad A\cap B=4$$
$$B-A=5$$

Figure 18.21

Children were then asked to interpret figures such as 18.20 and 18.21 and to employ their knowledge of areas of triangles as in Figures 18.22 and 18.23. Solve 18.23 yourself.

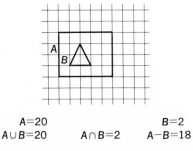

$$A=20 \qquad\qquad B=2$$
$$A\cup B=20 \qquad A\cap B=2 \qquad A-B=18$$

Figure 18.22

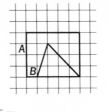

A= —   B= —
  A∪B= —   A∩B= —   B−A= —

Figure 18.23

The challenge was increased by using three polygons with various intersections. (See Figures 18.24, 18.25, 18.26, and 18.27.) You are encouraged to complete these problems and then compare your answers.

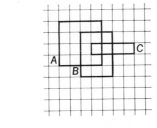

A=16   B=12   C=4
  A∪B=22   A∩B=6   A∪C=19
  A∩C=1   B∪C=14   B∩C=2
  A∪B∪C=24   A∩B∩C=1

Figure 18.24

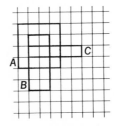

A= —   B= —   C= —
  A∪B= —   A∩B= —   A∪C= —
  A∩C= —   B∪C= —   B∩C= —
  A∪B∪C= —   A∩B∩C= —

Figure 18.25

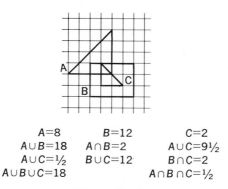

A=8	B=12	C=2
A∪B=18	A∩B=2	A∪C=9½
A∪C=½	B∪C=12	B∩C=2
A∪B∪C=18		A∩B∩C=½

Figure 18.26

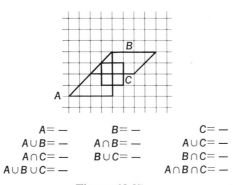

A= —	B= —	C= —
A∪B= —	A∩B= —	A∪C= —
A∩C= —	B∪C= —	B∩C= —
A∪B∪C= —		A∩B∩C= —

Figure 18.27

Children found a stimulating challenge in these examples and were quite accurate in their responses.

BIBLIOGRAPHY

Heddens, James W. *Today's Mathematics.* Chicago: Science Research Associates, Inc., 1964.

Johnson, Donovan A., and Glenn, William H. *Sets, Sentences and Operations.* St. Louis: Webster Publishing Company, 1960.

Osborn, Roger, *et al.* *Extending Mathematics Understanding.* Columbus, Ohio: Charles E. Merrill Books, Inc., 1963.

Peterson, John A., and Hashisaki, Joseph. *Theory of Arithmetic.* New York: John Wiley & Sons, 1963.

Suppes, Patrick. *Sets and Numbers, Books 1–6.* Syracuse, N.Y.: The L. W. Singer Company, 1964–65.

Topics in Mathematics for Elementary School Teachers, Twenty-Ninth Yearbook of the National Council of Teachers of Mathematics. Washington, D.C.: The National Council, 1964.

Answers to the problems in Figures 17, 23, 25, and 27

Figure 18.17

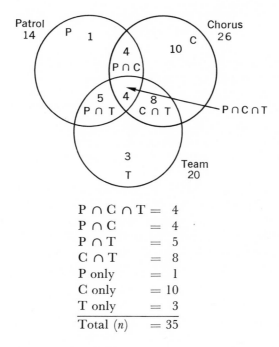

$$P \cap C \cap T = 4$$
$$P \cap C \quad\quad = 4$$
$$P \cap T \quad\quad = 5$$
$$C \cap T \quad\quad = 8$$
$$P \text{ only} \quad\quad = 1$$
$$C \text{ only} \quad\quad = 10$$
$$T \text{ only} \quad\quad = 3$$
$$\overline{\text{Total } (n) \quad = 35}$$

Figure 18.23

$$A = 20 \quad\quad\quad\quad\quad B = 6$$
$$A \cup B = 20 \quad A \cap B = 6 \quad B - A = \{ \ \}$$

Figure 18.25

$$A = 16 \quad\quad B = 10 \quad\quad C = 5$$
$$A \cup B = 20 \quad A \cap B = 6 \cup A \cup C = 18$$
$$A \cap C = 3 \quad B \cup C = 13 \quad B \cap C = 2$$
$$A \cup B \cup C = 22 \quad\quad\quad A \cap B \cap C = 2$$

Figure 18.27

$$A = 8 \quad\quad B = 8 \quad\quad C = 4$$
$$A \cup B = 14 \quad A \cap B = 2 \quad A \cup C = 10$$
$$A \cap C = 2 \quad B \cup C = 10 \quad B \cap C = 2$$
$$A \cup B \cup C = 15 \quad\quad\quad A \cap B \cap C = 1$$

LETTER TO THE EDITOR[1]

Dear Editor:

There are errors in my article "Venn Diagrams Strengthen Children's Mathematical Understanding" which appeared in the February, 1966, issue of The Arithmetic Teacher.

All of the material appearing before the treatment of polygons was used during in-service education sessions with teachers. The material and experiences reported on pages 151 through 161 were conducted with teachers only. Teachers, not children, were asked to shade drawings as reported for Figure 18.8. Teachers made the generalizations referred to on page 156. The class that shaded the diagrams " . . . such as those in Figure 18.8," referred to on page 156, was composed of teachers.

The second sentence of the second paragraph on page 151 is the key to the intent of the article. "The efforts to help teachers grasp the full significance and meaning of this approach led to the illustrations and explanations reported in this article." The experiences did much to help teachers who, in turn, were better able to help children.

In the answer section the union symbol should be ignored which appears under Figure 18.25 between the separate answers A $\cap$ B $=$ 6, and A $\cup$ C $=$ 18.

Thank you for noting these corrections.—Lewis B. Smith, *Madison, Wisconsin.*

[1] Appeared in *The Arithmetic Teacher*, vol. 13, no. 5 (May 1966), p. 348.

19 PATTERNS AND PROPERTIES IN ADDITION AND SUBTRACTION

Lola May

BEFORE YOU READ   A child develops an understanding of a fundamental concept such as addition or subtraction slowly and over a sus-
tained period of time.   During this interval several factors shape the degree
of understanding a child will achieve.   First, there must be a consideration of the types, the numerousness, and the number of variables the child
must add or subtract.   For example, the child might, in successive fashion
over a period of time, perform computations such as:

$$5 + 3 = n; \quad 27 + 18 + 38 + 69 + 95 = n; \quad 5261 - 2489 = n;$$

$$5/6 - 8/9 = n; \quad 16.289 - 1.592 = n; \quad \text{and}$$

$$n^2 + 2n - 6 + 3n^2 - 9n = 15.$$

Second, there must be a consideration of the rationale used to
facilitate addition and subtraction.   Ideally, the rationale should be based
on properties of number rather than rules, because the properties are
fewer in number than the rules and they are applicable to many different
number systems.   Rules simply do not have this kind of applicability.

Third, there must be a consideration of the referents to which
notions of addition and subtraction are attached.   The illustrations and
concrete materials used to develop meaning must be carefully chosen.

The following article by Dr. May does all these things by discussing
and illustrating the use of patterns, properties, frames, and the number
line for addition and subtraction of whole numbers in primary grades.

After reading this article the teacher should be able to use the
number line to represent any addition of the form $n + m = \Box$, or any
subtraction of the form $k - j = \Box$ where j, k, n, and m are whole
numbers and k is greater than or equal to j; and write a paragraph
describing the ways frame arithmetic can be used to teach addition and
subtraction facts.

Primary teachers have always known the value of using manipulative
materials in developing the idea of number.   The age-old problem is going

---

Reprinted from *Grade Teacher*, vol. 85, no. 2 (October 1967), pp. 41, 44, 46, 48, 50. **Dr. May**
is the Mathematics Consultant for the Winnetka, Illinois, Public Schools.

from the stage of using manipulative materials to the abstract stage of knowing the facts without developing "finger counters." Children need help in developing a mental process that will help them learn the facts so they do not have to resort to counting. The properties and patterns in mathematics can build that bridge.

Children who have been exposed to the use of the number line in the early grades learn to start on the number that represents the first addend and then count the number of spaces represented by the second addend. It is easier to do $7 + 3$ on the number line than $3 + 7$ because you have to count fewer spaces. The commutative property of addition states that the order of the addends can be changed and the sum is the same. Often in the primary grades this is known as the "buddy" property. $5 + 8$ is the buddy of $8 + 5$. If children know this property, they can imagine a number line and count only two spaces in doing the fact $2 + 6$. Knowing the property will give the students confidence to place the smaller addend second when they add.

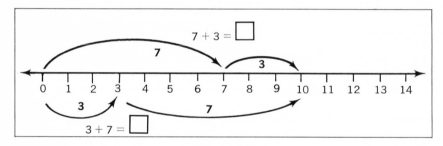

Figure 19.1

RENAMING ADDENDS

In adding three or more addends, the addends can be grouped in any order and the sum is the same. This is known as the associative property of addition. This property is useful in adding facts with larger numbers. In adding $8 + 7$, the seven can be renamed as $2 + 5$, and then you can add eight and two and then add five: $8 + 7 = (8 + 2) + 5$. This mental process can replace counting on fingers because it is what children do when they count on their fingers. To the teacher this appears harder than memorizing $8 + 7 = 15$, but this is only true if you already know $8 + 7 = 15$. It is very important that teachers spend time in helping children learn how to rename one addend. Confidence needs to be developed so they feel free to rename one addend and then add the three addends.

ZERO COMBINATIONS

Children need experiences with zero combinations. Zero is a special number in addition. When you add zero the sum is the same as the other addend. Knowing that zero is the identity element of addition becomes important later in mathematics. In playing games, children know it is important to record the "0" when one side has not made any points to indicate the side has had a turn, but did not score. Zero is used in real life situations as an addend, and children should learn how to add with zero as one of the addends.

PATTERNS

Generalizations or patterns are developed through exploratory exercises. These generalizations help children to develop patterns which make their work in mathematics easier. There are some patterns children can learn concerning the basic addition facts.

1. Children learn that adding one is equivalent to counting by ones. This is rather simple, but useful in adding.
2. Adding doubles for most children is easy. They learn $2 + 2$, $3 + 3$, etc., long before they know other facts. The doubles can be used in patterns to learn other facts. For example, $8 + 9$ is the same as $(8 + 8) + 1$. The pattern is the sum of a number when the next number larger is one more than the sum of the double of the first, or smaller number: $6 + 7 = (6 + 6) + 1$.
3. Another pattern is to use the idea of doubles and *subtract* 1: $8 + 9 = (9 + 9) - 1$. The pattern here is to double the larger number and then subtract one.
4. Nine can become a special number in adding by linking it to 10. For example, $8 + 9 = (8 + 10) - 1$ which shows the pattern of adding nine is the same as adding 10 and then subtracting one.

Mathematically inclined students find all these patterns or generalizations on their own. They call them shortcuts. The need is for the teacher to provide enough experiences so the average and below average student become aware of the patterns and can use them. The most important activity is learning to rename numbers so parts consist of 10 and some number.

SUBTRACTION

The most important generalization to remember in the operation of subtraction is to remember it is the inverse of addition. In addition, the parts are called addends and the answer is called the sum.

$$6 \qquad + 4 \quad = \quad 10$$
(Addend) (Addend) (Sum)

In addition, you are always given the addends and you find the sum. In subtraction, you are always given the sum and one of the addends, and you find the missing addend. Therefore, use the words addend and sum in subtraction, not minuend and subtrahend, which are meaningless.

$$10 \quad - \quad 4 \qquad = 6$$
$$\text{(Sum) (Addend) (Missing Addend)}$$

Practice is needed in analyzing sentences and having the children point out which number represents the sum, and which numbers represent the addends. A key question to ask is, "What are we finding, the sum or an addend?" Every subtraction problem can be rewritten as an addition problem, with a missing addend:

$$15 - 7 = \underline{\quad}$$
$$7 + \underline{\quad} = 15$$

To rewrite a sentence from a subtraction exercise to an addition exercise, you must know which number is the sum and which number is the addend. This is the type of practice that is needed as much as finding the answer.

There are other related patterns in subtraction that should help in learning the basic facts.

1. When zero is subtracted from a number, the number is unchanged: $9 - 0 = 9$. This is true because zero is the identity element of addition. First, you must know that $9 + 0 = 9$, and then from this you get $9 - 0 = 9$. In this case, the sum and one of the addends are the same.

2. Subtracting a number from itself leaves zero: $8 - 8 = 0$. Again, this comes from knowing that zero is the identity element of addition.

3. Subtracting ones from a number is equivalent to counting backwards by ones.

4. When you are subtracting more than one number from a given number you can add the numbers you are subtracting and then subtract them at one time.

$$(18 - 5) - 3 = ?$$
$$18 - 8 = 10$$

5. The number to be subtracted can be renamed and then each part subtracted. $(18 - 9) = (18 - 8) - 1 = 9$. For some children it is easier to subtract 8 and then subtract 1. This is possible because you can rename 9 as $8 + 1$.

Today's programs of teaching mathematics give the children in the primary grades an opportunity to explore all the addition and subtraction combinations. In the traditional programs, they were limited to the mastery of the facts with the sums of 10 or less. The emphasis today upon looking for many ways of solving problems provides for individual differences and also develops the confidence of the student. It is far better that children can find the right answer with a clumsy method, than be forced to use one method and get the wrong answer.

FRAME ARITHMETIC

The use of frame arithmetic in the elementary grades provides for many worthwhile addition and subtraction exercises. The two rules of frame arithmetic are:

1. When the frames are alike in a sentence, the number that replaces them must be the same.

$$\boxed{3} + \boxed{3} = 6$$

   The only answer is three because frames are alike.
2. When the frames are different in a sentence, the numbers that replace them can be the same or different. These are the same rules used with variables in algebra:

$$\boxed{1} + \triangle\!\!5 = 6 \text{ or } \boxed{3} + \triangle\!\!3 = 6$$

In doing an exercise such as box plus triangle equals nine, the children can find many different ways to name nine with whole numbers.

Figure 19.2

$\square$	$\triangle$
1	8
2	7
3	6
4	5
5	4
6	3
0	9
etc.	etc.

Figure 19.3

The more mathematically inclined may even use fractional numbers. Exercises like this show children a problem can have more than one answer, and a number has many names. Also, the emphasis is on nine as the sum, and you are finding the parts that make nine.

The frame on the left side of the equal sign is difficult at first for some children in the primary grades. The teacher needs to realize that in writing an exercise this way, you are really teaching the *meaning* of the addition fact:

$$6 + \square = 9$$

To work the problem, you must first find the sum. After you recognize nine as the sum, then six becomes an addend. You are finding the missing addend or the other part. If a child can tell you 6 + 3 equals nine but cannot tell you six plus what equals nine, you can be almost sure he has memorized the fact and does not understand what he is doing.

In doing an exercise such as box plus triangle plus cloud equals 12, the children will find many answers that will make the sentence true. By looking at the solutions they have used, it becomes evident that the commutative and associative properties of addition have been employed. They are learning to add numbers in any order to get the same sum.

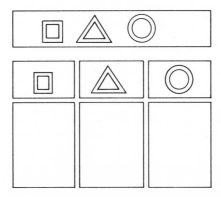

Figure 19.4

In discussing an exercise such as box plus triangle minus box equals six, the children will see that the number which replaces the first box must be used to replace the second box, because the frames are alike in the sentence.

When you take a number and subtract it from itself, the answer is zero. Now, the problem is, "What do you add to zero to get six?" The answer is six. Therefore, the triangle must always be replaced by six and any number can be used to replace the boxes. Much of mathematics can be learned from one frame arithmetic problem, and children can have the fun of unwinding it.

Figure 19.5

Lucky are the children who have teachers who help them to employ patterns and properties of mathematics in learning the mental processes that will make all of their computation easier. Only those who really know the rules of the game called mathematics can become skilled players in using these rules. Our main objective in elementary mathematics should not be mastery of the facts but learning more about the game so we can become better players. What we need is more ways of getting the correct answer.

20 SOME IDEAS ON SUBTRACTION AND DIVISION: PARTS I-II

Thomas C. O'Brien

BEFORE YOU READ   Subtraction and division are difficult concepts for children to grasp, especially when large numbers are involved. Procedures for performing these operations should, to the extent that is possible, be based on both an intuitive and a mathematically correct rationale. The next article in two parts by Mr. O'Brien meets these criteria. This article contains both characteristic and specific examples of the two operations, which will enable the teacher to see what subtraction and division look like both in a general and a specific sense. The author suggests consistent ways in which subtraction and division can be done. A pupil does not have to use drastically different procedures when he performs computations involving different sets of numbers.

As a result of reading this article, the teacher should be able to describe the mathematically correct rationale for the operations of subtraction and division and be able to convert a subtraction or division exercise to a related addition or multiplication exercise, subsequently solving the equivalent exercise.

PART I

Anyone who has taught mathematics in the elementary school—or the high school or the college—is likely to support the idea that the so-called inverse operations, subtraction and division, are particular trouble spots for students. The trouble may be due to the way students first approach the operations. This article suggests a possible alternative to the approaches currently being taught in the elementary school. In the first part of the article, subtraction is considered; in the second . . . division is discussed.

SUBTRACTION—WHOLE NUMBERS

$7 - 4$ is the number you add to 4 to get 7. What do you add to 4 to get 7? 3. So $7 - 4$ equals (is) 3.

$8 - 1$ is the number you add to 1 to get 8. 7 is the number you add to 1 to get 8, so $8 - 1 = 7$.

Reprinted from *School Science and Mathematics*, vol. 67, nos. 6 and 7 (June 1967, October 1967), pp. 521–522 and pp. 650–654. Thomas C. O'Brien is a Research Associate for the Educational Research Council of Greater Cleveland, Ohio.

In general, $a - b$ is the number you add to b to get a. That is, $b + (a - b) = a$. While this approach to subtraction conveys the mathematical essence of subtraction, it is not generally used in classrooms save for a brief mention in the coverage of basic subtraction "facts."

Why not use the approach in developing subtraction algorisms? For example, just as $7 - 4$ is the number you add to 4 to get 7, so $74 - 58$ is the number you add to 58 to get 74.

A student might proceed as follows:

```
  74
- 58
———
   2   74 − 58 is the number I add to 58 to get 74. I'll try adding 2 to 58.*
```

That gets me to 60.

```
  10   Now I'll try 10. That gets me to 70.
+  4   And I'll go 4 more.
———
  16   I added 2, 10, and 4 to 58 to get 74. 74 − 58 is 2 + 10 + 4.
```

Similarly, a student might solve the following exercise as follows:

```
 10,004
—    968
————
     32   If I add 32 to 968 I get 1000.
   9000   I want more than 10 thousand, so I'll add 9 thousand more.
      4   Now another 4 and I have 10,004.†
————
   9036   9036 is the number I add to 968 to get 10,004.
```

Discussion   At first glance, it would seem that the approach suggested is vastly inefficient when compared with computational methods in current use. A systematic rule-bound procedure for computation may in fact be quicker. Yet it is possible that the very freedom of the approach suggested here will permit students to develop their *own* systematic computational procedures which may, in fact, be more efficient than any of those currently being force-fed to students. On the other hand, the approach as it stands may not be so inefficient and uneconomical as it seems. How, almost universally, do cashiers make change when given a dollar bill for a pack of cigarettes?

SUBTRACTION—INTEGERS

One advantage of the approach to subtraction suggested above is that it does not have to be unlearned or at least put on the shelf when the student leaves the set of whole numbers.

---

* What other possible starts might the student make? There may be as many solutions as there are students.

† Again this is not the only solution. What other solutions are possible?

In the set of integers the difference $^+7 - {}^-3$ is the number you add to $^-3$ to get $^+7$. What do you add to $^-3$ to get $^+7$? If you add $^+3$, you get 0. Then if you add $^+7$ more, you get $^+7$. So

$$^+7 - {}^-3 = {}^+3 + {}^+7.$$

Similarly, $^-5 - {}^+3$ is the number you add to $^+3$ to get $^-5$. If you add $^-3$ to $^+3$ you get 0. And adding $^-5$ more gets you to $^-5$, so

$$^-5 + {}^+3 = {}^-3 + {}^-5.$$

In general, for any integers a and b, $a - b$ is the integer you add to b to get a. If you add ^-b to b you get 0 and adding another a gives you a. So, for any integers a and b

$$a - b = {}^-b + a.$$

And, since addition is commutative in the set of integers,

$$a - b = a + {}^-b,$$

which is what was meant by the old rule, "to subtract an integer, add its opposite."

PART II

In the first part of this article it was claimed that $12 - 3$ is the number you add to 3 to get 12 and, in general, $a - b$ is the number you add to b to get a. Then a new approach to the teaching of subtraction was discussed. In this part, a similar treatment will be given to division.

Just as $12 - 3$ is the number you add to 3 to get 12, so $12 \div 3$ is the number you *multiply* by 3 to get 12. What do you multiply by 3 to get 12? 4. So $12 \div 3 = 4$. In general, $a \div b$ is the number you multiply by b ($b \neq 0$) to get a. That is, if

$$a = bx \qquad \text{(if } x \text{ is the number you multiply by } b \text{ to get } a\text{)}$$

then

$$a \div b = x.$$

And if

$$a \div b = x,$$

then

$$a = bx \qquad (x \text{ is the number you multiply by } b \text{ to get } a).$$

This approach to division is often used in the development of division "facts," but it has application in children's study of division as a whole.

COMPARING NUMBERS

Given two rational numbers, there are three basic approaches to comparing the numbers. The numbers may be compared additively, multiplicatively, or by a combination of multiplication and addition.

For example, 12 and 3 may be compared by the equation $12 = 3 + 9$, thus saying that 12 is 9 more than 3. Since both 9 and $12 - 3$ are the number which you add to 3 to get 12, 12 and 3 can also be compared by the equation $12 - 3 = 9$. Both these equations and the six others of the kind ($12 = 3 + 9$, $3 + 9 = 12$, $12 - 9 = 3$, $3 = 12 - 9$, etc.) express additive comparisons of 12 and 3.

A multiplicative comparison can be shown between the numbers 12 and 3 by the equation $12 = 3 \cdot 4$. Since both $12 \div 4$ and 3 are the number which you multiply by 4 to get 12, the numbers 12 and 3 can also be compared by the equation $12 \div 4 = 3$, or by any of six other equations ($12 = 3 \cdot 4$, $4 \cdot 3 = 12$, $12 \div 3 = 4$, $4 = 12 \div 3$, etc.).

In the set of whole numbers, two numbers can always be compared additively. Given any whole numbers a and b, one of the two equations

$$a + x = b \text{ or } a = b + x$$

will do the job. That is to say, one of any two numbers is always a whole number more than the other.

On the other hand, in the set of whole numbers a multiplicative comparison between two numbers is not always possible. 12 and 3 can be compared, for example, by the equations $12 = 3 \cdot 4$ or $12 \div 4 = 3$, but no multiplicative comparison exists in the set of whole numbers for 13 and 3. There is no whole number x such that

$$3x = 13 \text{ or } 13x = 3.$$

There is, however, a third method of comparison which uses both multiplication and addition. For 13 and 3 there are four essentially different comparisons involving multiplication and addition. They are

$$13 = 4 \cdot 0 + 13 \quad 13 = 4 \cdot 1 + 9 \quad 13 = 4 \cdot 2 + 5 \quad 13 = 4 \cdot 3 + 1.$$

In general, it is possible to compare two whole numbers a and b by an equation of the form

$$a = bx + r \text{ or } b = ax + r$$

where x and r are whole numbers.

DIVISION—WHOLE NUMBERS

In computing the quotient $15 \div 3$ the student is dealing with a multiplicative comparison of 15 and 3. He wants to compute the number which when multiplied by 3 is 15. He wants the x of

$$15 = 3x.$$

Similarly, to compute the quotient $798 \div 38$, the student is computing the x of

$$798 = 38x.$$

He is computing the number which when multiplied by 38 is 798.
Using trial-and-error techniques, he may try 10 to get the inequality,

$$798 > 38 \cdot 10$$

or the multiplication-addition comparison

$$798 = 38 \cdot 10 + 418.$$

He wants a multiplicative comparison, so 10 is too small. If he tries 20, he gets the inequality

$$798 > 38 \cdot 20$$

or the equation

$$798 = 38 \cdot 20 + 38.$$

Next, he may try 30 to get

$$798 < 38 \cdot 30$$

or

$$798 = 38 \cdot 30 - 342.$$

So 30 is too great and 20 is too small. The x of $798 = 38x$ is between 20 and 30. By trial-and-error, the student finally arrives at the multiplicative comparison,

$$798 = 38 \cdot 21.$$

So $798 \div 38$, which is the x of $798 = 38x$, is 21. That is $798 \div 38 = 21$.

Had the student computed $799 \div 38$, he would have arrived at the multiplicative-additive comparison expressed by the equation

$$799 = 38 \cdot 21 + 1$$

with 21 as the "quotient" and 1 as the remainder.

Multiplicative-additive comparisons are useful in obtaining straight multiplicative comparisons, that is, in computing quotients. Here is $798 \div 38$ computed again.

$$798 = 3q + r$$
$$798 = 38 \cdot 10 + 418$$
$$418 = 38 \cdot 10 + 38$$
$$38 = 38 \cdot 1$$

So

$$798 = 38 \cdot 10 + 38 \cdot 10 + 38 \cdot 1$$
$$= 38(10 + 10 + 1) \text{ because of the distributive property}$$
$$= 38 \cdot 21$$

A convenient device for keeping track of the computational steps is the algorism below.

$$
\begin{array}{r|l}
38)\overline{798} & \qquad 798 = 38x \\
380 \quad 10 & \qquad 798 = 38 \cdot 10 + 418 \\
\hline
418 & \\
380 \quad 10 & \qquad 418 = 38 \cdot 10 + 38 \\
\hline
38 & \\
38 \quad 1 & \qquad 38 = 38 \cdot 1 + 0 \\
\hline
0 & \qquad 798 = 38 \cdot 10 + 38 \cdot 10 + 38 \cdot 1 \\
& \qquad\quad = 38(10 + 10 + 1) \\
& \qquad\quad = 38 \cdot 21
\end{array}
$$

DIVISION—RATIONAL NUMBERS

One great advantage the multiplicative interpretation of division has is that it does not have to be unlearned or shelved when the student leaves the set of whole numbers.*

* Division of whole numbers is often approached in terms of repeated subtraction. How does this approach apply in division of rational numbers?

In the set of rational numbers, $a \div b$ is still the number which we multiply by b to get a. It is still the x of $a = bx$ ($b \neq 0$, of course). For example, $\frac{3}{4} \div \frac{1}{2}$ is the number we multiply by $\frac{1}{2}$ to get $\frac{3}{4}$. In multiplication of rational numbers we compute by multiplying numerators then denominators, so if

$$\frac{^{-}3}{4} \div \frac{1}{2} = \frac{a}{b},$$

then a is the number which we multiply by 1 to get $^{-}3$ and b is the number we multiply by 2 to get 4. Clearly a is $^{-}3$ and b is 2, so

$$\frac{^{-}3}{4} \div \frac{1}{2} = \frac{^{-}3}{2}.$$

In the case of

$$\frac{3}{4} \div \frac{3}{5} = \frac{a}{b},$$

we have some trouble. a is the number we multiply by 3 to get 3, so a is 1. But b is the number we multiply by 5 to get 4, and there is no such integer.

What we do is to use a fraction equivalent to $\frac{3}{4}$ in which the denominator is divisible by 3 and the numerator by 5. Such a fraction is

$$\frac{3 \cdot 5}{4 \cdot 5}$$

and so we have:

$$\frac{3}{4} \div \frac{3}{5} = \frac{a}{b}$$

and

$$\frac{3 \cdot 5}{4 \cdot 5} \div \frac{3}{5} = \frac{a}{b}.$$

So,

$$\frac{5}{4} = \frac{a}{b}$$

$\frac{5}{4}$ is the number which we multiply by $\frac{3}{5}$ to get

$$\frac{3 \cdot 5}{4 \cdot 5},$$

which is $\frac{3}{4}$, so $\frac{3}{4} \div \frac{3}{5} = \frac{5}{4}$.

In general, if a/b and c/d are rational numbers and $c \neq 0$, then

$$\frac{a}{b} \div \frac{c}{d} = \frac{a \cdot c \cdot d}{b \cdot c \cdot d} \div \frac{c}{d}.$$

Now

$$\frac{a \cdot c \cdot d}{b \cdot c \cdot d} \div \frac{c}{d}$$

is the number which we multiply by

$$\frac{c}{d} \quad \text{to get} \quad \frac{a \cdot c \cdot d}{b \cdot c \cdot d}.$$

And

$$\frac{a \cdot c \cdot d}{b \cdot c \cdot d} \div \frac{c}{d} = \frac{ad}{bc},$$

so in general for rational numbers

$$\frac{a}{b} \quad \text{and} \quad \frac{c}{d} \, (c \neq 0).$$

$$\frac{a}{b} \div \frac{c}{d} = \frac{ad}{bc}.$$

This, of course, is a rationale for the old "invert and multiply" rule.

21 MULTIPLICATION WITHIN THE SET OF COUNTING NUMBERS

J. Fred Weaver

BEFORE YOU READ   This article by Professor Weaver contains a comprehensive treatment of the operation of multiplication. There are numerous referents in the article which can be used by the teacher to promote understanding. The properties that apply to multiplication are stated, and there is a systematic concern for the achievement of knowledge of the properties by the use of arrays. Very complete, mostly substantive in nature, the article contains vocabulary a teacher should know in order to help children understand and use multiplication.

Upon completion of the article the teacher should be able to write an interpretation of multiplication in terms of repeated addition, arrays, and Cartesian products, and to partition an array to show the use of distributive property in doing a multiplication exercise.

Recently the professional literature on mathematics instruction for the elementary school has included a variety of discussions and research reports pertaining to multiplication. More often than not, a focus of attention has been one or another of three ways in which this operation may be characterized or defined: (1) the so-called *repeated addition* interpretation, (2) the *array* interpretation, and (3) the *cartesian product* interpretation.

Such discussions and reports hopefully have clarified some of the issues inherent in these characterizations of multiplication. Undoubtedly, however, these presentations also raised new issues and reopened old ones! In any event, there are several points regarding each of the three interpretations of multiplication that continue to warrant consideration.

In the present discussion of these points we shall restrict ourselves almost exclusively to the operation of multiplication within the set of counting numbers:

$$C = \{1, 2, 3, 4, 5, 6, 7, 8, 9, 10, 11, 12, 13, \ldots\}.$$

Except for a brief concluding "Postscript," this will be our universal set throughout the discussion.

Reprinted from *School Science and Mathematics*, vol. 67, no. 3 (March 1967), pp. 252–270. Professor Weaver is at The University of Wisconsin in Madison, Wisconsin.

MULTIPLICATION AND REPEATED ADDITION

Of the three interpretations mentioned at the outset, the characterization of multiplication as "repeated addition,"—i.e., as the successive addition of equal addends,—is the one most commonly used in the past. It also is the one that is avoided very deliberately in some of our contemporary programs.

According to this interpretation of multiplication, we may *define* the product of two counting numbers, *a* and *b*, as

$$a \times b = \underbrace{b + b + b + b + b + b + b + b + \cdots}_{a \text{ addends}^1}$$

This, in turn, may be associated with the *union of equivalent, disjoint* sets, where we specify the number of members in the union of *a* such sets, each having *b* members or elements.

For instance, in keeping with this definition we may interpret the product 7×5 to mean

$$7 \times 5 = \underbrace{5 + 5 + 5 + 5 + 5 + 5 + 5}_{7 \text{ addends}} = 35.$$

That is, there are 7×5 or 35 members in the union of 7 disjoint sets, each of which has 5 members.

It is this "repeated addition" interpretation of multiplication that Rappaport (1965), for one, does not want to see slighted or lost in comtemporary programs of mathematics instruction for the elementary grades.

Before we set forth several aspects of a major concern regarding this interpretation of multiplication, let us be sure that our thinking will not be sidetracked by a somewhat arbitrary choice of interpretation that has been made. We may, in truth, define the product of two counting numbers, *a* and *b*, to mean either of two things in terms of the successive addition of equal addends. That is, we may define $a \times b$ to mean *either*

(1) $a \times b = b + b + b + b + b + b + b + \cdots$ [to *a* addends], or

(2) $a \times b = a + a + a + a + a + a + a + \cdots$ [to *b* addends].

Specifically, for instance, we may view 7×5 as meaning *either*

(1) $7 \times 5 = 5 + 5 + 5 + 5 + 5 + 5 + 5$, or

(2) $7 \times 5 = 7 + 7 + 7 + 7 + 7$.

---

[1] According to an older and now archaic terminology, the *first b* is called the *augend*, and each subsequent *b* is called an *addend*. Here, however, we have used the more familiar terminology now in vogue and have referred to *each b* as an addend.

This side issue is not unique to the interpretation of multiplication as "repeated addition." Some persons, e.g., Kushta (1966),—in effect have expressed a preference for the second meaning of $a \times b$ or 7×5 over the first one. It is admitted that a substantial argument [much more compelling than Kushta's] can be advanced in support of such a preference. However, since the *first* meaning is the more familiar one in relation to elementary-school mathematics instruction, that is the one that we elected to use initially and that we shall continue to use in this section of the discussion. As Cunningham (1965) has indicated, it is not difficult to reconcile these two interpretations of $a \times b$ as the successive addition of equal addends. The points to follow are valid under either meaning, and we shall continue to abide by the *first* one.

Now let us turn to several illustrations of significant aspects of concern regarding the "repeated addition" characterization of multiplication within the set of counting numbers. From a mathematical standpoint, the essential *disadvantage* of this interpretation is that it does not establish multiplication as an operation in its own right, *independent* of addition. Consequently, the *properties* of multiplication are not wholly independent of the nature and properties of addition. Not only is this undesirable mathematically, but from the standpoint of elementary-school pupils, it may be less effective than if the properties of multiplication are "discovered" and explored without *necessarily* involving the successive addition of equal addends. In fact, it even may lead to problems that otherwise would not be encountered. Let us illustrate this in two ways.

1. Consider first the *commutative* property of addition within our universal set. For every counting number a and every counting number b, it is true that

$$a \times b = b \times a.$$

When multiplication is defined in terms of "repeated addition," the essence of the commutative property of multiplication is far from being "intuitively obvious" to young children. Consider, for example, this specific instance:

$$4 \times 3 = 3 \times 4.$$

The "repeated addition" characterization of multiplication asserts that

$$4 \times 3 = 3 + 3 + 3 + 3, \text{ and}$$
$$3 \times 4 = 4 + 4 + 4.$$

However, it is *not* "intuitively obvious" to young children that

$$3 + 3 + 3 + 3 = 4 + 4 + 4,$$

and hence that

$$4 \times 3 = 3 \times 4.$$

Surely, we can show rather easily that this specific instance of commutativity is true by associating arrangements or groupings of sets of objects with these multiplications. In the illustration to be cited, the circular discs have been numbered[2] to clarify their rearrangement.

First, 4×3 may be associated with 4 sets of 3 discs each:

① ② ③   ④ ⑤ ⑥   ⑦ ⑧ ⑨   ❿ ⑪ ⑫

Then, these same discs may be rearranged as 3 sets of 4 discs each, and the resulting representation associated with 3×4:

① ② ③ ④   ⑤ ⑥ ⑦ ⑧   ⑨ ❿ ⑪ ⑫

Through illustrations such as these, children *do* learn to generalize the commutative property for multiplication within the set of counting numbers. [This is *not* meant to imply, however, that children should learn to verbalize or symbolize this generalization when they first become aware of it!] Nevertheless, the fact remains that in virtually all such instances, during early stages of learning it is *not* "intuitively obvious" to young children that one sum is equal to another sum [e.g., that $5 + 5 + 5 + 5 + 5 + 5 + 5 = 7 + 7 + 7 + 7 + 7$], and consequently that one product [7×5] is equal to another product [5×7]. Thus, commutativity of multiplication is not sensed as easily as it might be if multiplication were characterized independently of addition. We shall see an explicit illustration of this in a later section of this discussion.

2. Now let us consider the "repeated addition" meaning of multiplication as it relates to the *multiplicative identity* property. Here we encounter a problem of much greater conceptual consequence,—one that has been touched upon by D'Augustine (1966) and merits amplification here.

The multiplicative identity property governs our use of the number 1 as a factor. Within our universal set this property asserts that for every counting number, n, it is true that

$$n \times 1 = n \quad \text{and} \quad 1 \times n = n.$$

For $n > 1$ we encounter no problem with 1 as the *right*-hand multiplicative identity; i.e., with $n \times 1 = n$. In terms of the successive addition of equal addends we may view this as meaning

$$n \times 1 = 1 + 1 + 1 + 1 + 1 + 1 + \cdots [\text{to } n \text{ addends}] = n.$$

[2] This writer simply refuses to say that the discs have been "numeraled"!

In a specific instance such as 8×1, we may construe this to mean

$$8 \times 1 = 1 + 1 + 1 + 1 + 1 + 1 + 1 + 1 = 8.$$

But suppose that $n = 1$. How do we interpret 1×1 as "repeated addition?"

Or consider the use of 1 as the *left*-hand multiplicative identity; i.e., $1 \times n = n$. How do we interpret 1×6, for example, as the successive addition of equal addends? We can't have just *one* addend,—whether it be 6 or any other counting number,—and still speak of addition. As a binary operation, addition is an operation on *two* numbers,—on *two* addends.

So, whenever the first or left-hand factor is 1, we observe that the "repeated addition" characterization of multiplication simply cannot apply. Yes, we do have ways of "getting around" this difficulty, to be sure. But it is an inescapable fact that the interpretation of multiplication as successive addition of equal addends is *not* applicable for *all* ordered pairs of counting numbers. The definition fails utterly for all ordered pairs of the form $(1, n)$, which lead to products of the form $1 \times n$, where 1 is the left-hand multiplicative identity and n is any counting number.

Why use a definition subject to limitations of the nature we have discussed, when it is possible to characterize multiplication independently of addition in a way that does not have such limitations? This leads us directly to the next section on Multiplication and Arrays.

MULTIPLICATION AND ARRAYS

The interpretation of multiplication of counting numbers in terms of *rectangular arrays* is quite common in contemporary programs of mathematics instruction for the elementary grades. There is little doubt that the emphasis upon arrays reflects the influence of curriculum innovators such as the School Mathematics Group [SMSG] and the sample texts prepared by SMSG writing teams (1963b, 1965a, 1965b). Also, we now see arrays involved to one degree or another in research on the learning of multiplication by elementary-school pupils, such as that reported by Gray (1965), by Schell (1965), and by Hervey (1966).

Let's be sure at the outset that we understand the way in which the term *array* will be used in this discussion. By an *array* we shall mean a *rectangular*[3] arrangement of objects in rows and columns, with the same number of objects [or *elements* or *members*] in each row. We do not restrict the elements of an array to any particular kind of object, nor do we insist that all the members of a given array be alike. However, we frequently

---

[3] Arrays may be triangular, for instance, as well as rectangular. In this paper, however, we use "array" to mean *only* a *rectangular* array. Some persons e.g., [Moise (1966)] use *matrix* in the same sense that we here use *array*.

find it convenient to use dots or the like in array representations, as illustrated in Figure 21.1.

Figure 21.1 A 5-by-8 array

The array shown in Figure 21.1 has 5 rows and 8 columns; i.e., 5 rows of elements, with 8 elements in each row. We shall refer to this as a 5-*by*-8 array, in which we follow the convention of *first* specifying the number of *rows* and then specifying the number of columns [i.e., the number of elements in each row].

By contrast, an 8-by-5 array is shown in Figure 21.2.

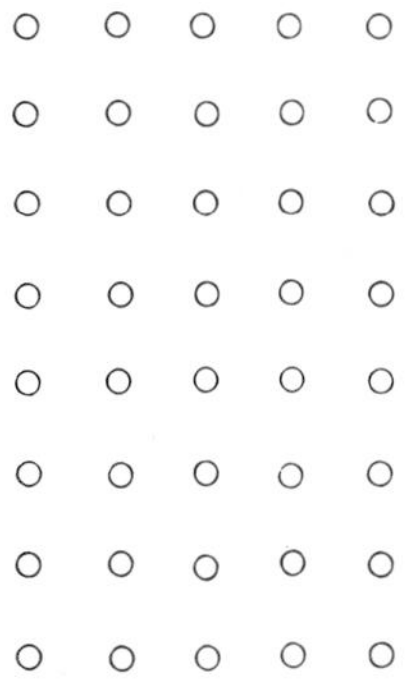

Figure 21.2 An 8-by-5 array

This 8-by-5 array,—and every 8-by-5 array,—has 8 rows and 5 columns. In our discussion we shall continue to use this "rows-by-columns" convention

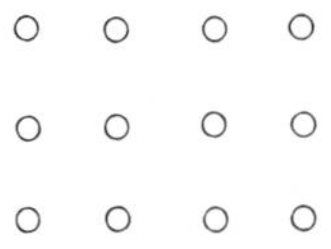

Figure 21.3 A 3-by-4 array

to name arrays. Thus, if we speak of a 3-by-4 array, we know that its pattern is like the one illustrated in Figure 21.3 rather than in Figure 21.4.

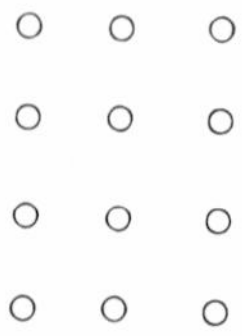

Figure 21.4 A 4-by-3 array

There are five things which the writer wishes to emphasize regarding arrays and multiplication within the set of counting numbers.

1. The use of arrays in connection with multiplication is *not new*. We can look in elementary-school texts, etc. of quite a few years ago and observe that multiplication is associated with arrays, particularly in relation to work with "multiplication facts." Admittedly, such representations were not called arrays. Furthermore, they were used in conjunction with the "repeated addition" characterization of multiplication rather than as the basis for establishing multiplication as an operation in its own right.

Here we have the crux of the significant contribution that arrays can make to the study of multiplication. A distinguishing feature of certain contemporary programs of mathematics instruction for elementary-school pupils is not the fact that these programs use arrays,—and call them by that name! Rather, a distinguishing feature of these programs is the principal *way* in which arrays are used: as the basis for characterizing multiplication independently of addition, and for exploring the properties of multiplication as an operation in its own right.

We very easily,—and very profitably,—may *define* the *product of two counting numbers, m and n, to be the number of elements in an m-by-n array*. Thus, *by definition*, the product of the numbers 2 and 6, for example, is the number of elements in a 2-by-6 array, such as:

There are 2×6 or 12 members in this array. And so, with this array and with every 2-by-6 array we may associate the number sentence

$$2 \times 6 = 12.$$

Similarly, *by definition*, the product of the numbers 9 and 7 is the number of elements in a 9-by-7 array, such as

$$\begin{matrix}
\Delta & \Delta & \Delta & \Delta & \Delta & \Delta & \Delta \\
\Delta & \Delta & \Delta & \Delta & \Delta & \Delta & \Delta \\
\Delta & \Delta & \Delta & \Delta & \Delta & \Delta & \Delta \\
\Delta & \Delta & \Delta & \Delta & \Delta & \Delta & \Delta \\
\Delta & \Delta & \Delta & \Delta & \Delta & \Delta & \Delta \\
\Delta & \Delta & \Delta & \Delta & \Delta & \Delta & \Delta \\
\Delta & \Delta & \Delta & \Delta & \Delta & \Delta & \Delta \\
\Delta & \Delta & \Delta & \Delta & \Delta & \Delta & \Delta \\
\Delta & \Delta & \Delta & \Delta & \Delta & \Delta & \Delta
\end{matrix}$$

Figure 21.5

There are 9×7 or 63 elements in this [and every] 9-by-7 array; so we may write

$$9 \times 7 = 63.$$

"But wait just a minute!", you say. "In the first example, 2×6, I very definitely *added* 6 and 6 to realize that there were 12 members in the 2-by-6 array. And in the second example, 9×7, to find the number of elements in the 9-by-7 array I *counted by 7's*,—which in effect is adding. So, I have *not* been working with multiplication independent of addition."

Good for you! This leads directly to the second of the five things we wish to emphasize regarding arrays and multiplication.

2. In terms of arrays, the product of two counting numbers may be defined directly, without recourse to addition. But this does not mean that multiplication is unrelated to addition. It may be *convenient to use addition* to find the number of elements in an array. Or we may elect simply to "count by ones" to find the number of elements in an array. However, the *use* of such procedures does not imply that the product of two counting numbers has been *defined* in terms of addition or counting.

Until a pupil has memorized certain "basic multiplication facts," he very well needs *some* procedure that will enable him to find the number of members in an array and, thus, to find the product of two counting numbers.

$$\begin{matrix}
\circ & \circ & \circ & \circ & \circ \\
\circ & \circ & \circ & \circ & \circ \\
\circ & \circ & \circ & \circ & \circ
\end{matrix}$$

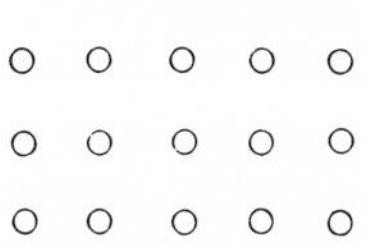

Figure 21.6

For instance, when finding the product of 3 and 5 by using a 3-by-5 array this procedure may take a variety of forms. A pupil may count by 1's; or he may count by 5's; or he may add three 5's; or he may count by 3's; or he may add five 3's; etc. But the use of such procedures does *not* mean that the operation of multiplication therefore has been *defined* in terms of addition or counting. No. The product of 3 and 5, for instance, is defined as the number of elements in a 3-by-5 array. And, as Phillips (1963, 1965) has pointed out, there are stages in children's mathematical development when things such as counting and addition are very appropriate ways to ascertain that number.

With larger numbers, such as 24 and 36, children learn to use properties of multiplication and techniques of computing as means to find the "standard name," 864, for the product 24 × 36. But our essential characterization of multiplication remains unchanged. The product of 24 and 36 is, *by definition*, the number of members in a 24-by-36 array,—regardless of whether or not such an array has been used or shown explicitly.

3. This matter of an *explicit* array representation leads to a significant point regarding the application of multiplication in the solution of "word problems." In order to clarify this point, first consider the following problem statement:

a. The chairs in a room are arranged in rows and columns. There are 6 rows of chairs, with 8 chairs in each row. How many chairs are there in this room?

A 6-by-8 array is *explicit* in the statement of the problem,

```
h  h  h  h  h  h  h  h
h  h  h  h  h  h  h  h
h  h  h  h  h  h  h  h
h  h  h  h  h  h  h  h
h  h  h  h  h  h  h  h
h  h  h  h  h  h  h  h
```

and the number of chairs in the room may be associated directly with the number of elements in a 6-by-8 array,—and hence, with the product of the numbers, 6 and 8.

But now consider this problem:

b. John has 4 packs of lollipops, with 5 lollipops in each pack. How many lollipops does John have in these four packs?

Clearly, an array is *not* explicit in this problem statement. However, it is both very easy and very convenient to *think* of the lollipops as arranged in a 4-by-5 array: as 4 rows [packs] of lollipops, with 5 'pops in each row [pack].

Figure 21.7

Thus, in view of the array characterization of multiplication, it is quite reasonable to associate the total number of lollipops with the product of the numbers 4 and 5.

Also consider this problem:

c. Ball point pens were on sale for 9¢ apiece. Sally bought 3 of them. How much did Sally pay for these three ball point pens? [Excluding any sales tax that might apply!]

Again, no array is explicit in the statement of the problem. But, as with problem *b*, the essential features of the situation may be represented as an array. With each of the 3 pens we may associate a row [set] of 9 cents, thus thinking in terms of a 3-by-9 array such as

Figure 21.8

Thus, it is quite appropriate to associate the number of cents that Sally paid for the ball point pens with the product of the numbers 3 and 9.

[It is true that the preceding problem *b* could have been interpreted in terms of a 5-by-4 array (5 lollipops in each of 4 *columns*) rather than in terms of a 4-by-5 array as illustrated. It also is true that problem *c* could have been interpreted in terms of a 9-by-3 array (9 cents in each of 3 *columns*) rather than in terms of a 3-by-9 array as shown. The respective products would be unaffected, of course, by these alternative interpretations.]

Frequently we wish to apply multiplication to problem situations that, in effect, involve the union of equivalent disjoint sets. Regardless of whether or not arrays are *explicit* in the statements of such problems, we find it to be both reasonable and appropriate to apply to these problems the definition of the product of two numbers, *m* and *n*, as the number of elements in an *m*-by-*n* array.

4. Now let us turn to the contention that arrays facilitate an understanding of properties of multiplication. We shall illustrate this with (a) the *commutative* property of multiplication, (b) the *multiplicative identity* property, and (c) the *distributive* property of multiplication over addition.

a. There is reason to believe that the commutative property of multiplication is more "intuitively obvious" to young children when that operation is characterized in terms of arrays than when it is defined in terms of the successive addition of equal addends. In this connection, consider Figures 21.9 and 21.10. Figure 21.9 shows an array that may be associated with the product of the ordered pair of numbers, 4 and 7. Figure 21.10 shows this array after it has been rotated through 90°. Thus, Figure 21.10 shows an array that may be associated with the product of the ordered pair of numbers, 7 and 4.

O   O   O   O   O   O   O

O   O   O   O   O   O   O

O   O   O   O   O   O   O

O   O   O   O   O   O   O

Figure 21.9 A 4-by-7 array

O   O   O   O

O   O   O   O

O   O   O   O

O   O   O   O

O   O   O   O

O   O   O   O

O   O   O   O

Figure 21.10 A 7-by-4 array

Since all that we have done is to rotate one array [Figure 21.9] to form another array [Figure 21.10], the number of elements in the second array must be exactly the same as the number of elements in the first array.[4] There

---

[4] We often display an array such as Figure 21.9 on a card, and then rotate the card through 90° to show the array of Figure 21.10.

is no need at all to appeal to the not-so-obvious fact that

$$7 + 7 + 7 + 7 = 4 + 4 + 4 + 4 + 4 + 4 + 4$$

in order to make it clear that

$$4 \times 7 = 7 \times 4.$$

The latter statement is "intuitively obvious" to most children as a direct consequence of the array rotation, without any recourse to addition. Yes, we may wish to use addition to *verify* the observation that $4 \times 7 = 7 \times 4$. But addition is not at all necessary when initially we derive the statement that $4 \times 7 = 7 \times 4$.

It is significant to note something here in passing. On occasion we may use an array with the intent of showing an instance of commutativity of multiplication, and yet fail to do so! This is illustrated in Figure 21.11.

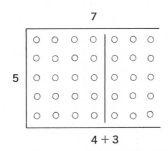

Figure 21.11 Finding and verifying the number of elements in a 3-by-5 array

Figure 21.11 shows by two different additions that this 3-by-5 array has 15 elements. But Figure 21.11 does *not* illustrate commutativity for the instance, $3 \times 5 = 5 \times 3$. Figure 21.11 shows just *one* array, not two arrays. Hence, Figure 21.11 does *not* show that a 3-by-5 array and a 5-by-3 array have the same number of elements,—unless we retract our original agreement regarding the *unique* rows-and-columns interpretation of an array, and now regard an array such as the one in Figure 21.11 as being either a 3-by-5 array or a 5-by-3 array [or both].

Such an ambiguous interpretation of an array may be advantageous at some later stages of mathematical learning, but it can be confusing to young children who are first learning about arrays and multiplication. At this earlier stage we prefer to associate 3×5 and 5×3 with *different* arrays rather than with the same array. Consequently, an illustration of commutativity necessitates showing *two* arrays,—each one being, in effect, a 90°-rotation of the other one.[5]

---

[5] Of course, when an n-by-n array is rotated through 90°, we still have an n-by-n array of the same order, e.g., when we rotate through 90° an 8-by-8 array, the resulting array is also an 8-by-8 array.

b. Earlier in this discussion we pointed to a problem of interpretation regarding 1 as the multiplicative identity, if we defined multiplication in terms of "repeated addition." No such problem exists, however, when the product of two counting numbers is characterized in terms of an array. There is *no* conceptual difficulty whatever in conceiving of either an n-by-1 array or a 1-by-n array, where n is any counting number. It makes very good sense, for instance, to have a 9-by-1 array,—an array with 9 rows, and 1 element in each row. And it makes equally good sense to have a 1-by-9 array,—an array with 1 row of 9 elements. Furthermore, even· a 1-by-1 array poses no conceptual problem. This simply is an array with 1 row, and with 1 element in that row. This single-element condition does not disqualify it as an array.

Thus, since we have no conceptual problem with either an n-by-1 or a 1-by-n array [regardless of which counting number n represents], we have no conceptual problem with 1 as the multiplicative identity in either the form $n \times 1 = n$ or the form $1 \times n = n$.

c. Finally, in connection with properties of multiplication, let us illustrate very briefly the power of arrays when working with the distributive property of multiplication over addition.

First consider the partitioning of a 5-by-7 array, for example, into a 5-by-4 array and a 5-by-3 array:

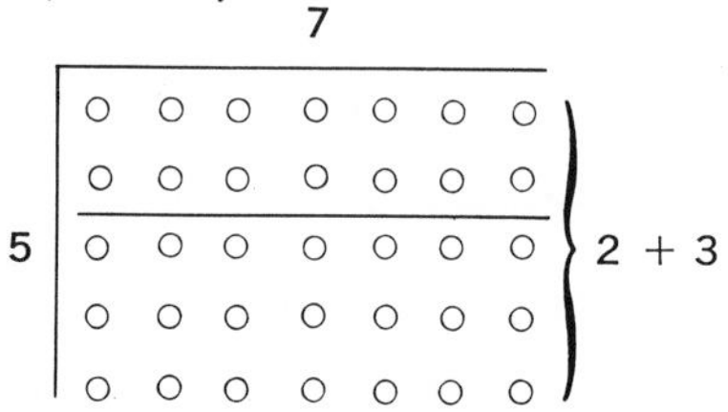

Figure 21.12

This partitioning illustrates effectively the fact that

[1] $5 \times 7 = 5 \times (4 + 3) = (5 \times 4) + (5 \times 3)$. $[20 + 15 = 35]$

Now consider the partitioning of a 5-by-7 array, for example, into a 2-by-7 array and a 3-by-7 array:

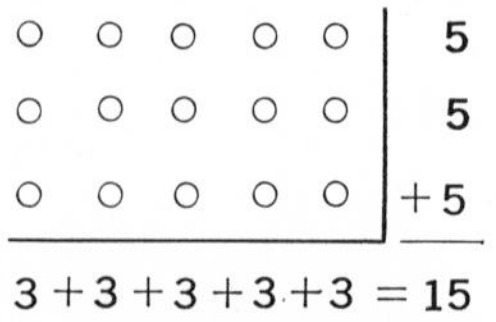

Figure 21.13

This partitioning illustrates effectively the fact that

[2] $5 \times 7 = (2 + 3) \times 7 = (2 \times 7) + (3 \times 7)$. $[14 + 21 = 35]$

In general, depending upon the way in which arrays are partitioned, we may use them effectively in the development of either form of the distributive property for all counting numbers a, b, and c:

[1] $a \times (b + c) = (a \times b) + (a \times c)$.

[2] $(a + b) \times c = (a \times c) + (b \times c)$.[6]

We are not contending that the distributive property of multiplication over addition should be stated for elementary-school pupils in the generalized forms just cited. Rather, we are concerned that these pupils have some degree of understanding of the *essence* of this property and its applications. We believe that the definition of the product of two counting numbers in terms of an array facilitates such understanding.

5. The last point to be clarified here regarding arrays and multiplication is the fact that the use of arrays does *not* mean that multiplication consequently has been defined in terms of *cartesian products*. It is true that at least some cartesian products may be displayed as arrays. But it does not follow from this that every array is necessarily a cartesian product. In fact, not one of the arrays used thus far has been derived from such a product.

We shall discuss this point in detail in the following section.

MULTIPLICATION AND CARTESIAN PRODUCTS

First, let us be sure that we recall the meaning of a *cartesian product*. We shall use A and B to designate any two sets. [We do not restrict these to disjoint sets, nor do we exclude the possibility that $A = B$.] Also, we shall use a to designate a member of set A, and we shall use b to designate a member of set B; i.e., $a \in A$ and $b \in B$. Then, *by definition*, the *cartesian product* of sets A and B, designated as $A \times B$ [read as "A cross B"], is the *set of all ordered pairs* of the form (a, b) such that the *first* component, a, of each pair is a member of set A, and the *second* component, b, of each pair is a member of set B.

Frequently we write this definition as

$$A \times B = \{(a, b) \mid a \in A, b \in B\}.$$

To cite a specific illustration, suppose that $A = \{1, 2\}$ and $B = \{5, 10, 15\}$.

---

[6] Forms [1] and [2] correspond to the forms involved in the preceding illustrative examples. However, there is no intention of implying that $a \times (b + c) = (a + b) \times c$ for any particular a, b, and c. Such an assertion is *not* valid and has *not* been made; e.g., $6 \times (5 + 4) \neq (6 + 5) \times 4$. It *is* true, of course, that $a \times (b + c) = (b + c) \times a$, and that $(a + b) \times c = c \times (a + b)$.

[The members of sets A and B could have been other kinds of things, of course.] Then, in this instance,

$$A \times B = \{(1, 5), (1, 10), (1, 15), (2, 5), (2, 10), (2, 15)\}.\ [7]$$

The product of two counting numbers is related to the cartesian product of two sets in the following way. If $n(A)$ represents the number of elements in set A, and $n(B)$ represents the number of elements in set B, then it is true that

$$n(A) \times n(B) = n(A \times B),$$

where $n(A \times B)$ represents the number of elements in the cartesian product of sets A and B.

For the specific illustration we just use, $n(A) = 2$ and $n(B) = 3$; also, $n(A \times B) = 6$; i.e., set A has 2 members, set B has 3 members, and the cartesian product, $A \times B$, has 6 members. Then,

$$n(A) \times n(B) = n(A \times B)$$
$$2 \times 3 = 6.$$

It likely is obvious that a cartesian product interpretation of the multiplication of two counting numbers is more mathematically sophisticated than either of the other two interpretations we have considered in this discussion. In fact, persons such as Fehr (1963) and Van Engen (1963) consider it to be *too* sophisticated for general use with elementary-school pupils. They also emphasize that relatively few "social situations" involving cartesian products have any particular significance for these pupils.

Let us avoid the *skirts-and-blouses* problems that have been over-worked to the point of triteness and, instead, use the following setting to extend our consideration of multiplication and cartesian products.

Suppose that Hank and Maria are candidates for the office of president in a school election. We shall let

$$A = \{\text{Hank, Maria}\}.$$

Also suppose that Cathy, Jose, and Sue are candidates for the office of secretary in the same election. We shall let

$$B = \{\text{Cathy, Jose, Sue}\}.$$

We wish to know how many different president-secretary combinations are possibilities for winning this election.

[7] Keep in mind that since each member of $A \times B$ is an *ordered* pair, it is true that $(1, 5)$ is a member of $A \times B$; but $(5, 1)$ is *not* a member of $A \times B$. Actually, $(5, 1)$ is a member of

$$B \times A = \{(5, 1), (5, 2), (10, 1), (10, 2), (15, 1), (15, 2)\}.$$

We may approach this by finding the number of members in the cartesian product, $A \times B$. Let us assume that we do not already know the fact that $n(A) \times n(B) = n(A \times B)$. So, we shall actually list the members of the product set:

$1 \times B = \{$(Hank, Cathy), (Hank, Jose), (Hank, Sue),

(Maria, Cathy), (Maria, Jose), (Maria, Sue)$\}$.

Thus, we see that there are 6 such possible combinations for election.

We should keep in mind that the members of $A \times B$ are *ordered* pairs; i.e., the *first* name in a particular pair indicates a nominee for *president*, and the *second* name in that pair signifies a nominee for *secretary*. Notice that the pair (Sue, Hank), for instance, is *not* a member of $A \times B$. This pair would imply that *Sue* is nominated for *president* and that *Hank* is nominated for *secretary*,—and this is not so!

Sometimes we find it convenient to display a product set, $A \times B$, in such a way as to suggest an *array*. We have done this in Table 21.1, but we have abbreviated things a bit. Each ordered pair is designated by a pair of letters instead of names. For example, in place of (Hank, Cathy) we used simply (H, C). Thus, the members of this particular $A \times B$ may be represented as:

Table 21.1

Using $A \times B$ to suggest an array

| | | Set B | | |
		Cathy	Jose	Sue
Set A	Hank	(H, C)	(H, J)	(H, S)
	Maria	(M, C)	(M, J)	(M, S)

We may go one step further, as in Table 21.2, and simply use something such as a *dot* to *represent* each member [ordered pair] of $A \times B$:

Table 21.2

Using Dots for $A \times B$ to suggest an array

| | | Set B | | |
		Cathy	Jose	Sue
Set A	Hank	.	.	.
	Maria	.	.	.

We notice that in both Table 21.1 and Table 21.2, a 2-by-3 array is suggested. The number of elements in any 2-by-3 array is 2 × 3 or 6. However, an important distinction related to Tables 21.1 and 21.2 should not be overlooked.

The representation in Table 21.1 does not obscure the composition of each ordered pair that is a member of $A \times B$. [The fact that single letters were used to stand for names is immaterial and irrelevant.] Even if we had displayed only the array

$$(H, \ C) \ (H, \ J) \ (H, \ S)$$
$$(M, \ C) \ (M, \ J) \ (M, \ S)$$

each element of this array is clearly an ordered pair, and each element of this array is clearly a member of the cartesian product $A \times B$ [and there are no elements of $A \times B$ that are not elements of the array]. We do not need the row and column headings to show this.

In Table 21.2, however, the composition of each ordered pair of $A \times B$ is indicated by the *position* of a particular dot in the array with reference to the row and column headings, but *not by any dot per se*. If we had displayed in isolation, as it were, the array

$$\cdot \quad \cdot \quad \cdot$$
$$\cdot \quad \cdot \quad \cdot$$

we could not infer that this *necessarily* represented $A \times B$ or even *any* cartesian product. In itself, *each dot is not an ordered pair of any sort;* however, each dot may have been used to *represent* an ordered pair that is a member of some product set. But the *form* of this representation is not the form of an ordered pair.

If we are interested in the *specific members* of a cartesian product, we simply may list them. Or we may elect to list them in an array form as in Table 21.1 [with or without row and column headings], where each element of the array explicitly designates an ordered-pair member of a particular cartesian product.

On the other hand, if our concern is chiefly with the *number* of elements in a product set, we may elect to represent the situation as in Table 21.2. The resulting *array of dots* has the same *number* of elements, *but not the same elements* per se, as does the cartesian product it represents.

We observed in the preceding section on Multiplication and Arrays that some arrays may arise quite independently of, or apart from, any cartesian product idea. Here in this present section, however, we have considered arrays that may be associated with cartesian products. In some instances [as in Table 21.1] the elements of an array signify explicitly, by their form, the elements of a particular product set. In other instances [as in Table 21.2] the form of the elements of an array does not suggest that they represent elements of a product set. Discrimination must be exercised concerning the use of each of these two forms of representation.

IN CONCLUSION

We have sought to clarify some aspects of multiplication within the set of counting numbers as it relates to three things: (1) a characterization of multiplication as the successive addition of equal addends; (2) a definition of the product of two counting numbers in terms of arrays; and (3) a relation between both multiplication and arrays and the concept of a cartesian product.

We have given reasons why this writer rejects "repeated addition" as the basis upon which multiplication within the set of counting numbers can be defined to best advantage. We also have given reasons why this writer favors defining the product of two counting numbers in terms of arrays.

In light of the more sophisticated concept involved and the limited applications that are of significance to elementary-school children, we recognize that it would be unwise to attempt to use cartesian products as the basis upon which multiplication is characterized for these children. However, the definition of the product of two counting numbers in terms of arrays is not at all inconsistent with the cartesian product concept. In fact, we should not rule out the possibility of *introducing* this concept to at least some pupils within the elementary grades,—not as the basis upon which multiplication is characterized but as a higher level concept to which the multiplication operation may be related and applied. This puts product sets in a quite different perspective.

Finally, it may be worthwhile to recognize two additional things regarding the use of arrays.

1. Some persons favor a more explicit use of *mappings* in connection with the several arithmetic operations. For instance: multiplication is the operation which *maps* the ordered pair of counting numbers (7, 5) onto the counting number 35. This fact may be written as:

$$(7, 5) \xrightarrow{\times} 35.$$

[By way of contrast, addition maps the ordered pair (7, 5) onto the number 12; i.e.,

$$(7, 5) \xrightarrow{+} 12.]$$

But on what basis do elementary-school children decide that 35 [and not 12, or whatever] is the counting number onto which (7, 5) is mapped by *multiplication?* The definition of the product of two counting numbers in terms of an array provides just such a basis. Arrays do not inhibit a mapping interpretation of multiplication. They facilitate this for elementary-school pupils.

　　2. The use of arrays with multiplication of counting numbers extends very easily to the use of rectangular regions with multiplication of rational numbers greater than zero. We may pave the way for this extension by showing arrays not only in the form shown in Figure 21.14, but also in the form shown in Figure 21.15.

Figure 21.14

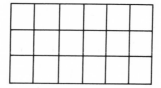

Figure 21.15

In each instance we have a 3-by-6 array. Considerable experience with the form shown in Figure 21.15 provides a desirable readiness for using a somewhat similar representation with multiplication of positive rationals.

REFERENCES

Cunningham, George S. "Three Views of the Multiplier." *Arithmetic Teacher* 12: 275–76; April 1965.

D'Augustine, Charles H. "Letters to the Editor," *Arithmetic Teacher* 13: 25; January 1966.

Fehr, Howard F. "Modern Mathematics and Good Pedagogy," *Arithmetic Teacher* 10: 402–11; November 1963.

Fehr, Howard F. "Sense and Nonsense in a Modern School Mathematics Program." *Arithmetic Teacher* 13: 83–91; February 1966.

Gray, Roland F. "An Experiment in the Teaching of Introductory Multiplication." *Arithmetic Teacher* 12: 199–203; March 1965.

Hervey, Margaret A. "Children's Responses to Two Types of Multiplication Problems." *Arithmetic Teacher* 13: 288–92; April 1966.

Kushta, Nicholas. "Horizontal and Vertical Presentation." *Arithmetic Teacher* 13: 106; February 1966.

Morse, Edwin E. *The Number Systems of Elementary Mathematics* (Counting, Measurement, and Coordinates). Reading, Mass.: Addison-Wesley Publishing Co., 1966.

National Council of Teachers of Mathematics. *Topics in Mathematics* (for Elementary School Teachers). Twenty-ninth Yearbook. Washington, D.C.: The Council, 1964.

Phillips, Jo McKeeby, "The Baby and the Bath Water." *School Science and Mathematics* 63: 291–304; April 1963.

Philips, Jo. " 'Basic Laws' for Young Children." *Arithmetic Teacher* 12: 525–32; November 1965.

Rappaport, David. "Multiplication *Is* Repeated Addition." *Arithmetic Teacher* 12: 550–51; November 1965.

Schell, Leo Mac. "Two Aspects of Introductory Multiplication: The Array and the Distributive Property." *Dissertation Abstracts* 25: 1561–62; March 1965.

School Mathematics Study Group. *A Brief Course in Mathematics for Elementary School Teachers*, Revised Edition. Studies in Mathematics, Volume IX. Stanford, Calif.: Stanford University, 1963. (a)

School Mathematics Study Group. *Mathematics for the Elementary School Grade 4: Teacher's Commentary*, Revised Edition. New Haven, Ct.: Yale University, 1963. (b)

22 PRIMES AT THE PRIMARY LEVEL

Sister M. Ferrer

BEFORE YOU READ   One aspect of the modern mathematics movement has been introduction of new content. Included in this is number
theory designed to increase pupils' understanding of the structure of
mathematics. To some extent this may have been overdone, yet there are
aspects of number theory that children can understand and that are
especially important, aspects which contribute directly to learning more
about basic concepts in mathematics. While a study of primes and
composites may not appear to belong in a section discussing basic operations, such a study can help pupils to attain an enriched understanding
of both multiplication and division. The reasons for this are made clear
in the following article by Sister Ferrer.

Recall that the final article in Section I dealt with flow charting
the components of a teaching strategy. The preface stated that each
article in Sections II through VI dealt with content and, at least implicitly, with methodology. As an illustration of how the content and
pedagogy of this book may be combined, this presentation by Sister
Ferrer has been translated into a lesson plan written in flow-chart form.

The transition period of school mathematics is being felt on the elementary
level. It is true that most teachers realized that work must be done at this
level, but attention was given to the high school because of their proximity
to collegiate work.

The chief purpose of elementary arithmetic is to introduce the number
system and provide a tool for further mathematics and sciences. Thus the
first principles of arithmetic are identical with the first principles of all
mathematics. Hence, an understanding of some of the first principles of
numbers provides meaning and understanding of what must be taught to
the students at the elementary level. This article considers at least one or
two of the principles of number, taken from number theory. The first is the
classification of the numbers according to the number of divisors possessed
by the numbers. This classification can be used in many ways in elementary
mathematics to provide meaning, understanding, and pleasure in the doing
of arithmetic exercises.

Reprinted from the *Catholic School Journal*, November 1961, pp. 48–49 with permission of the
publisher. This article is copyrighted. © *1961* by CCM Professional Magazines, Inc. All
rights reserved. Sister M. Ferrer is at St. Xavier College, Chicago, Illinois.

Flow Chart Lesson Based on Article 22.

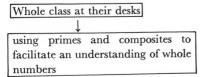

| Whole class at their desks |
| ↓ |
| using primes and composites to facilitate an understanding of whole numbers |

Exposition

Talk about a whole number as a combination of other whole numbers.

Get at factors and products

3 and 7 → 3 × 7 = 21 and

21 ÷ 7 = 3 and

21 ÷ 3 = 7

———— do same with 12

↓

Exploration

Drill sheet on finding all factors of

———— 18, 9, 7, 14, 20, 36

↓

Discussion—illustration

on board 1, 2, 3, 4, 5, 6, 7, 8, 9, 10

Questions—pursue factors
———— of each

↓

Exposition

Give verbal definition of prime and composite numbers

The classification of natural numbers (1, 2, 3, ...) into three classes according to the number of their divisors is as follows:

1. One: It is in a class by itself since it has only one divisor, itself.
2. Primes: Primes are those numbers having only two divisors, itself and one. For example: 2, 3, 5, 7, 11.
3. Composite Numbers: Composite numbers are those numbers having more than two divisors. For example: 6 = 2 × 3. The divisors of 6 are 1, 2, 3, and 6.

If a number is a composite number, it can be written in terms of its factors, i.e., 6 = 2 × 3 — 2 and 3 are factors of 6; 12 = 3 × 4 = 2 × 6 = 2 × 2 × 3 = 12 × 1.

The classification with respect to the number of divisors as well as the concept of factor can be applied to elementary mathematics at various levels. This classification can affect the operations of multiplication, division, the least common multiple, fractions, the least common denominator for the addition and subtraction of fractions, percentage, and elsewhere, and thus provides a continuity through various grade levels.

A second number theory concept that proves to be a handy tool for teaching understanding in elementary arithmetic is known as the division algorithm. It provides a means of writing an answer to a division problem when the divisor is not a factor, and hence, there exists a remainder.

These two concepts, the classification of whole numbers according to the number of their divisors, and the division algorithm were presented to a small number of elementary teachers for the purpose of experimentation. The teachers studied the material and returned for a second meeting at which they asked many questions. After this, they experimented in their classes and found that more meaning was conveyed to the students than had been done by their former methods. Their own reactions were mirrored in their enthusiasm and anxious willingness to do further experimentation. Three typical results were presented to a meeting of about 100 fourth-, fifth-, and sixth-grade teachers. The meeting fired most of these teachers with enthusiasm to try the material themselves. As a result, the Saint Xavier College faculty, who instigated this experiment, is besieged for more and more material.

The following is an outline summary of the presentation made by Sister Mary Armella, fourth-grade teacher at Christ the King Elementary School, Chicago, Ill., to the teachers assembled:

READINESS FOR HIGHER MATHEMATICS IN THE FOURTH GRADE

We are attempting to show this afternoon how some basic mathematical principles which the child will use in his higher mathematics courses in high school and college may be presented in the intermediate grades.

At the primary level, children learn the sequence and meaning of numbers, from one to ten, and later understand and use these ten different number symbols, or digits, in two-place numbers, in three-place numbers, and so on. Then they begin to separate numbers into groups. They count numbers by 2's, by 10's, by 5's, and then by 3's. They even classify numbers into odd and even. In this way they are given a firm understanding of our basic number system.

Upon this solid foundation can be laid a further classification of numbers. This classification of *natural numbers*, known in arithmetic as *whole numbers*, depends on the factors, or divisors, of a number. Within this classification whole numbers will fall into three groups . . . the groups being: *one*, *primes*, and *composites*.

1. The *number one* would be in a class by itself since it has *only itself* as a divisor or factor. $1 \div 1 = 1$.

2. A *prime number* has no divisor except itself and one. $2 \div 1 = 2$; $2 \div 2 = 1$.

   Other primes are 3, 5, 7, 11, ...

3. All other whole numbers that are neither one nor prime would be in the third group. This group consist of composite numbers, i.e. numbers having more than 2 divisors. A composite has more than two divisors (itself, one, and others) $4 \div 1 = 4$; $4 \div 2 = 2$; $4 \div 4 = 1$. 12—divisors are 1, 2, 3, 4, 6, 12.

A QUIZ TO TEACHERS

Here is a quiz that Sister Mary Armella gave to the teachers. Test yourself on the classification of numbers

$a)$ 5 $b)$ 18 $c)$ 1 $d)$ 17 $e)$ 49 f) 51 $g)$ 47 $h)$ 16

Answers

Number	Classification	Divisors
5	prime	1, 5
18	composite	1, 2, 3, 6, 9, 18
1	one	1
17	prime	1, 17
49	composite	1, 7, 49
51	composite	1, 3, 17, 51
47	prime	1, 47
16	composite	1, 2, 4, 8, 16

Presentation to fourth grade Now I'm sure the questions that are uppermost in your minds are: When do I present this classification of numbers to fourth graders? And what will be my teaching procedures? When you receive a group of fourth graders in September, most of them have been exposed to the multiplication and division facts of the 5's, 2's, and 3's, which have been taught both simultaneously, and as inverse operations, i.e. one undoing the other.

Using the example of $3 \times 4 = 12$, the following is a manner of presentation.

$$
\begin{array}{cccc}
1\ 1\ 1\ 1 & 3 & 3 & 4 \quad 4 \\
1\ 1\ 1\ 1 & 3 & \underline{\times 4} & 4 \quad \underline{\times 3} \\
1\ 1\ 1\ 1 & 3 & 4 \\
 & \underline{3} & \underline{12} \\
 & \overline{12} &
\end{array}
$$

Further recognition of products and factors were given at the board to the students such as:

This is the way I presented the material: Boys and girls, no matter what number you think of, it will be a combination of some numbers. All of our whole numbers are made up of one or more numbers. Any number you think of in this fashion is a whole number. You have already learned that when you multiply a whole number by another whole number, your answer is called a *product*. Formerly you called the two numbers you multiplied together, the multiplicand and the multiplier. Today we are going to use a term for these two numbers that you will continue to use through the grades, and even in high school and college. We are going to call the numbers we multiply together, *factors*.

7 and 3 are numbers. If I multiply 7 and 3 together, they become factors, and the product of these factors is 21. The factor of a number is the same as the divisor of a number.

$$21 = 7 \times 3; \quad 21 \div 7 = 3; \quad 21 \div 3 = 7.$$

The product is 12. 6 and 2 are factors of 12.
The product is 12. 4 and 3 are factors of 12.
The product is 15. 5 and 3 are factors of 15.

When pupils were able to recognize the factors and products, practice in supplying missing factors was introduced. For example, 12. The product is 12. One factor is 6. We can find the missing factor by dividing the product by the given factor.

Finally, as a means of drill, the children were given just a *product*, and had to give the factors of the product. 12: 6 and 2 are factors of 12; 3 and 4 are factors of 12.

To re-enforce the teaching of factors and products, I made several drill sheets. After the drilling, when I felt that the children understood products and factors, they were ready for the further classification of numbers . . . one, prime, and composite.

I placed the ten digits on the board: 0 1 2 3 4 5 6 7 8 9.

Does the number 1 have any factors? No, just itself. $1 \times 1 = 1$; $1 \div 1 = 1$. So 1 is a special number, and is in a class all by itself.

How about 2? Does it have any factors? $2 \times 1 = 2$; $1 \times 2 = 2$; $2 \div 1 = 2$; $2 \div 2 = 1$. We are going to call 2 a prime number. That means that it has for its divisors itself and 1. Other examples are: 3, 5, 7, 11, 13, ...

Some children became confused and thought all odd numbers were primes. To clarify this, reference was made to 2 and 15. Many exercises were given to re-enforce this teaching process.

In conclusion, the terms I have presented this afternoon: *factors*, *product*, *prime*, and *composite numbers*, etc., when presented at the fourth grade level prepare the child to accept the teaching of fractions in a meaningful way. It equips him with terminology for later mathematics courses.

What was the result of this experiment? What was the reaction of the children? The children were interested in the new work. They had the feeling of satisfaction and also satisfied their ego by believing they were learning arithmetic that other boys and girls learn in high school and college. It is true that some students at these upper levels are learning this material that could be taught at any earlier level.

My own reaction is that this material has provided understanding, as a result of which I found it possible to cover *more* material *faster* and with greater meaning than in previous classes. The better fourth graders are now doing fractions and are making use of primes, composites, and factorization for the operations of addition and subtraction of fractions.

23 FRACTIONS

E. Glenadine Gibb

BEFORE YOU READ   A consistent theme of this book has been the active engagement of children in the learning of mathematics. Children also need to become increasingly mature with regard to the abstractions of mathematics. One of the problems encountered in teaching fractions is that of finding meaningful semiabstract referents which will enable children to conceptualize the meaning of fractions better.

The article by Professor Gibb contains several appropriate referents for fractions and a description of how they may be used to facilitate addition and multiplication of fractions. The type of referents shown in the article can be easily reproduced on overlays and displayed on an overhead projector.

Through reading the article the teacher should be able to draw several psychologically sound and mathematically appropriate illustrations demonstrating the concept of fractional numbers, and describe two specific procedures which utilize drawings in portraying operations with fractions.

Typical approaches to the study of fractions in today's schools make it difficult for children to learn about fractions. Certainly, learning about fractions needs our special attention. If we are to improve our instructional program in the teaching of fractions, we must give careful consideration to the selection of experiences which exhibit the common property we are attempting to identify. These experiences must be not only mathematically sound but also psychologically appropriate for elementary-school children.

Let us think about ways of helping children develop sound under-standing of some of the ideas about what we shall in this article refer to as *fractional numbers*. Let us think about what part of our present program may well be retained. Also, let us think about what part of our present program should be replaced.

THE CONCEPT OF FRACTIONAL NUMBER

We may confess that in helping children to learn about the natural numbers (whole numbers beginning with 1), we confine our efforts to having them

---

Reprinted from *Grade Teacher*, vol. 79, no. 8 (April 1962), pp. 54, 95–97. E. Glenadine Gibb is a professor in the Department of Curriculum and Instruction at the College of Education of the University of Texas, Dallas, Texas.

learn a process for finding names of those numbers. We spend time on counting. We spend too little time and thought on the selection of activities designed to help children develop concepts upon which an understanding of the properties of natural numbers can be built. We become "skill minded" instead of "idea minded" as we have children find ways to name something about which they know little.

We may be guilty of repeating this emphasis as we help children learn something about fractional numbers. For example, we ask children to tell what pair of numbers describes the fractional number. We use such exercises as the following:

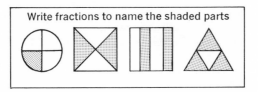

Figure 23.1

What misunderstanding have we invited? Let us name the fractional number-represented in each of the figures below:

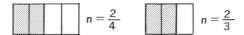

Figure 23.2

If we traced the shaded part of one and placed it on top of the other, we would see that they are the same size. But they represent different fractional numbers. Why? The unit has changed. *The unit and subunits are important aspects of learning about fractional numbers.* We see this same idea represented in a different way in Figure 23.3.

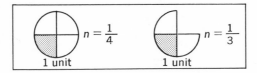

Figure 23.3

Another experience which helps children learn more about the fractional numbers is illustrated in Figure 23.4. The two parts of Figure 23.4 show the same relationship between the shaded part and the whole.

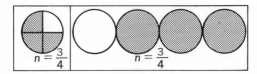

Figure 23.4

Notice that the common number property of the two parts of the figure is described by the same fraction numeral, namely 3/4.

To develop a richer concept of fractional numbers, a child must do more than learn how to name them. We must help him to *think of units* and then to *think in subunits of that unit*. We must help him to learn to symbolize the relation between the subunits or parts and "the whole" by using a new kind of numeral, namely the fractional numeral. This numeral names the measure of the part being considered with respect to the whole.

DIFFERENT NUMBER PAIRS EXPRESS THE SAME RELATIONSHIP

Have you ever asked the children in your class to "reduce a fraction" or to "change to lowest terms"? What did you expect them to do?

We should give children many experiences in using manipulative materials to represent fractional numbers. As they use these materials we should guide them to make certain observations. They should notice that each of these pairs of numerals [2, 4; 4, 8; 1, 2] may be used to describe the same fractional number.

The number line pictured in Figure 23.5 helps a child to visualize this idea.

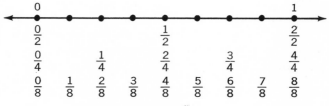

Figure 23.5

Many different pairs of numerals name the same fractional number. All of these pairs describe the same property.

We may ask children to list some other members of the set each of whose elements is a name for the fractional number 1/2. They learn to write [1/2, 4/8, 5/10, 6/12 . . .], using ". . ." to express the idea that there are many, many more names. In fact, the list of names is endless. Likewise, the set of numerals [2/3, 4/6, 6/9, 8/12, . . .] all name the same fractional number which may be expressed "in lowest terms" as 2/3.

When we ask children to "reduce a fraction," we really are asking them to select the simplest pair of numerals that may be used to name that particular fractional number. Notice that the numbers of this simplest pair will have no common factors other than 1. You are familiar with the techniques for determining this pair; you also know how to find other members of the set each of whose elements names a particular number. You should lead children to discover these techniques, and to notice that each pair belongs to only one set. Each such pair describes one fractional number.

OPERATION

Let us think now about operations with fractional numbers. How do you teach addition, subtraction, multiplication and division of fractional numbers? Do the expressions "like denominators," "unlike denominators," "whole number times a fraction," "fraction times a fraction" and "whole number divided by a fraction" sound familiar?

Yes, our texts classify exercises according to the type of name used to express a fractional number. Then they proceed to develop specific techniques for each type. The real idea to be developed—the meanings of these operations with fractional numbers—gets lost among the details of computation.

How might we help children to learn about addition of fractional numbers? Surely we should not begin to develop separate skills for several kinds of problems identified by the form of the fractional numeral.

To learn about addition of natural numbers, we view the operation of addition as describing the number property of the union of appropriate sets. We should follow a similar procedure in teaching the addition of fractional numbers.

Suppose we have two pieces of wood.

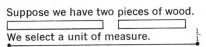

We select a unit of measure.

We use this unit of measure to express the length of the pieces of wood. We see that the first piece is $\frac{1}{2}$ unit long. The second piece is $\frac{1}{3}$ unit long.

We put the two pieces of wood together. We use our unit of measure to measure the length of the union of these pieces.

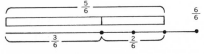

Figure 23.6

We can write this mathematical sentence to describe this action:

$$1/2 + 1/3 = \frac{m}{n}$$

We wish to determine this sum. To accomplish this, we select a suitable subunit of our original unit. What subunit is appropriate for both 1/2 and 1/3?

Another name for 1/2 is 3/6. Another name for 1/3 is 2/6.

We write: 3/6 + 2/6 = m/6 and determine the sum to be 5/6.

Likewise, we consider the operation of multiplication. In our opinion, we would not begin with problems like 3 × 3/4 = 3/4 + 3/4 + 3/4, for we cannot extend this approach to products as 2/3 × 3/4. We prefer an approach that reflects the full meaning of operations with fractional numbers.

We use the operation of multiplication of natural numbers to describe the number property associated with Figure 23.7.

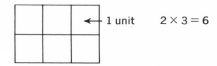

Figure 23.7

We use the same approach with fractional numbers.

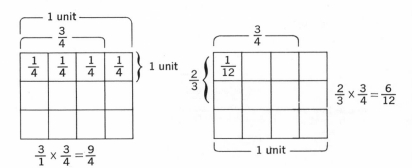

Figure 23.8

Computational skills, as we commonly know them, should find their place in the shortcuts we devise to speed up computation. These shortcuts can grow out of an understanding of the properties of fractional numbers and operations with fractional numbers.

These are the kinds of things we should be thinking about: What are our goals? Are we interested in developing mathematical ideas for permanent framing in mathematics? Are we more interested in teaching children facts that lead quickly to right answers to questions in a test?

I believe that we have, in any elementary-school mathematics program, responsibility for developing mathematical ideas. We also have a responsibility for developing skill and proficiency in computation. This is not an "either or" proposition. By what approaches can we best achieve our goals? Are certain approaches better than others? These are among the questions we should ask ourselves as we consider new ways to meet our responsibilities.

24 DIVISION OF FRACTIONS FOR UNDERSTANDING

Thomas V. Baucom

BEFORE YOU READ   By the time children are ready to begin
division of fractions they should have a firm knowledge of factors and
products. They should also be shown meaningful illustrations of this
process. A child's understanding of division of fractions is made easier by
a meaningful use of the number "one" and the "multiplicative inverse of
a number." This is consistent with the idea that as a pupil gains mathematical maturity, and as he becomes capable of more abstract conjectures, his reliance upon concrete referents becomes less important.
Translating the type of progress children should make into appropriate
lessons is a difficult task. Some suggestions on how this may be done in
more than one manner are shown in the article by Professor Baucom.

The procedures for dividing fractions described by the author
should be particularly helpful to pupils who demonstrate some ability in
conceptualizing numbers mentally. To obtain a better idea of what is
meant by gaining increased mathematical maturity the teacher may compare this article with the previous one by Professor Gibb.

As a result of this reading the teacher should be able to illustrate
the division of fractions in three different ways and describe the rationale
for the "invert the divisor and multiply" rule.

There are few social applications of dividing a proper fraction by another
proper fraction, so the teacher may be reluctant to spend much time on this
topic. The amount of time available and the degree of understanding
desired will determine the approach which should be used. Several approaches will be considered.

A general understanding of the reasonableness of the expected
answer is necessary before developing a particular technique. The following
generalizations stress this point:

1. The quotient of a number divided by itself is 1.

Reprinted from *School Science and Mathematics*, vol. 65, no. 5 (May 1965), pp. 432–435.
Thomas V. Baucom, who is at Frostburg State College in Frostburg, Maryland, presented
this article first as a paper at the annual CASMT Convention in Detroit, Michigan, on November
28, 1964.

2. The quotient of a number divided by a smaller number is greater than 1.
3. The quotient of a number divided by a larger number is less than 1.
4. Any number multiplied or divided by 1 has the same value.
5. Multiplication and division are inverse processes.
6. 1 is the identity element for multiplication and division.

There should be some discussion of the meaning of a fraction. The fraction $\frac{3}{4}$, for instance, could be interpreted as:

1. Three parts of the whole which has been broken into four equal parts.
2. A quotient of two numbers $(3 \div 4)$.
3. A ratio of two numbers $(3 : 4)$.
4. One of four parts of three things.

If the common denominator method has been used in teaching the addition and subtraction of fractions, it would be easiest to use the same approach to the division of fractions if the problem is one of measurement. The common denominator approach can be regarded as going from one unit to a smaller unit. This was man's early approach to this troublesome problem.

1. Example:
$$\frac{2}{3} + \frac{3}{5} = \frac{10}{15} + \frac{9}{15} = \frac{19}{15}$$

$$\text{or } 10\left(\frac{1}{15}\right) + 9\left(\frac{1}{15}\right) = 19\left(\frac{1}{15}\right)$$

or 10 fifteenths + 9 fifteenths = 19 fifteenths

Thus the change has been made to smaller units (fifteenths). If this concept is understood, then the problem of division of fractions is relatively easy.

2. Example:
$$\frac{2}{3} \div \frac{4}{5} = \frac{10}{15} \div \frac{12}{15} = \frac{10}{12}$$

$$\text{or } 10\left(\frac{1}{15}\right) \div 12\left(\frac{1}{15}\right) = 10 \div 12 = \frac{10}{12}$$

$$\text{or } 10 \text{ fifteenths} \div 12 \text{ fifteenths} = \frac{10}{12}$$

This method changes the problem from one of division of fractions to division of whole numbers in a smaller unit.

The social applications are rather infrequent. Mueller[1] uses the illustration of a hamburger weighing $\frac{2}{9}$ lb. and raises the question of the

[1] Mueller, F. J., *Arithmetic, Its Structure and Concepts*, Prentice-Hall.

number of hamburgers which can be made from $\frac{2}{3}$ lb. of ground meat. The common denominator approach gives

$$\frac{2}{3} \div \frac{2}{9} = \frac{6}{9} \div \frac{2}{9} = 6\left(\frac{1}{9}\right) \div 2\left(\frac{1}{9}\right) = 6 \div 2 = 3.$$

This can be confusing unless the interpretation is clearly shown that $\frac{6}{9}$ lb. equals $3 \times \frac{2}{3}$ lb. or 3 hamburgers can be made from the $\frac{2}{3}$ lb. of meat.

If this method is not liked or desired, the complex form of the fractions may be used and the complex fraction may then be multiplied by unity in the form of C.D. $\div$ C.D.

3. Example:
$$\frac{2}{3} \div \frac{4}{5}$$

$$\frac{\dfrac{2}{3} \times 15}{\dfrac{4}{5} \times 15} = \frac{10}{12} = \frac{5}{6}$$

Newsweek magazine says the Russians are using this approach.

If the complex form of fraction is understood, this is an easy approach to the problem. If the students will later take algebra, this approach is almost a "must" at some point in the education of such students.

A slight variation is to use the common denominator approach with the problem in complex form and then follow the same procedure.

4. Example:
$$\frac{2}{3} \div \frac{4}{5}$$

$$\frac{\dfrac{10}{15} \times 15}{\dfrac{12}{15} \times 15} = \frac{\dfrac{10}{1}}{\dfrac{12}{1}} = \frac{10}{12} = \frac{5}{6}$$

The method in general use in this country is the simple inversion of the divisor before multiplication.

5. Example:
$$\frac{2}{3} \div \frac{4}{5}$$

$$\frac{2}{3} \times \frac{5}{4} = \frac{10}{12} = \frac{5}{6}$$

The teacher is not bound to one explanation. If the problem is put into complex form, the multiplication of the numerator and denominator by the inverse of the denominator over itself may be used.

6. Example: $\dfrac{2}{3} \div \dfrac{4}{5}$

$$\dfrac{\dfrac{2}{3} \times \dfrac{5}{4}}{\dfrac{4}{5} \times \dfrac{5}{4}} = \dfrac{\dfrac{10}{12}}{\dfrac{20}{20}} = \dfrac{\dfrac{10}{12}}{1} = \dfrac{10}{12} = \dfrac{5}{6}$$

This method without explanation of the meaning of multiplicative inverse or reciprocal does not improve the situation although the student easily sees and understands why it works without the use of the large words (multiplicative inverse and reciprocal).

Many teachers believe the topic is well worth careful development through the use of the multiplicative inverse or reciprocal approach. Stress is placed on 1 as the identity element for multiplication and division and that they are inverse processes.

If any number is either multiplied or divided by 1, the result is the original number. Inverse is another number which when multiplied or divided by the given number yields 1 as the product or quotient, respectively. It is necessary that the students understand that division is always exactly equivalent to multiplication by the reciprocal of the divisor.

7. Example: $\dfrac{2}{3} \div \dfrac{4}{5}$

$$\dfrac{2}{3} \times \dfrac{1}{\dfrac{4}{5}} = \dfrac{2}{3} \times \dfrac{5}{4} = \dfrac{10}{12}$$

The "Cross Multiplication" method is a very old form of manipulation. It is confusing to use because the divisor is written first.

8. Example: $\dfrac{2}{3} \div \dfrac{4}{5}$

$$\dfrac{4}{5} \times \dfrac{2}{3} \begin{array}{l} \rightarrow 10 \\ \rightarrow 12 \end{array} = \dfrac{5}{6}$$

Another manipulative method was used many years ago. The fractions were first written in complex form, then the outside numbers were multiplied to give the numerator of the answer, while the inside numbers were multiplied to give the denominator of the answer.

9. Example: $\dfrac{2}{3} \div \dfrac{4}{5}$

$$\mathrm{N}\left(\dfrac{\dfrac{2}{3}}{\dfrac{4}{5}}\right)\mathrm{D} = \dfrac{2 \times 5}{3 \times 4} = \dfrac{10}{12} = \dfrac{5}{6}$$

The inversion method is an easy manipulative method but involves little understanding unless accompanied by an adequate approach. One of the approaches shown in Examples 2, 3, 4, 6, 7, or variations of them, may appeal to the teacher.

The illustration used throughout has been the most troublesome part of the problem, i.e., division of one fraction by another. The same methods may be used with division of a whole number by a fraction or a fraction by a whole number if the whole numbers are given in fractional form.

A special case was used throughout in order to simplify the understanding. The same procedure could be followed using the general case.

25 UNDERSTANDING NEW MATH

Robert W. Plants

BEFORE YOU READ   In a sequence of courses in algebra the coefficients of polynomials are typically whole numbers, integers, rational numbers, and undesignated real numbers, in that order. A sequence of examples is

$$3X + 5 = 0, \; {}^{-}2X^2 + 3X - 6 = 0, \; 4/3X - 2/5 = 0, \text{ and } y = m \cdot X + b.$$

For some reason, which could probably not be justified in the light of present knowledge of what children can learn, there is virtually no consideration of negative integers in elementary school programs. Integers are the numbers . . . , $^{-}2$, $^{-}1$, 0, 1, 2, . . . Negative integers are the numbers $^{-}1$, $^{-}2$, $^{-}3$, $^{-}4$, . . . This neglect is unfortunate because children use both positive and negative numbers in their conversation and play in and out of school.

The next article by Professor Plant discusses the problem of developing rules which govern the multiplication of signed numbers in a meaningful manner. The article deals only with multiplication of signed numbers.

As a result of reading the teacher should be able to enunciate the rationale that governs the multiplication of signed numbers and provide a number line illustration for each case.

Here is a letter I received from a perplexed 7th grade math student. The question he asks is rather common, but as it is not answered concisely in most textbooks, I'm including my answer.

264 Arthur St.
Shreveport, La.

Dear Uncle Bob:

My mother and I are having a controversy over the alleged fact that "a minus number $\times$ another minus number = a plus number." She has a book on her side, but I say that if you have a hole in the ground you can't make a hill out of it by digging it deeper. Could you tell us which one is right and then explain by the use of a number line?

Love,
Mark Stephenson
University, Mississippi

Reprinted from the *Mississippi Educational Advance*, vol. 58, no. 7 (April 1967), pp. 16–17. Robert W. Plants is Associate Professor of Education at the University of Mississippi.

Dear Mark:

We have all enjoyed your question and your letter. Your mother and her book are correct. You ask for a meaningful explanation to an abstract operation that many authors do not consider. You must remember that arithmetic books are not written by students who are learning arithmetic, but by professionals who write in terms of axioms and laws that have been discovered during hundreds of years of work with problems.

The first problems were not too difficult as they were related to everyday life, but today more than ever—our problems are related to problems related to life *today*.

The higher you go in school the more you will find books and teachers who present axioms and expect students to understand the underlying number operations and concepts from which these axioms are gleaned. We might call this a "putting the cart before the horse" way of teaching.

There is an attempt today in the new arithmetic programs to return to the inductive or discovery method of teaching. Many teachers, however, find it difficult to allow enough classroom time for the discussion and exploration needed in the new programs to discover the laws or axioms related to the problems their students are studying.

We therefore find ourselves hurrying through our textbooks with all of their axioms and laws, drilling and memorizing bits of this and that and hoping that understanding will come later.

You ask that I use the number line to show you the answer to this operation of multiplication in which you are using "signed" numbers. The number line is related to life. It is a picture, model, and measuring device that we can see and talk about meaningfully. (Writers refer to it as "directed" or "ordered" numbers.)

Your difficulty does not lie in the mathematics of multiplying "signed" numbers, but in an understanding of how to read your problems so that you can understand its relationship to what you already know about life.

EXAMPLES HELP YOU UNDERSTAND

Neither the numerals nor operation signs involved convey the understanding you seek. I'm enclosing four number sentences that involve the operation of multiplication and "signed" numbers. Each number sentence is a number line—picturing the solution.

It's possible that the use of the general term "factor" in the new arithmetic books instead of multiplier and multiplicand increases the student's difficulty in determining which number of a number pair is the operator.

In the number pair $(-2) \times (-4)$ the second number is operated on by the first number or (to say this another way) the first number does the work. This distinction is conveyed by the word "multiplier" more so than by the more general term, "factor," currently being used. It is not too difficult to understand a problem if we know how to read it. We are concerned with the negative or inverse of *two* negative (multiplier) *fours* (multiplicand).

Mark, I hope this clarifies your problem. Arithmetic and more comprehensively, mathematics, can be fun, but we have to learn how to read it.

Give my regards to your folks and write again.

Your Uncle Bob

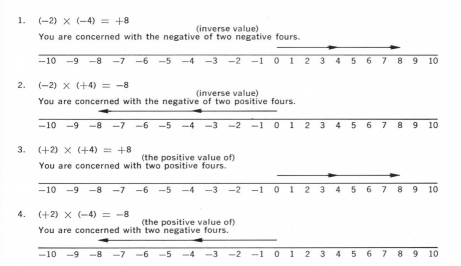

1. (−2) × (−4) = +8
    (inverse value)
    You are concerned with the negative of two negative fours.

2. (−2) × (+4) = −8
    (inverse value)
    You are concerned with the negative of two positive fours.

3. (+2) × (+4) = +8
    (the positive value of)
    You are concerned with two positive fours.

4. (+2) × (−4) = −8
    (the positive value of)
    You are concerned with two negative fours.

Figure 25.1

Dear Uncle Bob,

Thank you for the answer. Thank you from my mother also. She knew that −△ × −□ equals plus ○, but she did not know why.

Mark Stephenson

SECTION V

Geometry: Examining Spacial Relationships

> *"In mathematics he was greater than Tych Brahe or Erra Pater; For he by geometric scale, Could take the size of pots of ale."*
>
> Samuel Butler, *Hudibras*, Part I

Introduction

INTRODUCTION

The fact that numerical aspects of mathematics are emphasized while geometry continues to receive much less attention in most elementary school programs is indeed an enigma when one considers what children can learn as well as the presence of shape and form in man's environment. The concrete nature of a plexiglass disk, the semiabstract nature of the coordinate plane, and the abstract nature of Euclid's parallel postulate indicates that Euclidian and non-Euclidian geometries can be investigated by elementary school pupils in nearly perfect accordance with the mental development described by Piaget. Never before has man been so surrounded by geometric shapes, especially those other than triangles, circles, squares, and rectangles. The teacher has available an environment which offers numerous and exciting possibilities for active exploration and conjecture.

The primary school child can demonstrate considerable ability to work with the coordinate plane. He can locate points; identify open and closed curves; determine a set of ordered pairs which, if plotted on graph paper and connected by line segments, form a polygon; and he can play games of tic-tac-toe. These activities must become more prominent in primary classrooms.

The intermediate school pupil has the ability to do geometric constructions by following a sequence of fairly complex directions given in notational form. Yet a check of the materials available in a classroom often fails to produce sets of rulers, compasses, and protractors—the tools children could be using to do these constructions. It may be that there is a "geometry gap."

Most attempts to upgrade the mathematics education of teachers in the mid-1960's did not include comprehensive recommendations regarding geometry. Perhaps the abstract nature of geometry courses traditionally offered in secondary schools has caused prospective elementary teachers to avoid the subject. Perhaps the tendency of the past to require pupils to memorize a seemingly endless list of formulas for computing perimeters, areas, and volumes has been a contributing factor. Uncertainty in the minds of mathematicians regarding what geometry is may be partially responsible. Whatever the cause, the study of geometry does not seem to have taken its rightful place in elementary school mathematics programs. The ideas advanced in Section I regarding learning and the teaching of mathematics lend support to the notion that we should no longer exclude geometry from the elementary school.

Much current thinking about how children learn is especially appropriate to geometry. The emphasis on a laboratory approach in which pupils actively work with concrete materials and attempt to discover basic geometric and numerical relationships has cast geometry in a new light. This is appealing because the ideas explored are concrete instead of abstract, intuitive instead of logical, and active instead of passive. As a consequence the work is more rewarding for children and more interesting to the teacher.

As an example, consider a group of children who have been given geo-boards and some rubber bands. They can be asked to fit bands over the pegs in such a way that several triangles are formed. They may then be asked to examine their triangles to see whether any of them "appear to have" the same shape. Following this, pupils can examine the respective units of length associated with the sides of the triangles. Pupils might make conjectures about why certain triangles have the same shape. If guidance is skillful, the pupils can be led to discuss relationship between proportion and similarity. There are other directions the lesson might take, but regardless of what the children do, interesting patterns can be discovered and the students will want to state what they observe. In this setting children are encouraged to experience the excitement of self-discovery. The teacher's function is to coordinate discussion and guide exploration as a coequal in the learning enterprise.

This Section contains articles which treat geometry in the spirit described here. While each article is self-contained, there are themes which run throughout the Section. When combined, these themes are characterized by an emphasis on pupil activity, on discovery, and on the need to use concrete materials as referents for abstractions to be encountered later.

26 GEOMETRY FOR THE ELEMENTARY SCHOOL

Charles Buck

BEFORE YOU READ   The word "simple," when used by mathematicians and teachers, appears to have interpretations that differ. A mathematician is inclined to view something which is highly abstract, logical, and elegant as being "simple." In the elementary school "simple" is thought of as something which is concrete and obvious. This dichotomy is pursued and clarified by Mr. Buck in Part I of his article when he discusses fundamental ideas regarding points, lines, planes, and measurement. After reading Part I the teacher should be able to describe an intuitive meaning of the terms point, line, and plane.

In Part II the author describes specific ways to engage children actively in the investigation of points, points and distance, and regular polyhedra. As a result of reading Part II the teacher should be able to define the terms triangle, inequality, collinear, and coplanar, as well as describe and construct each of the five regular polyhedra.

PART 1:   A PHILOSOPHY FOR ELEMENTARY SCHOOL GEOMETRY

It is an educational platitude that we should start with the familiar and concrete when we wish to teach the unfamiliar and abstract. Another way of saying much the same thing is that we should start with the particular when we wish to teach the general.

A precisely contrary statement asserts that we should start with the simple in order to teach the complex. This is nonsense. The particular and concrete is always complex. It is the general and abstract that is simple. The particular box on the floor is brown, it is made of pasteboard, it has printing on it, and it has torn flaps. By abstracting from the particular box, ignoring its color and other complexities, we can use it as a model for a rectangular prism, a concept beautiful in its simplicity. In teaching children we start, of necessity, from the complex (the box) and proceed toward the simple (the rectangular prism).

Let us apply the platitude of the first paragraph to the planning of an elementary school geometry program. We must always bear in mind the

---

Reprinted from *The Arithmetic Teacher*, vol. 14, no. 6 (October 1967), pp. 460–467. Charles Buck is Research Associate for the Greater Cleveland, Ohio, Mathematics Program.

booby trap indicated in the second paragraph. (I actually saw a publisher's blurb that claimed that a certain textbook proceeded simultaneously from the concrete and simple to the abstract and complex; hence I conclude that boobies can fall into the trap.)

What do I mean by elementary school geometry? I do not mean high school geometry brought down to elementary school. Neither do I mean empty drill in geometric vocabulary, although there are some who seem to regard this drill in vocabulary as the essence of elementary instruction in geometry. By teaching geometry in the elementary school I mean teaching geometric concepts extracted from the child's experience with familiar objects. What geometric objects are familiar to children? Blocks, balls, the chalkboard, the classroom, sheets of tablet paper. Here is where we should start.

For example, a sheet of tablet paper is a *rectangle*. It is not helpful to ask whether the rectangle is the region or the union of four segments. Much geometry can be done before it is profitable to consider metaphysical questions. Metaphysics concerns itself with what things *really are*. It has no place in the school room. When we find ourselves worrying the students about what a thing "really is," we should examine our objectives and see if they cannot be better served by ignoring the metaphysical problem. Basically, the concern about distinguishing between a polygon and its interior comes from exposure to a beginning course in analytic geometry. Because of our preference for equations over inequalities, we often prefer, in analytic geometry, to emphasize the circumference of a circle rather than its interior. In some courses in higher mathematics, however, this manner of speaking is abandoned, and the word circle is used to apply to a disk.

The concern with "what things really are" is a sophistry that has no place in the classroom. The elementary school child is strong on imagination and, like most of the rest of us, is impatient with logic-chopping. Rather than fussing (and it is fussing) about whether a circle is a disk, its interior, or its rim, it would be better to introduce the child to such fundamental geometric forms as point, line, and plane. Here he can exercise his imagination.

It should be a fundamental educational principle that, where possible, we should exploit the student's strong points rather than, in our approach, emphasize his weaknesses. The elementary school child is not mature enough for deductive geometry, nor has he the dexterity to manipulate a ruler and compass effectively. His familiarity with the space in which he lives and with the objects in that space, plus his imagination, are the raw materials for building into the child a strong geometric intuition. This should be the purpose of elementary school geometry. The elementary school child is capable of developing a strong feeling for geometric relationships in space. Too often, by the time he gets into high school his feeling for geometric space will have been flattened out by years of work at the two-dimensional blackboard and on two-dimensional sheets of paper.

What should the content of elementary geometry be? I mentioned the geometric forms: points, lines, and planes. Let us examine these things in turn.

Points   A *point* is the precise answer to the question "Where?" With experience and need, the answer becomes increasingly precise. The three questions "Where is Buckingham Palace?" "Where is Westminster Abbey?" and "Where is the Greenwich Observatory?" have different appropriate answers according to who is asking them. An American school child would be satisfied with the answer "London." The question "Where is London?" could be answered by pointing to a spot on a globe or map. An astronomer might answer "London" to the first two questions; he would probably stress the zero longitude of Greenwich in answering the third question. A historian or a tourist guide might point out that the Greenwich Observatory no longer exists; it has been turned into a museum.

In a room the notion of point as an answer to "Where?" can be illustrated thus: two feet from the east wall, three feet from the north wall, and four feet from the floor. This illustration exhibits the point as the result of three measurements.

Another approach to the idea of point is a consideration of the corners of a rounded rectangular block. To understand this notion, think of the corners of the rounded rectangle in Figure 26.1. The pupil is to indicate where the corners would be if they had not been rounded off. The rounded rectangular block is the figure in space which corresponds to the rounded rectangle. The place where the corner would be if it had not been rounded off is quite clear to the child. The *point* answers this "Where?"

Figure 26.1

There are many rounded corners, such as the corners of desks in your classroom. As a matter of fact, there is no corner that is not rounded. It is important to get the children to *see* the points where these corners would be.

This approach to the concept of point avoids two errors that are often made in trying to teach the concept. The first error consists of stressing the notion that a point cannot be seen. If "seeing" consists of sensing a stimulation of the optic nerve, then a point cannot be seen; if "seeing" means comprehending (as in the expression "I see"), then the child sees the point. To say that a point cannot be seen puts the emphasis in the wrong place.

The other error is stressing the infinitesimal size of a point. Infinite and infinitesimal are concepts understood by mathematicians, but never correctly learned by school children. The best way to avoid giving the children the wrong notions of infinite and infinitesimal is to avoid using the words or alluding to the concepts. Nothing will set children off on useless, wild verbalizations as will a mention of *infinity*. At least one university professor of mathematics has forbidden his precalculus students to use words like "infinity" because they are so regularly abused. Never ask students how many points there are in a line segment or in the room. "More than can be counted" is the only acceptable statement that can be made, but I do not quite know what a child has in his mind when he makes this verbal remark. Possibly he is thinking about the number of hairs on his head (about 2,000) or the number of visible stars (about 4,000). Probably he is just thinking, "More than I would like to count."[1]

Lines   We often hear it said that a straight line is the shortest path between two points. If we stop and think, we see that this involves more than two points and that it involves the concept of distance as well. The child has a good rudimentary concept of distance. We can build on this to strengthen his feeling for geometry. Let us consider three points, A, B, and C. The distance between A and B we will designate as $d(AB)$. The distance between B and C and between A and C is written $d(BC)$ and $d(AC)$. (See Figure 26.2.) In general, the sum of any two of these distances will be greater than the third distance. This is the so-called triangle inequality.

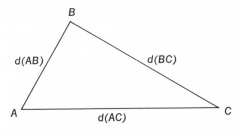

Figure 26.2

In exceptional cases the sum of two of the distances will exactly equal the third. In that case, we say the three points A, B, and C are on a line. If $d(AB) + d(BC) = d(AC)$, we say B is between A and C. (See Figure 26.3.)

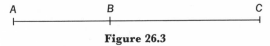

Figure 26.3

This is a starting point for talking about lines, but there is more interesting material to come. Suppose A and C are points in the classroom, and B is a

---

[1] Archimedes, in *The Sand Reckoner*, estimated the number of grains of sand (actually grains of fine powder) that could be contained in a sphere of radius 6 million-million miles. His figure was a 1 with 63 zeros after it. This is still not comparable to the number of points on a line segment.

point outside, possibly visible through a window. Furthermore, suppose that $d(AB) - d(BC) = d(AC)$. (See Figure 26.4.) If we rewrite this as $d(AB) = d(AC) + d(BC)$, we see that this is against the condition that A, B, and C lie on a line, but this time C is between A and B. B could be any point whatever in the line determined by A and C. It could be a point on the moon, the sun, or any star, provided it is in a line with A and C. (How could you get two points that would be collinear with the sun?)

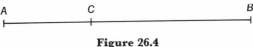

A   C   B

Figure 26.4

Two points do determine a line, but it is a relationship among three points that brings out this most important property of a line: if A, B, and C are on the same line, with B between A and C, then $d(AC) = d(AB) + d(BC)$.

Planes   Consider now three points, A, B, and C, that do not lie on a line. They determine three line segments, AB, BC, and AC, and the triangle ABC. Now consider a point D in the interior of $\triangle ABC$. Notice that the line AD cuts the side BC of the triangle. (See Figure 26.5.) In the case of a line, we went from a relation involving a point in the segment to a relation involving a point outside the segment but collinear with its end points. In the same way, we are going here from a relation involving points inside a triangle to a similar relation involving certain points outside the triangle.

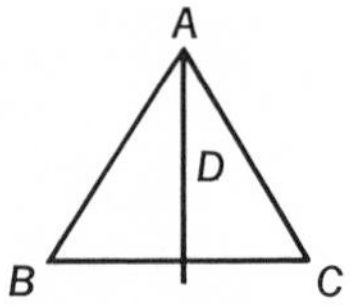

Figure 26.5

If a point E is such that the segment AE intersects the segment BC, we say that E is the plane of the triangle. (See Figure 26.6.) Indeed, more generally we can say that E is the plane of the triangle either if it lies on a line containing any side of the triangle or if the line joining it to one of the vertices of the triangle intersects the other side.[2]

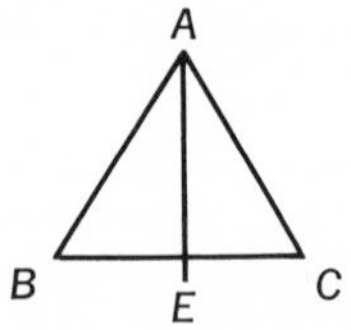

Figure 26.6

---

[2] We may make the following formal definition of coplanarity: Four points are coplanar if any three are collinear or if the four points determine a fifth point.

These points, lines, and planes that we have been discussing are abstract concepts, but they are made concrete by relating them to things in the child's everyday experience. They are more concrete than the numbers of arithmetic. These latter are highly abstract.

To make geometric notions more concrete, there are many activities involving geometric concepts that can be introduced into elementary classes. One of these, for example, might be making models for the regular polyhedra for a classroom exhibit. Patterns for these models can be found in most high school solid-geometry texts and will be given in Part II of this paper. The children's interest in geometry can be used to help develop their physical coordination. For example, the geometry can be used to develop a little skill in using straightedges, rulers, and compasses.

Measurement We have talked about distance in connection with lines, and we have just mentioned rulers as a tool. This brings us to another subject that is properly a part of geometry: measurement. A sophistry has come also into the teaching of measurement. In measurement the number concept somehow comes to be taken as fundamental. Length is defined as a function whose domain is the set of line segments and whose range is the real numbers. This is all very well and can be beautifully done—after a unit segment has been defined. In teaching measurement to children, it is no place to start. This approach is useless prior to the consideration of equivalence classes of congruent segments, a concept from more advanced mathematics.

It is not always realized that the notion "is the same length as" precedes the notion "length" both educationally, historically, and logically. To know that my sword is as long as yours, we don't have to know the measure of either; to know that two children are same height, we stand them back to back—we don't measure them. Not only do the notions "the same length as" and "the same height as" precede measurement, but so do the notions "longer than," "taller than," and "shorter than."

Logically, measurement of length comes about when we fix on a standard of length and refer to it, or to anything with the "same length," as having length *one*. This standard becomes our *unit* of length. When we measure the length of any object, we apply the notions listed in the previous paragraph to the object and to a numerical multiple of the unit of length.

Conclusion I have been stressing geometry as an intuitive and easy subject. It should be used in the elementary classroom as a relief from the formalism and rigor of arithmetic. This should be a welcome change for both the teacher and the pupil.

PART 11: GEOMETRY FOR THE ELEMENTARY CLASSROOM

Can geometry be meaningfully and enjoyably taught in the elementary classroom? In Part I of this paper I developed a philosophy for elementary school geometry with a few indications of the way the philosophy can be applied. The main purpose of Part I was, however, to express a point of view on the type of geometry that is appropriate for the elementary school. This article is devoted to showing how this geometry may be introduced.

One point   A point is the precise answer to the question "Where?" Part I shows how the teacher could introduce the children to the notion of point as a point on the earth or on a globe, a point in the classroom, or the point where the corner of the desk would be if it had not been rounded off. From this discussion it might appear that introducing the notion of point is entirely a matter of teacher exposition. This is not the intention, and this is not the way children learn. Professor George Polya, in speaking of the way learning is done (and he was essentially concerned with college students) says, "All real knowledge begins with perception and action." In learning, perception and action are inextricably mixed.

How do we direct the pupil's action so that learning takes place? In teaching the idea of point, we direct it by asking the question "Where?" We say, "I am thinking of a point," and then go on to give a description of a point in the classroom. You may describe it by giving the distances from two walls and above the floor; you may give insufficient information, such as "I am thinking of a point two feet above the floor," or "I am thinking of a point two feet above the floor and three feet from the west wall." You may overdescribe the point. For example, you might say, "I am thinking of a point five feet above the floor, two feet from the west wall, two feet from the south wall, and ten feet from the ceiling." If your classroom has fifteen-foot ceilings, you have given more information than is needed to locate your point. If your classroom does not have fifteen-foot ceilings, your point does not exist; you have given an inconsistent description of it.

The "I am thinking of a point" game brings out the important information that, in general, three measurements are required to characterize a point. The idea of a point as an exact location in space is an empty idea. It has no meaning. A point can be located only with respect to something else. If you locate a point on a piece of paper on your desk and then drop the paper to the floor, the point on the paper is still on the paper, and the point on your desk, where the paper was when you marked it, is still on your desk. Your room and the desk and the paper have been traveling about 900 miles an hour eastward as the earth turns on its axis, and the earth itself has been traveling about 18,000 miles per second in its orbit around the sun. The sun has a velocity of its own with respect to the fixed stars, and so on. You may think that the matters I have been discussing are of no concern to your pupils. However, they learn about the rotation and revolution of the earth in geography class, and they live in an age of earth satellites and of spacecraft that go to Venus and Mars.

To bring out these ideas and to stimulate the children to think correctly about the location of points, you might ask them to imagine that, before the Mariner II spacecraft left Cape Kennedy on its trip past Venus, a workman had marked a point on the very tip of the spacecraft. Where is that point now? The point 300 feet above the ground at Cape Kennedy is still 300 feet above the ground at Cape Kennedy. The point on the spacecraft is still on the spacecraft and has traveled several times around the sun. Discussion of the many meanings of these questions could be exciting and instructive. The teacher would have to be prepared to admit the limitations of his knowledge. No one could answer all the questions the children might raise. An outstanding characteristic of the mature teacher is willingness to admit the limitations of his knowledge.

A single point has only one attribute: location with respect to some object taken as fixed.

Two points: distance   In addition to the location of each of its points, a pair of points has an additional attribute, the distance between them. The distance between the points A and B we designate as $d(AB)$ or as $d(BA)$, which shall mean the same thing.

Two points determine the position of a line, but the most important property of lines involves three points. Each point of a triple of points has location; each pair of points in the triple has a distance assigned to it. The triple itself may consist of three points in a line or of three points that are not in a line. You may designate any three points along the baseboard of your room as A, B, and C. If B is between A and C, then $d(AB) + d(BC) = d(AC)$. Let your children verify this by individual measurements of the distances. If C is between A and B, then $d(AC) = d(AB) - d(BC)$. Let your children also verify this by direct measurement of the three distances. Now, mark on the floor or on the blackboard three points that are not in a line; call these points A, B, and C also. Now it will always be the case that

$$d(AB) + d(BC) > d(AC),$$
$$d(AC) + d(BC) > d(AB),$$

and so on. The sum of any two is always greater than the third. We now have a metric criterion for collinearity. If three points are so arranged that the sum of the distances associated with two of the pairs is equal to the distance between the third pair, the points are collinear. Otherwise, the sum of the distances between two of the pairs will always be greater than the third distance. The latter relation is called the triangle inequality.

If A and B are two points, then X is a point on the line AB if

$$d(AB) = d(AX) - d(XB),$$

or if

$$d(AB) = d(BX) - d(AX),$$

—in other words, if among the three distances $d(AB)$, $d(AX)$, and $d(BX)$, two may be selected whose sum is the other distance. It is thus clear that the fixed points A and B uniquely determine their line.

We found in the last paragraph that the relation of collinearity was a relation among triples of points, but that two points were sufficient to determine a line. We shall now find that the relation of coplanarity is characterized by conditions on four points, but that three noncollinear points are sufficient to determine a plane.

Just as we started out to derive the condition for collinearity by examining the properties of three points along the baseboard of the classroom, so to get a condition for coplanarity, we shall examine four coplanar points, no three of which are collinear, and arrive at a condition that we can use to characterize coplanarity. Let A, B, C, and D be four points on the blackboard, no three of which are collinear. For most choices of A, B, C, and D, the line AB and the line CD will intersect in some point and we have four points determining a fifth. If AB and CD do not intersect, perhaps AC and BD do. If these lines should be parallel also, then certainly AD and BC intersect. Hence, in all cases the four coplanar points of which no three are collinear have determined at least one additional point. As a general rule, we say that A, B, C, and D are coplanar, provided they determine a fifth point. If A, B, and C are noncollinear, we say the point X is in the plane ABC, provided X is on one of the lines AB, BC, or AC, or that X together with A, B, and C determines a fifth point.

If four points do not determine a fifth point, then they are not in the same plane; they are the four vertices of a tetrahedron, a triangular pyramid. (See Figure 26.7.) As well as four vertices, the tetrahedron has four triangular faces. The four vertices have six lines joining them. These lines are also the intersections of the planes of the four triangular faces.

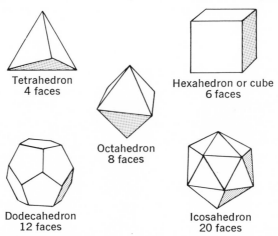

Tetrahedron
4 faces

Hexahedron or cube
6 faces

Octahedron
8 faces

Dodecahedron
12 faces

Icosahedron
20 faces

Figure 26.7

We see in the tetrahedron some illustrations of several important geometric relations. Two points always determine a line. Two planes, if they intersect, determine a line. Three noncollinear points determine a plane. Three planes in general position determine a point. (By general position we mean that the three planes do not all contain the same line and that the three lines in which the pairs of planes do intersect are not parallel to each other.)

The regular polyhedra   If a tetrahedron has all of its edges equal to one another, it is called a regular tetrahedron. The faces of a regular tetrahedron are all equilateral triangles, and every vertex is just like every other vertex. (See Fig. 26.7 for illustrations.)

In the plane there are regular polygons of any given number of sides. It is an important fact of solid geometry that there are only five regular polyhedra. A regular polyhedron has all faces of the same size and shape and all vertices of the same shape; all of the faces of a regular polyhedron are regular polygons; the regular tetrahedron has four equilateral triangles for faces. If you put two regular tetrahedra of the same size together so that a face of each coincides with a face of the other, you would have a figure with six equilateral triangles for faces. Is this a regular polyhedron?

The cube is sometimes called a regular hexahedron, referring to the fact that it has six faces. These faces are squares. When you build the cube out of d-sticks,[3] you will find that it is not a rigid figure; if you want a rigid figure, you will have to make the faces out of plastic or cardboard. The cube has six faces, twelve edges, and eight vertices. The regular octahedron, or eight-face, has eight equilateral triangles for faces. It has six vertices and, like the cube, twelve edges. Unlike the cube, when the octahedron is made out of d-sticks, it is a rigid figure without further reinforcement. The regular dodecahedron, or twelve-face, and the regular icosahedron, or twenty-face, are related somewhat the same way as the cube and octahedron. The dodecahedron, having pentagons for faces, is rigid only if reinforced.

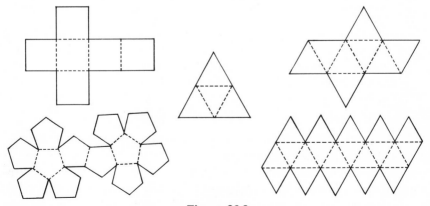

Figure 26.8

[3] Available from Edwards Scientific Company, Barrington, N.J. 08007.

The icosahedron, having equilateral triangles for faces, is a rigid figure. The twelve-face has twenty vertices, the twenty-face has twelve vertices. They each have thirty edges. There are many important and interesting facts concerning these polyhedra; probably the most important and possibly the most interesting is that there are only five of them. (By the way, look at the polyhedron made by fastening two tetrahedra together. Why is it not a regular polyhedron? All faces are congruent equilateral triangles. Are all the vertices the same?)

To help strengthen their feeling for geometry in general and the regular polyhedron in particular, the children should build the tetrahedron and other regular solids, using (1) d-sticks or (2) cardboard, scissors, and paste, guided by the diagrams in Figure 26.8.

The Euler polyhedral formula is almost always brought up in connection with the regular polyhedra. It asserts that the number of vertices minus the number of edges plus the number of faces is equal to two. This formula is true of much more general configurations than the regular polyhedra. It is true of any polyhedron that does not have a hole in it.

CONCLUSION

Throughout Part II, I have emphasized the importance of pupil activity: in the first section the children were making simple measurements; in the second section they were studying simple configurations on the blackboard; in the third section they were building regular tetrahedra out of d-sticks or with cardboard, scissors, and paste.

Whenever a treatment of any geometric or other mathematical topic appeals to us by its sophistication, it is almost certainly wrong for children. Naïve mathematics can be beautiful—this is what we strive for.

The previous discussion takes it for granted that we are going to teach more geometry in the elementary school than we have in the past. What purposes does geometry serve in the elementary syllabus? I see three such:

1. Geometry is a part of mathematics that is within the children's capacity and that will form an important part of their high school studies. Well-grounded geometric intuition is a big help in the study of the deductive geometry of the high school.
2. Geometry can motivate some of the developments in arithmetic.
3. Geometry furnishes a convenient field for the application of arithmetic.

I started this two-part paper with a platitude; I will end it with another. This one, too, I feel is often neglected.

The word "education" comes from the Latin *educare*, which in turn comes from *ex*, "out," and *ducere*, "to lead." Education, then, is the process of "leading out." If you would lead the children out, you must go to where the children are—but you must not stay there, and you must be leading them out to some definite goal.

27 GEOMETRY FOR THE PRIMARY

Donovan Johnson

BEFORE YOU READ   The primary grades are the ideal place to make
an intensive and concrete investigation of geometry. The article by
Professor Johnson identifies concepts children can learn by describing
several learning activities for teachers to utilize. In doing this the author
helps clarify the relationship between how one teaches geometry and what
children learn.

As a result of reading this article the teacher should be able to
translate suggested activities for teaching geometric ideas into a series of
lessons that would be especially appropriate for the primary grades.

Until recently we have assumed that mathematics for the primary grades
should consist of counting, reading and writing numerals, and learning the
basic number combinations. From several points of view, these may not be
the most appropriate ideas for an introduction to mathematics. The
psychologists would probably recommend that geometry would be a good
beginning topic since the opportunity for concrete and visual experiences are
abundant. The historians would point out that geometry was well developed
over a thousand years before our Arabic numerals appeared at the scene.
This order of invention might be suggestive of the order for presentation to
children. Finally, some mathematicians are suggesting that number
concepts might be developed through geometric representation, such as the
number line and geometric materials such as blocks, etc.

That many of the ideas of geometry *can* be developed at the primary
level is fairly well established. The experiments by Piaget suggest that many
geometric relations (nonmetric geometry) are understood more readily than
measurement (metric geometry). For example, young children rated the
volumes of objects by considering height only. The experiments by Hawley
and Suppes suggest that it is possible to teach a great deal of geometry in
the primary grades. In this experimental project, many primary grade
children learned the constructions typically taught in tenth-grade geometry.
These children became adept at constructing and talking about line segments, perpendicular lines, bisectors of lines and angles, circles, triangles,

Reprinted from *Grade Teacher*, vol. 79, no. 8 (April 1962), pp. 52, 92–95. Donovan Johnson
is Professor of Education at the University of Minnesota College of Education in Minneapolis,
Minnesota.

quadrilaterals, pentagons, hexagons and equilateral triangles. A series of English texts, *Geometry for Juniors* by Grace A. Moss, indicates that similar materials are being introduced into the elementary schools of England.

The fact that children can develop geometric ideas at the primary level does not, of course, mean that we should teach geometry. However, many of the current curriculum projects are recommending that more geometry be taught in the elementary grades. If we accept this suggestion, let us consider what geometric topics to present at the primary level and how to present them. We should begin with examples and a vocabulary that is related to the child's experiences. His experience with geometric forms such as blocks or balls, patterns in cloth or tiles, and measures of distances and time will provide beginning ideas.

If we are realistic about the abilities of primary children, we will not expect them to have achieved a mature, complete and highly organized pattern of relationships among geometric figures by the end of Grade 3. Young children can learn a great deal about geometric relations—some more than others, of course. A few meaningful relationships clearly understood and properly used will contribute more to future learning than routine memorized statements and forms.

An intriguing way of presenting many geometrical ideas is to fold paper. Forming straight lines and folding creases on a sheet of paper is a simple way of illustrating relationships of lines and angles. Although any paper is usable, heavy wax paper is most suitable. On wax paper, a crease becomes a distinct white line. The transparency of the paper makes it easy to fold a point upon a point, a line upon a point, or a line upon another line. Some teachers have found tracing paper suitable because of the ease of writing on it. The following folding exercises are appropriate for primary pupils:

1. A *straight line* is formed by folding a crease in the wax paper.
2. A *square corner* is formed by folding a straight line on the paper over on itself. The lines forming the square corner are *perpendicular* lines.
3. A line segment is *bisected* if the end points of the segment are folded one upon the other.
4. Two *parallel lines* are formed by folding two perpendiculars to the same line.
5. *The bisector* of an angle is formed by folding so that one side of the angle falls upon the other side.
6. By tearing off the corners (angles) of a paper triangle, we can fit these angles (corners) of the triangle to form a straight line.
7. By tearing off the corners (angles) of a quadrilateral, we can fit these angles of the quadrilateral to fill all the space around a point.
8. By folding to form the angle bisectors of each angle of a triangle, we find that these lines intersect in a common point.

9. The *diameter* of a circle is formed when a paper circle is folded upon itself.

10. The *center* of a circle is found when the diameter is bisected.

11. A *pentagon* is formed when a strip of paper such as adding machine tape is tied into a knot. Tie an overhand knot like the first knot in tying a shoestring. Tighten and crease flat. Cut the surplus length of paper.

12. *Symmetric* patterns are formed by folding and cutting the paper while it is folded. Fold two perpendicular creases, dividing the paper into four parts. Fold once more, bisecting the folded right triangles. Keep the paper folded and cut odd-shaped notches and holes. When the paper is unfolded, a symmetric pattern is apparent.

For instructions for more elaborate patterns and models, see a book on paper folding, such as *Paper Folding for the Mathematics Class*, available from the National Council of Teachers of Mathematics.

The marks we make on paper to represent a point, line, circle or cube are only pictures of these ideas. For example, a point is a location, it is invisible. The list below suggests geometric content that may be appropriate for the primary grade level. Other content can be added to this list. When these are presented, we should be careful to distinguish between the picture of the term and the idea.

1. *Lines and Curves*. Note the difference between pictures of straight lines, curves and jagged lines. Draw pictures of segments of straight lines. Draw illustrations of straight lines through one point. Illustrate straight lines through two points.

2. *Relationships of Lines*. Draw illustrations of lines that cross each other (intersect). Compare the angles formed by the crossing (intersecting) lines. Draw perpendicular lines and parallel lines.

   Illustrate the relationships of lines, curves and jagged lines, tacked at one point with a paper staple. Illustrate vertical and horizontal lines with a plumb line and a level.

3. *Comparison of Lines*. Compare the lengths of straight lines. Use the symbol $<$ for "less than" and $>$ for "greater than." Copy lines of equal length. Call straight lines of equal length congruent lines. Bisect a straight line. Divide a straight line into four equal parts.

   Double a straight line. Form a line which has a length equal to the sum of two lines. Form a line which has a length equal to the difference of two lines.

4. *Geometric Figures*. Connect points to form pictures of a triangle, rectangle, square, parallelogram, quadrilateral, pentagon and hexagon. Be able to identify different geometric figures. Compare the lengths of sides, length of diagonals, and the sizes of the angles of

geometric figures. Make models of geometric figures with cardboard strips as sides. Attach the strips with paper staples to form triangles and quadrilaterals. Cut geometric patterns out of cardboard to discover how to bisect geometric figures. Compare the sizes of cardboard figures by placing one upon another.

5. *Circles*. Learn to draw circles. Draw diameters and radii. Use the circle to draw hexagons and other symmetric designs.

6. *Solids*. Make cubes, prisms, pyramids, cones, cylinders and tetrahedrons out of cardboard. Learn to identify the objects. Compare the corners, edges, faces of each solid.

7. *The Number Line*. (This representation of number is somewhat abstract. It may be appropriate only for gifted children in the primary grades.) Draw a straight line. Locate a point to represent a zero point. Mark off equal lengths to the right of zero. Label these points with consecutive numbers from left to right beginning with one. Compare the distances between points. Use this number line to illustrate how numbers compare in value and the meaning of addition and subtraction.

In teaching these geometric concepts, we should capitalize on the opportunities to use concrete and visual illustrations. For discussion and illustration, the teacher should have a variety of charts and models. Geometric figures can be illustrated with cardboard models, with felt figures for the feltboard, with outlines in colored elastic thread on a pegboard, or by drawings on the chalkboard. Use color to identify different parts or make comparisons as well as to add attractiveness to the lesson.

Teaching geometric concepts lends itself very well to pupil participation in learning activities. With ruler, compasses, paper and pencil, your pupils are equipped for a variety of drawing exercises, measurement activities or paper folding. Whenever possible have the pupils discover geometric relations through learning activities and discussions. Supply the pupils with cardboard or construction paper so that they are able to make models. Attractive charts can also be made by forming lines with colored yarn moving through holes in cardboard.

It is not necessary to have a purchased compass for drawing circles. All you need is a stiff card or hard paper about an inch wide and about five inches long. Draw a line down the middle of this card. Beginning at a point P near one end of this line, mark off half inches. Make holes at the marks with a pin so that a pencil point will go through each hole. To draw circles with this strip, hold point P at a fixed point with a pin or sharp pencil point. Put another pencil through the hole and rotate the card around the point P. This card can also be used to draw straight lines as a substitute for a ruler. A loop of string can be used in place of this card if circles of a fixed radii are to be drawn. Some teachers use cardboard models as stencils.

28 STRING AND PAPER TEACH SIMPLE GEOMETRY

Lola May

BEFORE YOU READ   The extent to which children will eventually understand higher level and more abstract geometric concepts is dependent upon the extent to which basic concepts, such as curve and polygon, have been learned. A consistent appeal has been made to teachers asking that learning of basic ideas be accomplished in an environment which permits active pupil participation and which utilizes concrete instructional materials.

This article by Dr. May advocates the use of inexpensive materials, such as string and strips of paper, for developing an understanding of paths. The activities involve pupils in sorting and comparing tasks which help them discover special cases of paths, such as line segments and closed curves, and to discover special cases of closed curves, such as triangles, quadrilaterals, and circles. The activities suggested by Dr. May represent functional applications of the principle of active learning as it concerns the development of geometric concepts.

As a result of reading this article, the teacher should be able to utilize pieces of string to compare and contrast closed curves in order to identify conditions applicable to triangles, circles, and rectangles; and to describe the differences between path and line segment, open and closed curves, and triangle and polygon.

Geometry is a part of the total mathematics curriculum in every grade—even kindergarten. Children are aware of the physical world; therefore, part of their education should be to learn more about the physical objects they encounter.

Every grade needs a change of pace in mathematics, and geometry can provide this change of pace from the regular number work. Also, number work can be strengthened by finding application in the world of geometry. The type of geometry that children meet in the elementary school is known as intuitive geometry, in which they learn to investigate by looking, feeling, and building. The deductive geometry that is formal, logical proof is studied in high school.

Reprinted from *Grade Teacher*, vol. 84, no. 6 (February 1967), pp. 110–112. Dr. May is Mathematics Consultant for the Winnetka, Illinois, Public Schools.

In the primary grades, including kindergarten, the study of geometry should start by making paths. Paths in geometry are sets of points leading from one to another. Strings can be used to represent paths. The children should be given a string and told to make a path. Some of the paths will look like the drawings below. Then the children should discuss the different paths. As the teacher guides the discussion, the main objective is to notice that some of the paths are closed and others are not. All of the paths in geometry are called curves, and the children should learn the word "curve." Later, in the middle grades, students will learn that a curve is a set of points. Younger children, however, need only know that a path is a curve.

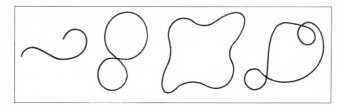

Figure 28.1

In the next lesson, each child should be given three strings of different lengths. Also, each child should be given a piece of paper having a large dot to the left with a house drawn by the dot and a large dot to the right with a kite drawn by the dot. The children are told they are going to make paths from the house point to the kite point. One of their strings should be just long enough to go from the house point to the kite point when it is straight. The other two strings should be longer. Then the children should lay the strings on the paper, making three paths from the house point to the kite point. The three paths might look something like this:

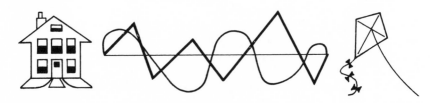

Figure 28.2

In the discussion about the paths, the teacher should ask the children which path is the shortest distance from the house point to the kite point. As the children point to the straight path, they should learn that the shortest path from one point to another is called a *line segment*. The concept of line segment will take many activities before the children are sure of it and learn the words. This is only the first introduction. All the paths made by the children are called *curves*, and a special curve is the *line segment*.

The next activity is to give the children another string and a piece of paper with just one dot and a picture of a balloon beside it. The dot should be drawn near the center of the paper. The children should make a path or curve that starts at the balloon point and comes back to the balloon point. This curve must be closed.

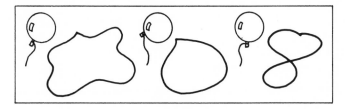

Figure 28.3

In discussing the various curves made by the children, the objective is to note that some of the curves crossed themselves and some did not. When a curve crosses itself, there are two or more insides, but when a curve does not cross itself, there is only one inside. Later in the grades, the students will learn that a closed curve that does not cross itself is known as a simple closed curve. The younger children do not have to learn this, but they are getting ground work for later work in geometry. What they are learning now is that the curve forms a boundary, and this boundary is the important idea. A geometric figure is only a set of points forming a boundary.

Each child should be given three narrow strips of paper of different lengths. In each set of three, it is important that one of the strips be longer than the other two. Have the children make a triangle with the three strips of paper. If possible, they should paste the strips of paper on a large sheet of paper. Then the teacher can hold up the sheets and discuss the different triangles.

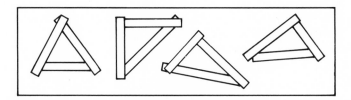

Figure 28.4

Each strip of paper is a path, but a special path called a line segment. How many line segments are needed for a triangle? Do all the triangles look alike? Is the figure still a triangle if it is a tall, skinny one or if it is a shorter, fatter one? Now the children are learning that a triangle is made up of three line segments and that triangles can be of many different sizes. Children should learn very early that a triangle does not always have to look like the figure below. It can be in many different positions and still be a triangle. Also, the children should note that the triangle has only one inside. Later they will learn to call this the interior region.

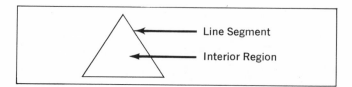

Figure 28.5

The study of the triangle can continue with the teacher giving the children three strips of paper the same length. The triangles made with these strips will all look the same. Why do all the triangles look alike now when in the other activity they were all different? From this discussion, the children will learn that there is a triangle family and that some of the triangles have special names because they have special properties. Triangles where the line segments are all the same length are called *equilateral triangles*. In the first and second grades, the children have learned the symbol = and know this means "is the same as." An equilateral triangle means the three sides are the same length.

Next, the children can be given three strips of paper where two strips are the same length and the third strip is a different length. The children should note that this triangle is different from the first triangles where all the line segments were different lengths and from the equilateral triangle where the line segments were all the same length. A triangle in which two sides have the same measure is called an *isoceles* triangle.

Learning the various names of different kinds of triangles is up to the teacher in the primary grades. More important initially is to learn that a triangle is a closed path or curve made up of three line segments.

For the next activity, the children should be given four strips of paper that are all different lengths. Have them paste the strips on paper, forming a closed figure. Although none of the figures is a square or rectangle, some of the children will use the words "square" or "rectangle" in discussing their pictures. How many line segments are there in each figure? How many interiors or insides? All of the figures are *quadrilaterals*. Quadrilaterals are the family of figures with four line segments.

Now give each child four strips of paper the same length. The children should then make a quadrilateral. During the discussion after the children have made the figures, the teacher should ask which figures are squares. The only figures that are squares will be the ones made with right angles. The younger children can call these "corner angles." The teacher can point out that when the line segments come together they form angles. How many angles in each figure? (4) How many line segments in each figure? (4) What are the properties of a square? The line segments are all the same size, and the angles form corners.

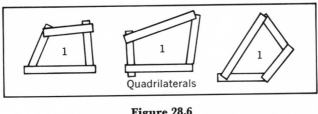

Quadrilaterals

Figure 28.6

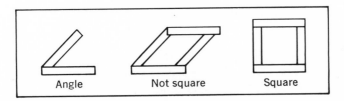

Angle   Not square   Square

Figure 28.7

The next four strips of paper should have two longer strips the same length and two shorter strips the same length. Once again the children are asked to make a figure by pasting the strips on paper. In looking at the various figures made by the children, can we find a square? No, because the sides or the line segments are not all the same length. Do we have any rectangles? Ask the children to point out the figures that are rectangles. Hold up the figures that are rectangles and have the children discover how these figures differ from the ones that are not rectangles. The children should observe that the short line segments are opposite each other and the long line segments are opposite each other. Also, all the angles are corners or right angles. What do rectangles and squares have in common? They both have angles that are all corners.

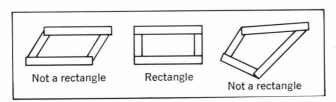

Not a rectangle   Rectangle   Not a rectangle

Figure 28.8

The teacher can make model figures for the geometry lessons by taking strips of oaktag and putting them together with brass paper fasteners. By manipulating the figures, the children will see that the triangle is a rigid figure, but that all the quadrilaterals are movable. The teacher can show that the model with four strips the same length can be moved to where the angles are not corners and the figure is not a square. The same type of activity can be done with the model that represents a rectangle. When the sides are moved and the angles are not corners or right angles, the figure is not a rectangle.

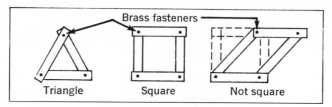

Figure 28.9

In the primary grades, the children should see that drawing a diagonal from one vertex to the opposite vertex in a quadrilateral divides the figure into two triangles. The children can do this by laying a string across one of the quadrilateral figures they have made. Some children may lay two strings across and then more triangles are formed.

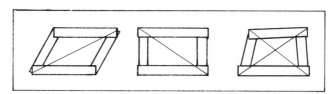

Figure 28.10

Using a string, the children can learn how to form a circle. The difference between a circle and an oval should be pointed out. Statements such as "A circle is round" or "It can roll" are good observations. Do you think an oval could roll as well as a circle? Once again it should be pointed out that the circle is the set of points represented by the string and the circle has an inside or interior.

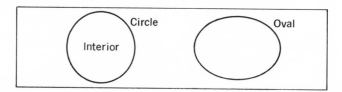

Figure 28.11

Children in all grades need to start geometry by making geometric figures and then making observations. What we do ourselves we do not forget. A lot of geometry has been taught in the few activities described in this article. The child who enters the middle grades knowing about paths, curves, line segments, triangles, quadrilaterals, circles, and ovals has a sound base to continue his study of geometry.

The article next month will continue the study of early geometry. The geometry to come later is built on these primitive but essential ideas.

29 SIMPLE CONSTRUCTIONS INTRODUCE GEOMETRY

Forrest Coltharp

BEFORE YOU READ   One technique that provides for active pupil participation is the making of constructions.   In this article Mr. Coltharp describes several important geometric constructions which are appropriate for elementary school children.

It was stated in the preface of this book that each article contained basic mathematical ideas which could be translated into a lesson or a sequence of lessons for use with children.   A lesson plan is given here, developed in flow-chart form and based on information from the article. Naturally, other strategies based on this article are possible, but before any lesson is developed, pupils should know how to use a ruler and compass and should be familiar with notations for points, line segments, rays, and distance.   The article should be read prior to reviewing the flow-chart lesson.

Upon completion of the reading the teacher should be able to define the terms bisect, median, and centroid.   In addition, through use of a compass and ruler, the reader should be able to construct congruent line segments, an equilateral triangle, and a perpendicular bisector of a line segment.

For many years now some people in the mathematics area, and especially those in mathematics education, have felt that a student must reach a certain level of maturity before he can "really appreciate the true beauty of geometry."   This is basically why a course in plane geometry has usually been offered at the sophomore level of high school.   It is my belief, however, that an appreciation can, and should, be developed over the years through some enjoyable experiences with a few of the simple concepts of geometry. True appreciation is derived from extensive contact, cooperation, and work over an extended period of time.

Almost without exception, the modern elementary mathematics programs include an intuitive introduction to geometry.   It is the purpose and intent of this article to discuss some of the basic construction techniques and how they can be used to establish concepts.   Through this approach, many sound geometric concepts can be formulated.

Reprinted from *The Instructor*, vol. 75, no. 2 (October 1965), p. 42.   Forrest Coltharp is Assistant Professor of Mathematics at Kansas State College of Pittsburg, Kansas.

Flow Chart Lesson Based on Article 29

(Note: This lesson was developed in accordance with the procedures outlined in the article by Professor Arnold from Section I.)

Whole class at desks with compass, ruler, pencil, and paper

↓

using compass and rulers to do geometric constructions

Exposition

(1.) Draw line segment $\overline{AB}$ and ray $\overrightarrow{CD}$ on your paper (make separate).

(2.) Set your compass to AB and mark this distance on $\overrightarrow{CD}$ using point C for your compass point. Label the intersection point F.

(3.) Check papers to see that they are correct.

↓

Discussion

What do you notice about $\overline{AB}$ and $\overline{CF}$? (Congruent.)

↓

Exposition

(1.) Now draw $\overline{AB}$ (about 2 inches long).

(2.) Set compass to AB and swing arc above $\overline{AB}$ using point A. Do same using point B. Label the arc intersection point C.

(3.) Complete line segments $\overline{AC}$ and $\overline{BC}$.

↓

Discussion

What kind of figure have you drawn? (Equilateral triangle.)

↓

Exploration

Try to draw a line segment, and then construct its perpendicular bisector.

Children are fascinated with the compass, and even drawing lines with the help of a straightedge becomes an adventure. A certain amount of play time should be allowed to create a sense of familiarity with the compass and the straightedge. But very soon work can start and certain facts be established; for example, the distinction between a line and a line segment. The fact that a line can be extended to infinity, and the limiting properties of a line segment, are discussed, with this conclusion: a line segment can be measured, copied, or reproduced in a different location, but always maintaining its unique distinction of length.

The length of a line segment should be established through the use of the compass. The straightedge may possess units of measurement, but they are mere approximations. The term used in a majority of the new programs to describe line segments equal in measure is *congruent*.

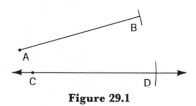

Figure 29.1

Here we have reproduced the line segment AB as line segment CD, maintaining the length of the segment. Therefore, $\overline{AB} \cong \overline{CD}$ should be read as, "Line segment AB is congruent to the line segment from C to D." The ability to copy a line segment will prove useful in the constructions we discuss.

Let us use this new-found ability in order to construct a triangle with all sides equal. With a compass, establish a length that will be the measure of the sides of the triangle. One line segment will be the base of the triangle. Swing an arc above the base from each endpoint. Connect the endpoints to the intersection of these arcs.

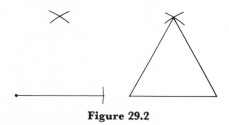

Figure 29.2

This triangle is called an *equilateral* triangle. One in which only two of the sides are equal is called an *isosceles* triangle.

BISECTING A LINE SEGMENT

We shall next *bisect* a given line segment. By this we mean to determine the midpoint of the line segment—the point located halfway between the endpoints of the segment. Take the given line segment and swing arcs having the endpoints of the segment as centers and a radius of any length greater than an estimated half of the line segment. This time, however, swing an arc above and one below the given line segment.

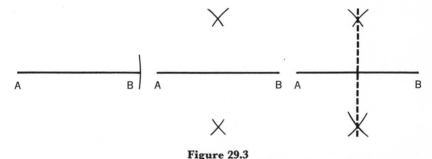

Figure 29.3

Connecting the intersections of these arcs we obtain the midpoint of the given line segment. This geometric fact is easy to see—every point along this line connecting the intersections of the arcs is an equal distance from the endpoints of the given line segment. Obviously then, the point where this line intersects the given line segment is the point midway between the endpoints.

Let us do a couple of interesting things with this newly developed ability. First, take any given triangle and find the midpoints of the sides (which in effect are three distinct line segments). Next, connect each midpoint with the vertex of the triangle opposite that side. The line segment connecting a vertex of a triangle with the midpoint of the opposite side is called a *median*. You notice that all three medians intersect in a common point. This is the *centroid* of the triangle, the center of balance of the triangular region enclosed by the triangle. This point of intersection divides a median into a ratio of 2:1; that is, it is located two-thirds of the way from the vertex to the midpoint of the opposite side.

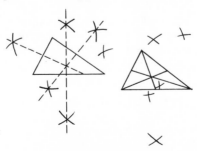

Figure 29.4

A second interesting outcome may be obtained by bisecting line segments. Take any four-sided figure (called a *quadrilateral*) and bisect all sides.

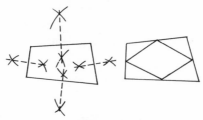

Figure 29.5

When the midpoints of the sides are connected in order, we obtain a special kind of quadrilateral called a *parallelogram*.

CONSTRUCTING PERPENDICULARS

Next, let us discuss the construction of a perpendicular to a line at a given point. Swing an arc of any radius with the given point as center so that it intersects the line on each side of the point. Lengthen the radius and swing arcs above the line using the obtained arc and line intersections as centers. Finally, connect the point and the intersection of the arcs above to obtain the perpendicular to the line at the given point.

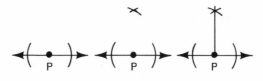

Figure 29.6

Perpendiculars should be used in the construction of squares and rectangles. Develop the understanding that all four sides of a square are congruent while only the opposite sides of a rectangle are. Through careful construction of perpendiculars it can be illustrated that all four angles of either a square or a rectangle are *right angles*, that is, the angle obtained by constructing a perpendicular.

An observation that might be made at this time is that when we bisect a line segment to locate the midpoint, the line connecting the intersections of the arc is also perpendicular to the line segment. In fact, this line is called the *perpendicular bisector* of the given line segment.

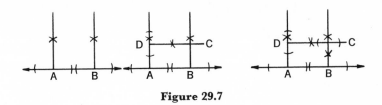

Figure 29.7

We now use this fact in another interesting construction. Again take any triangle and construct the perpendicular bisector of each of the sides. When these bisectors are extended, they all intersect in a common point. Taking this point as center and the distance to a vertex of the triangle as radius, draw a circle. This circle will *circumscribe* the triangle. By this we mean that the circle passes through the three vertices of the triangle. We might describe the triangle as being *inscribed* within the circle.

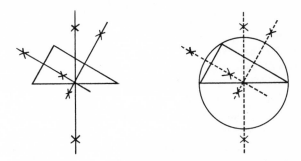

Figure 29.8

In this presentation we have discussed only two basic, simple constructions: bisecting a line segment, and constructing a perpendicular. Through the use of these constructions, however, we have established many sound geometric concepts. The most important outcome will be a familiarity with geometric shapes, tools, and basic concepts, creating an interest in further intuitive investigation of geometry.

30 A BEE ON A POINT, A LINE, AND A PLANE

Francis Sganga

BEFORE YOU READ   Probably no aspect of teaching mathematics better facilitates an understanding of concepts than the selection of appropriate referents for the concepts. The examples taken from the referent set for a concept can facilitate a pupil's understanding of a concept because the examples help to link what he is expected to learn with what he already knows.

Two ideas pupils ought eventually to understand are locations in relation to lines and planes. This article by Mr. Sganga uses the hypothetical movements of a bee to show how one-to-one correspondence and ordered number pairs can help pupils conceptualize locations on a line and a plane. The examples used by the author directly relate to situations children can easily visualize. This article can be translated into a single lesson or a series of related lessons for children.

As a result of his reading the teacher should be able to draw a number line and describe the movement of an animal with respect to changing locations, explain why the coordinate plane is an effective notion for indicating the location of an object on a plane surface, and create a hypothetical setting involving movement in such a way that children can invent a coordinate plane.

Most of the new elementary school mathematics programs place a great deal of emphasis upon such basic concepts as the number line, one-to-one correspondence, and number pairs. While there is general agreement that these concepts are important, a close study of how these concepts are developed indicates that it would be quite helpful to teachers and their students if greater emphasis were placed upon the *significance* of these concepts.

Why is one-to-one correspondence so important? Is the number line simply a more meaningful way to demonstrate the four basic operations on numbers? What about number pairs? Students may be able to list the number pairs whose sum equals 4 as (4, 0), (3, 1), and (2, 2), but the result may not seem very significant to them if further explanation is lacking.[1]

---

[1] This article deals only with number pairs that are sums.

Reprinted from *The Arithmetic Teacher*, vol. 13, no. 7 (November 1966), pp. 549–552. Francis Sganga is Coordinator of Mathematics and Science for Volusia County, Daytona Beach, Florida.

It is regrettable that so little is said about the *significance* of these concepts, since many children may miss the more interesting aspects of the mathematics involved. In addition, it seems that if children were provided with more "whys," they would tend not only to achieve greater understanding of mathematics, but also to remember better what they have learned.

Let's look at one of the interesting ways to show the significance of the concepts listed above and how they are related. Pose this problem to your students: A bee is perched on a line as shown below. How can you describe its exact location using arithmetic?

Figure 30.1

As they work on this problem, students should soon realize that they will have to first establish a *point of reference* (the "origin"), then divide the line into units of equal length:

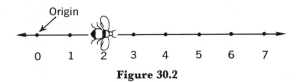

Figure 30.2

Now we can say, with some precision, that the bee is located two units to the right of the origin. However, some student may have established his origin at a different point. Is this permissible? Yes, and an important idea is driven home. The origin may be placed at *any* convenient point on the line. Hence, each of the following and many others are correct:

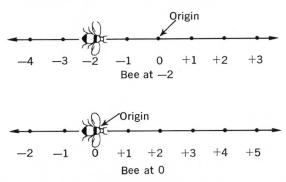

Figure 30.3

Quite probably, students will easily understand the reason for establishing a point of reference. However, some may wonder why it is necessary to mark off units of *equal length*. The importance of this is easily shown by assigning dimensions to the units making up the number line. If each unit represents one inch, then all of them must be the same length to give a true representation. Map-making is a good illustration of this idea. Every inch on the map represents the same given number of miles.

Now suppose the bee lands on a spot on the wall, where there are no lines, somewhat as follows:

Figure 30.4

How can the location of the bee be pinpointed now? This is a problem you may wish your students to ponder overnight. In this way more of them may be able to experience the delight of discovery for themselves as René Descartes did in 1619.

Hopefully, your students will remember how they located the bee on the number line. To locate the bee on a line, a plane (the wall), or in space requires the establishment of a point of reference. Let's choose the point where two of the line segments intersect in the "southwest" corner of the wall, and mark off units as was done before. (See Figure 30.5.)

Using a sketch such as this may lead to the realization that the bee cannot be located using only a single number. If we consider only "2 across," the bee can be anywhere "above" or "below" the 2 on the horizontal number line. A similar situation would result if we consider only "3 up" as the bee's location. Suppose both numbers and both directions were used? Run your pencil "2 across" from the origin, then "3 up." Right on target!

This is a clear demonstration of the fundamental idea that it takes two reference points to locate a point in a plane. The two reference points are called *coordinates*. In the above sketch the coordinates are (2, 3). To avoid confusion, the "across" coordinate is written first, followed by the "up" coordinate. The point represented by (2, 3) is entirely different from (3, 2). Since the *order* in which the coordinates are written is important, they are called *ordered pairs*. Many texts also refer to them as *number pairs*.

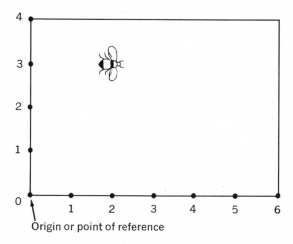

Figure 30.5

In choosing our origin, any of the four corners of the wall could have been used. However, this would mean that a new set of reference points would be needed, as seen in the following:

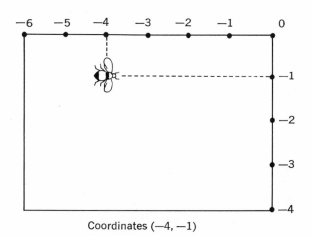

Coordinates (−4, −1)

Figure 30.6

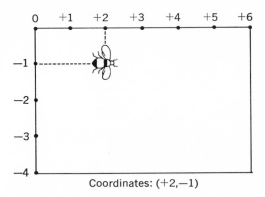

Coordinates: (+2,−1)

Figure 30.7

Both positive and negative numbers are used for convenience, since they quickly tell us the four main *directions* from the origin: left, right; and up, down. This is more easily seen from the conventional sketches used in mathematics:

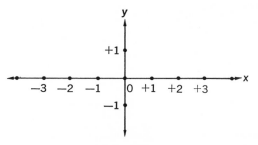

Figure 30.8

At about this time, students may be asked to relate what they have learned so far to such practical activities as locating ships at sea and plotting the paths of hurricanes, typhoons, and cold and warm fronts. What famous reference points are required for such activities? As your students reflect upon the question, they should soon realize the importance of the *prime meridian* and the *equator*. On a more personal basis, they could be asked to pinpoint where they live and the location of their seats in the classroom.

Now, what about one-to-one correspondence? Besides the association of this idea with the elements of sets, there is a one-to-one correspondence between the set of all numbers and the points on a line. This means that once the reference point and a unit of length have been established, any number can be represented by a unique point on a line, and any point on the number line may be assigned a unique number. However, the idea also applies to points in a plane such as the plane suggested by a wall. There is a one-to-one correspondence between a point in a plane and a number pair. Hence, if we think of the bee on the wall in Figure 30.5 as representing a point in a plane, there is only one number pair (2, 3) that corresponds to the point on that particular plane.

Since a bee is not likely to stay put for very long, it would be interesting, in the light of the above discussion, to see what would happen if he decided to stroll along the wall. A picture (graph) of his journey might look like this:

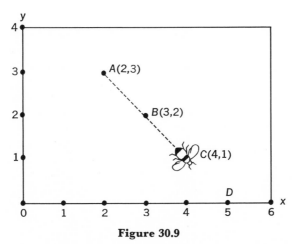

Figure 30.9

Starting at point $A(2, 3)$, the bee traveled through point $B(3, 2)$ and is at point $C(4, 1)$. What do you notice about the sum of each pair of coordinates? Each sum is 5. Suppose the bee moved to point D? The coordinates at that point are $(5, 0)$ and the sum is still 5. In fact, *any* point along the path taken by the bee has coordinates whose sum is 5. If we were to become mathematical and label the horizontal "axis" (x) and the vertical "axis" (y), we can identify the path with an equation as follows:

$$x + y = 5.$$

Some of the number pairs that "satisfy" the equation are

Points ⟶	A	B	C	D	?	?
x	2	3	4	5	6	7
y	3	2	1	0	−1	−2

Coordinates

Figure 30.10

Here, it is easy to see the one-to-one relationship between the points in a plane and their corresponding number pairs (coordinates). But wait, you may say, where are the points described by $(6, -1)$ and $(7, -2)$? It seems the bee turned out to be a termite and drilled a path right through the floor!

3 1   A LABORATORY APPROACH TO SPACE LOCATIONS

Douglas Cruikshank

BEFORE YOU READ   There has been much discussion in education of approaches to teaching. A recent addition to the list is the laboratory approach, of which a basic feature is the children's work with materials and apparatus. They collect data and attempt to use it to make discoveries. In doing this children also develop increased ability to take measurements and record information on tables.

Section I of this book explicitly deals with the need for a decisive and active methodology, one in which the teacher consciously makes decisions about construing the learning environment and choosing and sequencing learning activities. How these crucial elements may be combined with respect to determining and defining locations in space is described in this article by Professor Cruikshank. A focus is provided for the reader when the author asks, "How may a person determine and describe the location of a point in a contained space?"

Upon completion of the article the teacher should be able to answer this question for himself and the children.

The exciting new look in elementary school mathematics today is the look of action. Young children are investigating structures, patterns, shapes, and locations. These youngsters are measuring, comparing, sketching, discussing—in short, they are *doing* mathematics. Classrooms are emerging as laboratories with responsive environments, as opposed to yesterday's enclosures of silent, sedentary youngsters in straight rows of chairs. Students may move around the classroom, into the hallway, onto the playground, and into the world beyond. Modern programs of mathematics are generating new teacher attitudes and behaviors toward both teaching and learning. But let us picture the current scene with an illustration from geometry, a recent arrival in the elementary classroom.

We shall consider children's investigations of locations in space to lend emphasis and example to the concept of an active learning approach. Specifically, the question for student investigations will be: "How may a

---

Original material written especially for this book in the absence of adequate material relating to mathematical laboratories. Douglas Cruickshank is Assistant Professor of Mathematics Education at Temple University.

person determine and describe the location of a point in a contained space?" Such a question, with its concomitant side investigations, will challenge virtually any group of young children.

The particular topic chosen for exemplification is a natural outgrowth of common elementary school geometric experiences. That is, children are exposed very early to simple nonmetric and metric aspects of plane and space figures. Many of these early contacts with figures are quite necessary in developing a readiness to cope with locations in space. Several of these valuable prerequisite experiences are outlined below:

1. Number line
   Nonmetric—the concept of line in a plane and space.
   Metric—developing numerical scales, locating points and segments, familiarization with vertical as well as horizontal number lines.
2. Rectangular coordinate system
   Nonmetric—the concept of a rectangular coordinate system, patterns observed in the coordinate plane.
   Metric—numbering the "crossed number lines," locating points in the coordinate plane (drawing pictures, describing geometric figures with ordered pairs, ticktacktoe, and so on).
3. Geometric plane and space figures
   Nonmetric—description of shapes, characteristics of shapes.
   Metric—determining perimeters, diameters, area, edges, faces, surfaces, and volume based on a unit region.

Accompanying these experiences would be exercises and contests aimed at improving locational skills. For example, a strip of adding machine tape may be affixed to a hallway wall and a single point represented by a dot marked on it (*see* Figure 31.1). Three youngsters might be asked to go to the tape and describe precisely where the point is by writing a description or making a tape recording. Then the number line is brought to the classroom with the dot removed (or a congruent piece of adding machine tape is used). The description is read or broadcast to the remainder of the class, which attempts to locate the missing point. After several children have had an opportunity to locate the point, the original dot is placed or the original tape is compared. Discussion may center upon how accurately (or inaccurately) the description was presented, how it is interpreted, and how a description may be more effectively presented. Was the adding machine tape too wide? Would a baseline through the dot and parallel with an edge of the paper strip have helped? What are the advantages and disadvantages of measuring, as opposed to developing an independent scale to determine the exact position of the point? How could this exercise have been different if a taut string had been used in place of machine tape?

Figure 31.1 Point location on adding machine tape

Another activity involves locations on a plane. A child places a single checker on a checkerboard on one side of the classroom (*see* Figure 31.2). A second child or small group of children gives a written, taped, or oral description of the checker. Another child or group attempts to place the checker in the proper location. It is well to accept all descriptions that consistently result in locating the chosen spot. Again a discussion of how accurate and precise the descriptions were would be appropriate.

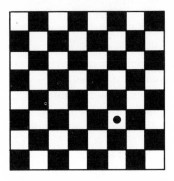

Figure 31.2 Point location on a checkerboard

A more sophisticated version of this same exercise would have the students describe the location of a dot on a classroom wall or floor, exchanging the description with another class. Still another challenge might focus on the location of a point in the interior of a square, triangle, or circle (*see* Figure 31.3).

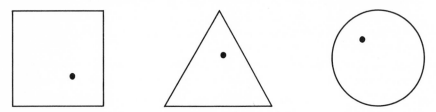

Figure 31.3 Point locations in the interior of plane figures

It is necessary to allow children to express creative responses in their investigations of line and plane locations. A youngster's description is likely to be most easily understood by his peers. The exploration of point locations in a contained space will be enhanced by varied prerequisite experiences in an active learning environment.

Gamelike, laboratory, or discussion approaches, among others, may be used to motivate the topic of locating points in space. At the introductory level one game which can challenge young thinkers involves suspending a washer, small ball, paper clip, or other small object plumb fashion from the ceiling of the room or a light fixture while a particular segment of the class is away (*see* Figure 31.4). The students in the classroom are to describe the precise location of the hanging object in the contained space of the room.

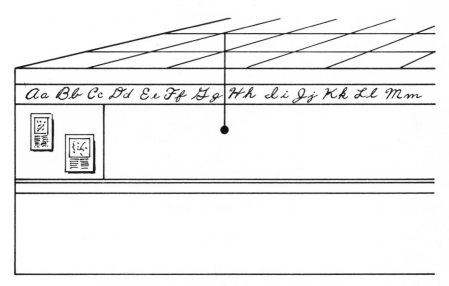

Figure 31.4 Point location in a contained space

After a few minutes, several descriptions could be prepared representing various opinions about the location. Descriptions may range from suggested visual sightings to an ordered triplet and designated base lines. The most successful descriptions will be determined by the youngsters who were away from the classroom.

The same activity could be pursued between two classes and would likely cause little problem, as many classrooms within a building tend to have identical shapes and sizes. A note from one class to another telling of suspending an object and describing its exact location in space could be interpreted by the second class and the results compared. Total physical involvement on the part of the youngsters would be needed in order to complete such an exercise.

The same activity in a laboratory setting might center upon an "activity card," as illustrated below:

MATHEMATICS LABORATORY

Locations in space   **Card 23**

1. Investigate the washer hanging from the light fixture in the back of the room. If you had a friend in another city and you wanted him to observe the washer in the identical location, how would you go about describing its position so that when he came to your city he could locate the same position precisely? Make two different and accurate descriptions. Check your descriptions by having another person locate the washer after you remove it.

2. Consider these questions:

(a.) How were numbers used in your description?

(b.) If you were to remove the washer and string, how could you be sure that a person had found the exact location again?

(c.) Name the smallest number of "tools" that would be needed for another person to determine the location of the washer.

(d.) What would it be like to describe an object such as the ball on top of a flagpole if you could not rely upon the flagpole in your description?

In a discussion setting the same activity would be under the direction of the teacher or a student to some degree familiar with the problem. The children would ponder collectively, but not inactively, how to describe the position of the point in space. Several descriptions could be recorded and tested by exchanging them with another class or by inviting an individual or small group to come in and follow the directions.

The identical concept which has been developed in the examples above may be illustrated on a different scale. A bead suspended by a thread from the top of a cardboard box may be used instead of the classroom and washers. With little effort the teacher or a student could construct the model from which to work (*see* Figure 31.5). If "windows" are included in the faces of the box, children could attack the problem of locating the bead in the contained space of the box. Various boxes could be exchanged among individuals or groups, and descriptions could be made and tested.

For the most highly motivated young minds, and those needing greater challenges, the teacher may wish to have the children explore locations in contained spaces other than the rectangular prism. He may ask the child to see if a position can be accurately described in the interior of a pyramid, cylinder, cone, or sphere (*see* Figure 31.6). The teacher should not pass up the opportunity to allow skillful pupils to construct figures such as those shown. By allowing opportunities for free thinking, the teacher may expect ingenious responses, as well as enthusiastic young investigators.

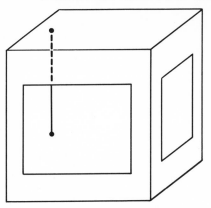

Figure 31.5 Point location in a box

In this consideration of a few geometric investigations, which should provide children with highly motivated mathematical experiences, we have attempted to illustrate the kinds of activities which can be seen in superior elementary school classrooms today. The children are encouraged to be actively involved in learning, to estimate and hypothesize, to test and confirm or reject, and to feel the satisfaction of having thought out an answer. The teachers are unafraid to improve their grasp of mathematics by working alongside their students.

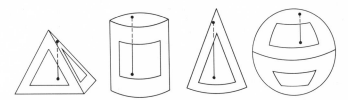

Figure 31.6 Point locations in various space figures

Geometry lends itself especially well to the more modern teaching and learning approaches, but should not be considered the only aspect of mathematics to be so used. Through continued effort on the part of teachers willing to extend themselves for professional growth mathematical experiences will become rewarding and exciting to most elementary school children.

SECTION VI

Problem Solving:
Motivating Ability
to Reason and Inquire

"When the Greek philosophers found that the square root of 2 is not a rational number, they celebrated the discovery by sacrificing 100 oxen."

Edward Kasner and James R. Newman,
Mathematics and the Imagination

Introduction

INTRODUCTION

To some extent that which is taught directly to children and learned on the basis of some criterion is of little value unless it can serve a useful end, for example, to help children solve problems. Children must have the opportunity to utilize as well as acquire knowledge and skill. A major objective of most elementary school programs is to help pupils learn the skills and attain the knowledge they need to function in adult society. As an example, in mathematics one does not learn computation for its own sake. Computation skills are developed so that ultimately one may keep bowling scores, verify advertising claims, check a monthly budget, or determine the gas mileage recorded on a trip, and so on.

Problem solving in elementary school mathematics centers around two types of problems, one could be called "mathematical" or "theoretical"; the other could be called "applied." In the first type of problem the emphasis is on a form of inquiry which will enable a child to discover a basic mathematical notion. Solving a mathematical problem generally requires an exploration of patterns or a manipulation of materials to discern relationship or generalization. For example, it is possible for second grade pupils to discover negative integers by investigating patterns in subtraction on the number line. Fourth grade pupils can discover, verbalize, and use many properties of the whole number system by examining sequences, series, or computations which reveal a pattern. Sixth grade pupils are capable of engaging in inquiry that leads them to discover the properties of the rational field.

The second type of problem is usually developed from a social or scientific basis. In the applied problem the emphasis is on an examination of given information. Some or all of the data is used to arrive at a quantitative solution. For example, when solving applied problems, first grade pupils can compute the cost of several candy bars, while fifth grade pupils can use indirect measurement techniques to compute the height of a tall building.

Many problems included in elementary school texts are of the applied variety, and are generally termed word or story problems. That a good deal of problem-solving activity still centers around the applied type is not too surprising, since they are designed to develop functional skills which are desirable in life outside of school.

The thoughtful reader should not get caught in the apparent dichotomy of applied versus mathematical problems, for this division need not be the distinctive feature of problem solving in the elementary school.

The special feature of problem solving *should* be to recognize that the process develops indirectly. That is, children must acquire this skill through consistently engaging in the process of solving problems over time and in a context that becomes increasingly complex. This position is extended in each of the articles of Section VI. Some of the articles focus on the extent to which certain variables facilitate the problem-solving process, while others offer a specific analysis of problem solving for different types of problems. Throughout, the focus is on the process and the notion that one learns to solve problems by solving them. Parenthetically, it is interesting to note that most articles use mathematical properties extensively in examples, as they make recommendations for improved problem-solving programs. If these examples are followed in the public school there is no real reason for continuance of the apparent dichotomy surrounding sound problem-solving programs.

3^2 PROBLEM-SOLVING—
ARITHMETIC'S PERSISTENT DILEMMA

N. Wesley Earp

BEFORE YOU READ   Three important concerns in developing
problem-solving ability are the nature of the problems presented to
children, the techniques a pupil can utilize to solve a problem, and the
guidance teachers can give to maximize a pupil's problem-solving ability.
In this article Professor Earp considers all three aspects and offers several
positive suggestions for approaching problem solving. The manner in
which the author has related the roles of teacher and pupil in problem
solving illustrates the importance of using a strategy to solve a problem.
That is, the pupils need to learn to employ a conscious pattern to solve
problems, and teachers must be aware of strategies that will help children
to do this.

    After reading the article the teacher should be able to list five
positive steps that can contribute to improved problem-solving ability for
children.

The term "problem solving" can be defined very broadly, even in the
restricted area of mathematics. Some take the view that the child faces a
problem solving situation any time he encounters a situation where he is not
sure how to proceed. This situation may be either realistic or fabricated.
This contrasts with the view that the only real problem a child may face is
that which arises in his own experiences. Still others point out that there
are two types of problems in math, those primarily mathematical in nature
and those with a social base, but asking a quantitative question. The first
of these might be demonstrated by the task of finding the number of possible
ways of representing the number nine by using numerals. The latter type of
problem might deal with the quantity of a commodity when the unit price
is known.

    The comments of this writing are concerned primarily with those
problems dealing with an issue of some social relatedness, hence one which
possibly may relate to the present or future everyday needs of the learner.
Not only are they to function in social situations but Van Engen[1] has pointed

[1] Henry Van Engen, "The Reform Movement in Arithmetic and the Verbal Problem,"
The Arithmetic Teacher, 10: 3–6, January 1963.

Reprinted from *School Science and Mathematics*, vol. 67, no. 2 (February 1967), pp. 182–188.
Professor Earp is at North Texas State University, Denton, Texas.

out that problems dealing with physical situations help the child to get a "toe-hold" in a mathematical operation; that physical situations via problem context provide a gateway to the concepts of the operations. At times these problems are also referred to as verbal problems, story problems, or even stated problems.

WHAT SEEMS TO BE THE PROBLEM?

Some forty years ago Stevenson[2] recorded these remarks of a child relative to her strategy for solving problems: "If there are lots of numbers I adds. If there are only two numbers with lots of parts I subtracts. But if there are just two numbers and one littler than the other, it is hard. I divides if they come out even, but if they don't I multiplies." The way some children approach problem solving in our present day is little if any more rational than this. At any rate, one does not have to look far to establish the fact that success in teaching problem solving procedures is very limited.

One of the most obvious obstacles children face in work with verbal problems is that of reading. It may seem a bit strange that reading and vocabulary study in arithmetic be undertaken, but this is likely to be necessary in improving problem solving. Teachers have long been known to admonish children to, "read the problem more carefully," and if such admonitions would significantly improve problem solving, there would be no need for the present writing. Although this is not the present focus, the reader is encouraged to provide needed instruction in both arithmetic reading vocabulary and comprehension.

Poor reading is only one handicap. Children who read quite well also do poorly in solving arithmetic problems. Other avenues must be explored to find the cause of their failures. Like the child quoted by Stevenson, many children have difficulty planning or arriving at a strategy for solving a problem. They rather uncritically take the numerals given and look for some cue as to the manner for processing them. There is no attempt to discern the action or direction of the problem. Consequently, the child searches rather randomly for an operation that "fits"—for a way of handling the numerals so that they are amenable or work out evenly. Most of the techniques used to try to remedy this problem have been somewhat ineffectual. Teaching the child to look for cue words and phrases will work in carefully designed or selected problems but is of doubtful value in more life-related problems. Many problems and problem situations simply contain no helpful cue words or may even be worded in such a way as to be detrimental to this aid. The procedure of following a well-defined series of steps such as deciding what is given, what is needed, what is to be done, etc.

[2] P.R. Stevenson, "Difficulties in Problem Solving," *Journal of Educational Research*, 11: 95–103, February 1925.

is a good analytical process. However, this process basically makes the child aware of the need for a strategy; it does not do much to help him develop one. Some good readers need help on strategy making for solving problems.

Arithmetic problems met in the context of life seldom have the well defined glibness of those found in arithmetic textbooks and worksheets. Children are often rather uncritical when given problems which contain unnecessary quantitative data. In the following problem the teacher is likely to be startled by some of the answers given:

> A group of 6 boys in Miss Carter's class collected old magazines for the paper drive. They worked on 9 different days in a two week period. They turned in 147 pounds the first week and 224 pounds the second week. How much paper did the boys from room 105 collect?

It hardly seems likely, but a number of children would simply be unable to ignore the unneeded data. Another deficiency likely to occur in children's approach to problem solving is the lack of experience with problem situations where not enough data are given. Children need work in such situations where they study the problem and decide what other information they need to know in order to plan a strategy that will work to provide the solution.

A deficiency which is related in part to a number of things, but particularly the use of unrealistic problems, and lack of strategy for solving problems is that of failure to seek or expect sensible answers. Seemingly, many children do not see the problem in a realistic light at all. The thought of a sensible answer does not enter into the picture—one simply looks for a neat way to juggle the numbers given in the problem statement. In answer to a routine question concerning computation of the routine federal income tax on a $5000 salary (with all essential information given) college students in certain of the author's mathematics classes have given answers ranging to more than $600,000.00; few are this far off, but far too many give completely exorbitant answers. Teaching children to seek realistic answers will prove to be effective practice not only in the problem solving context but also in teaching the computational processes.

CAN PROBLEM SOLVING BE TAUGHT?

Little progress seems to have been made in alleviating some of the deficiencies previously cited in the area of problem solving. Research studies such as those by Lindstedt[3] and Riedesel[4] indicate, however, that progress can be

[3] Sidney Axel Lindstedt, "Changes in Patterns of Thinking Produced by a Specific Problem Solving Approach in Elementary Arithmetic," Dissertation Abstracts, University Microfilms Inc.: Ann Arbor, Michigan, Volume XXIII, p. 2032.

[4] C. Alan Riedesel, "Verbal Problem Solving: Suggestions for improving instruction," The Arithmetic Teacher, May 1964, pp. 312–316.

made. Suggestions calculated to bring about such progress are made in the light of these research studies, the recommendations of arithmetic authorities, and numerous teaching experiences. In addition to the work in reading previously mentioned, special attention to the following suggestions is warranted:

1. Frequently the problems children are asked to work should come from their classroom or life situation. The teacher should often introduce new processes with such problems which she has devised. Some of the problem exercises should be largely comprised of this type problem.

   As part of this procedure some of the problems given should contain extraneous information. Children should have opportunity to discuss this type problem with emphasis on the fact that life situations are likely to be similar—one must often select from the several pieces of numerical data available that which is necessary to solve for the question asked. Discussions should center on what information is necessary, what is extra, and *why* this is the case. A related procedure is that of using problems which fail to incorporate all the needed information. The children must become aware that, in life, one must at times discern what is needed in additional numerical information and seek it out.

2. Children should be required in many instances to estimate what they believe to be a sensible answer to a problem. In fact they might be encouraged to do this quickly when beginning work on any problem. At times it will be worthwhile to discuss many problem examples, estimate sensible answers, give the method by which the estimate was made, and suggest a strategy for solving the problem. Perhaps it will seem a bit strange to suggest stopping at this point, but the goal of the lesson will have been accomplished without actually working the problem. This will focus the child's attention on logical estimation and procedure rather than always and only on the answer.

3. Since it is closely related to the previous suggestion, this idea may be briefly stated. Children should occasionally be asked to compose verbal problems of the type under study at that time. The experience of writing and discussing these will serve to reemphasize the essential parts of this type problem. Some children will not include enough information; others may be encouraged to put in more information than is needed. Hence practice and analysis of the type described in 2 above is accomplished; also, the child has likely developed insight into the problem and a workable strategy when he can write such a problem.

4. Flexibility in seeking the solution of problems is mandatory. Teachers sometimes tend to hinder the problem solving process by insisting

upon the use of one correct procedure. The child who is allowed to think out his own strategy and then who is gradually led to use more efficient procedures has an advantage. He may not always recall the most efficient procedure but the chances are good that he will always be able to work the problem in some way.

5. Related to flexibility in the solving of problems is the recommendation that the student receive instruction in drawing, diagramming, and/or using manipulative objects to represent a problem. As an example:

> The road crew on the new highway can pave $\frac{1}{3}$ of a mile each day. How far can they expect to pave this week if they work 5 full days?

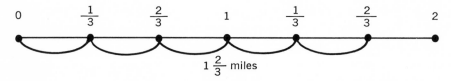

Figure 32.1

On the basis of such a diagram the child may make his strategy for solving the problem that of addition. In this case he will have to be led to multiplication. However he will certainly understand this situation and find the correct solution to the problem.

6. Much has been said in these comments about strategy for solving a problem. This, in the author's view is the paramount difficulty in the work of problem solving. The process in solving a problem has sometimes been referred to as programming and processing. The programming of the problem is a matter of arriving at a mathematical plan or statement for solving it. Usually it is a matter of deciding what type situation the problem entails, stating this in mathematical form, estimating the answer, and making a decision as to the needed processing. This "programming" is essentially what has been implied by the word "strategy." The processing is a matter of computing, relating and correctly labeling.

Encouraging children to use a carefully devised step procedure in looking at a problem is useful and may result, if applied by the child, in better problem solving. The very fact of a systematic approach is an improvement over the procedures most children use. However, as previously stated this is not, in effect, a means of teaching the child to devise a strategy.

In teaching children to devise a strategy for solving problems some of the most interesting of recent recommendations are made by Van Engen.[5] The reader interested in a comprehensive analysis of problem types and strategies should carefully examine this source.   In brief the strategy consists of analyzing the social situation to convert its language into a precise mathematical statement or statements of the problem situation.   In order to make this statement the analysis would consist of ascertaining if the problem involved action, and if so, what type of action.   By way of explanation, the problem that involves no action is one in which the answer situation is described by numbers without involving a mathematical operation to combine or separate the answer.   These are usually many-too-many correspondences; the numerous rate problems children meet are of this type.   The following example is a "no action" problem.

Example:

If John can buy candies at the rate of 5 for 1¢, how many can he get by spending 7¢?

In the example the task is to find a ratio proportional to that of $5:1$ where the second term is 7, hence $n:7$.   There is no actual combining, or separation, of the numerical quantities involved.   The child, by meeting numerous situations involving proportional ratios should recognize this type of problem and of course he can solve it oftentimes through a simple diagramming procedure.   As a more efficient procedure the problem can be set up thusly: $5/1 = n/7$.   The child finds n by completing the correct proportion—in other words, he ascertains that he must multiply 1 by 7 to produce seven; to complete the correct proportion the 5 must also be multiplied by 7.

In those problems involving action the child must be taught to analyze the type of action—combining or separating.   On the basis of this analysis the child attempts to write a mathematical sentence which correctly represents the problem.

Examples:

(a) Cindy had some stamps to begin her collection.   Ann gave her a sack of 25 stamps.   When all were placed in her album, Cindy had 123 stamps.   How many did she have to begin with?

(b) Mrs. Lockman put the hamburger rolls from 12 packages into the oven for the party.   If there were 96 rolls in all how many did each package contain if they were of equal size?

[5] Henry Van Engen, *et al.*, *Charting the Course for Arithmetic*, Chicago: Scott, Foresman and Company, 1960.

In (*a*) the action of the problem is quite definitely combining action. The two sets of stamps combine into the total set of 123. The sentence that accurately represents this situation is: $n + 25 = 123$. One of the complexities in problem solving is evident in this problem. The real action of the problem differs from the computation needed to solve it. However, with the statement of the problem in equation form the strategy has been developed and the student is ready to process. If he understands the relationship of the processes he recognizes that he has the numerals for one *addend* and a *sum* in his equation—the other *addend* in such a case is found by subtraction.

Problem (*b*) is also a combining action problem. To mathematically describe the situation the appropriate statement is: $12 \times n = 96$. Again the computation for solving the problem is not that implied in its action. The child must again recognize the inverse operation of division. If there is one *factor* and a *product* given then division will give the other *factor* which is needed to replace *n*.

Example problems such as these may be poor choices in that they deal with more than simple situations. Easier problems could have been chosen, yet these serve to demonstrate the necessity and importance of strategy quite well. It has always been puzzling to children that the computation teachers have urged them to use in solving these types of problems obviously contradict the situations of the problems. Many problems, of course, denote action and computational procedures which are the same. The strategies in these are much easier. The reader can envision numerous examples and mathematical statements of this sort in that they are reasonably obvious.

In regard to this type of procedure, studies by Lindstedt[6] and by Lerch and Hamilton[7] have indicated improved problem solving by children who were given instruction in developing such programming techniques. Children who are the better students seemed to benefit particularly from such teaching.

An interesting corollary of teaching children to make correct mathematical statements for problems exists. They can profit from working in the opposite direction. Several equation statements can be given and children given the task of exercising their ingenuity to write a problem which fits each statement. For example, the student given: $4 + n = 13$ might contribute in this manner:

> "I had 4 white mice, then I got some more white mice which made me 13. How many did I get?"

[6] Lindstedt, *op. cit.*, p. 2032.
[7] Harold H. Lerch and Helen Hamilton, "A Comparison of a Structured-Equation Approach to Problem Solving With A Traditional Approach." *School Science and Mathematics*, LXVI (March 1966), p. 241.

For additional ideas of value in developing strategies in solving problems the reader is directed to the work of May.[8] His suggestions will prove helpful to those who wish to emphasize this important step in problem solving.

SUMMATION

The very fact that teachers were cognizant of problem solving difficulties and placed special emphasis on this area in teaching has been shown to result in improved achievement by children. Some of these same studies indicate that through the simple expedient of giving children a good many well-chosen problems to solve, their abilities in this area were improved. It is safe, then, to predict an acceptable level of problem solving skill *if* the teacher will place emphasis on developing these skills and will apply the suggestions given to improving the skills.

[8] Frank B. May, "Three Problems of Using Equations in Elementary Arithmetic Programs," *The Arithmetic Teacher*, March 1964, pp. 166–168.

33 LABEL × LABEL = LABEL²—A POINT OF VIEW

Herbert Hannon

BEFORE YOU READ   A cardinal number is an abstraction that is based upon the establishment of one-to-one correspondences between finite sets which contain discrete elements. A unit of measure is an abstraction based upon marking off a distance, an amount of time, or an amount of weight. An operation on the cardinal numbers is, in one sense, an abstraction which is based on set operations. The extent to which these ideas should be distinguished is important for they help to differentiate between numbers and units in problems involving measurement.

In this article Professor Hannon discusses methods pupils can use to distinguish between numbers and units of measure in problem solving. He provides information regarding how pupils can solve verbal problems involving both numbers and units of measure, once the problem relationships have been written as mathematical statements.

The teacher should be able to describe a rationale for distinguishing numbers and units in measurement problems and be able to construct a measurement problem illustrating application of the rationale after reading the article.

As a student in elementary school and again as an elementary teacher with a limited background in mathematics I was taught, and taught in return, that all numbers used to represent measurements in a problem situation should be appropriately labeled and that these labels should be used in each step of the solution.

This fundamental error, if such it was, would seem to have been the result of confusion between set operations and operations on a well-defined system of numbers. In such a system the numbers, or elements, are expressed without labels. This is especially desirable since the number relationships can thus be abstracted and generalization developed. Such generalizations are needed in turn for their application to the practical side of mathematics—the problem-solving of our experiences.

In a practical sense a solution set may be interpreted as the end result of certain operations which are performed on the initial sets of the problem

---

Reprinted from *School Science and Mathematics*, vol. 68, no. 6 (June 1968), pp. 506–510. Professor Hannon is in the Mathematics Department of Western Michigan University, Kalamazoo, Michigan.

situation. Those operations include obtaining set unions, set intersections, duplicating sets a specified number of times, finding Cartesian products, obtaining appropriate subsets of the initial sets, and so on. No one would argue the necessity for distinguishing between these set operations and the operations upon the cardinal numbers of the sets specified. Mathematically we are interested in the relationship between the cardinal numbers of the original sets in the problem situation and the cardinal number or numbers named in the solution set—finding the simplest number names for the relationship.

However, it may be that we have overemphasized the distinction between set operations and number operations to the confusion of the teachers and students who will have to use both of these basic ideas in solving everyday life problems.

Number relations and operations are used in a practical sense to replace the set operations which would be needed, and the primitive operation of counting which would always be necessary to solve a problem if the operations on the numbers of the sets were not available.

Examples of practical problems will be used by the writer in the remainder of this paper to develop his point of view.

Mary has 24 inches of ribbon and Betty has 36 inches of ribbon. How much ribbon do they have together?

Question: 24 inches of ribbon and 36 inches of ribbon are how many inches of ribbon?

$$\text{Abstract relationship: } 24 + 36 = \square$$

The solution set:

$$\square = \{60\}$$

So together they have 60 inches of ribbon.

Now suppose we "define" inch as a numeral for the number one. The open sentence which expresses the relationship would be:

$$24 \text{ inches} + 36 \text{ inches} = \square \text{ inches}$$

By the distributive property of multiplication over addition, the solution pattern would be:

$$(24 + 36) \text{ inches} = \square \text{ inches}$$

Since $24 + 36 = 60$:

$$(24 + 36) \text{ inches} = 60 \text{ inches}$$

So the solution set is 60, the number of inches of ribbon they have together. Using the usual numeral for one:

$$(24 \times 1) + (36 \times 1) = \square \times 1$$
$$(24 + 36) \times 1 = \square \times 1$$
$$60 \times 1 = \square \times 1$$
$$\square = 60$$

Here, if the 1 stands for "inch" we may conclude that together the girls had 60 inches of ribbon.

The original problem might have been stated in feet. Then foot would be defined as a numeral for 1. So:

$$2 \text{ feet} + 3 \text{ feet} = \square \text{ feet}$$
$$(2 + 3) \text{ feet} = \square \text{ feet}$$
$$5 \text{ feet} = \square \text{ feet}$$
$$\square = 5$$

So the girls had 5 feet of ribbon together. In the above example the unit of measurement was changed to indicate that measurement units are arbitrary.

Certainly the 1's used in our system of numbers are abstractly defined also, but when the meaning of 1 is once accepted then the value of all other integers are immediately determined also.

This would seem to relate directly to our system of numeration where we arbitrarily define the grouping number used for the base of the system.

$(10)_{\text{base}}$ means one group the size of the base number which is used. $(333)_{\text{base}}$ means

$$[(3 \times 10^2) + (3 \times 10^1) + (3 \times 10^0)]_{\text{base}}$$

If the base number is ten, then $(333)_{\text{ten}}$ means

$$(3 \times \text{ten}^2) + (3 \times \text{ten}^1) + (3 \times \text{ten}^0)$$
$$\searrow (3 \times \text{one})$$

Here the word ten is used as a numeral and such words as thousands (ten^3), hundreds (ten^2), ten (ten^1), and ones (ten^0) are numerals also—names for numbers.

Similarly we might define all measurement units as numerals such as:

inch = inch	$1 = 1$
inch $\times$ inch = inch^2	$(1 \times 1) = 1^2$
inch $\times$ inch $\times$ inch = inch^3	$(1 \times 1 \times 1) = 1^3$

It is also necessary to define the following:

$$\text{inch} = \text{inch}$$
$$\text{inch}^2 = \text{sq. inch}$$
$$\text{and inch}^3 = \text{cu. inch}$$

An example will be used to illustrate the ideas involved.

Find the volume of a rectangular solid whose dimensions are: 3 inches by 4 inches by 5 inches.

The open number sentence would be:

$$3 \text{ in.} \times 4 \text{ in.} \times 5 \text{ in.} = \square \text{ in.}^3$$

By commutative and associative properties:

$$(3 \times 4 \times 5) \times (\text{in.} \times \text{in.} \times \text{in.}) = \square \times \text{in.}^3$$
$$(3 \times 4 \times 5) \times (1 \times 1 \times 1) \quad = \square \times (1)^3$$
$$60 \times 1^3 = 60 \text{ in.}^3 \text{ (by definition)}$$

60 is the number of inches.^{3} But also in.^{3} = cu. in., so the volume is 60 cu. inches.

Compare this pattern with:

$$30 \times 40 \times 50 = \square$$
$$(3 \times 10) \times (4 \times 10) \times (5 \times 10) = (3 \times 4 \times 5) \times (10 \times 10 \times 10)$$
$$= 60 \times 10^3$$

or

$$(3 \times \text{ten}) \times (4 \times \text{ten}) \times (5 \times \text{ten}) = (3 \times 4 \times 5) \times (\text{ten} \times \text{ten} \times \text{ten})$$
$$= 60 \times \text{ten}^3$$

The numeral ten^3 is defined in our system of numeration as 10^3 or 1000, so the number named is 60 × thousand = 60,000.

Perhaps we should note that our friends in the physical sciences have been using these basic definitions for many years and we "purists" of the mathematics cult have been reluctant to permit their use, in spite of the utilitarian aspects that are involved.

A final example will be used to indicate further the relation between set operations and number operations.

Mr. Brown has an orchard with 3 rows of trees. If there are 4 trees per row, how many trees are there in the orchard?

Since this means there are 3 sets of 4 trees, the practical problem can be solved by using set notation such as:

$$\{ \text{🌳 🌳 🌳 🌳} \} \cup \{ \text{🌳 🌳 🌳 🌳} \} \cup \{ \text{🌳 🌳 🌳 🌳} \} = \{ \text{🌳 🌳} \cdots \text{🌳 🌳} \}$$

3 sets of 4 trees = 1 set of □ trees.

We obtain the desired number by forming the set which is the union of the 3 sets of 4 trees and then counting to find the cardinal number of the set formed.

The equivalent number relationship is:

$$3 \times {}_n\{ \text{🌳 🌳 🌳 🌳} \} = {}_n\{ \text{🌳 🌳 🌳} \cdots \text{🌳 🌳} \}$$

or

$$3 \times 4 = 12$$

If we define the unit, tree, as 1, then:

$$3 \times (4 \text{ trees}) = \square \text{ trees}$$

By the associative property of multiplication:

$$(3 \times 4) \text{ trees} = \square \text{ trees}$$

or

$$(3 \times 4) \times 1 = \square \times 1$$
$$\square = 12$$

So there are 12 trees in the orchard.

SUMMARY

Three examples have been used to explore the desirability of using labels in problem solving. The point of view presented was that whenever measurement units were involved, these units might be defined as a numeral for 1. Number operations in the usual sense could then be used with the labels used as numerals, i.e., names for numbers.

First, $3a + 2a = (3 + 2)a$, where a is an arbitrary unit of measurement defined as 1.

Also, $3a \times 4a = (3 \times 4) \times (a \times a)$, where a^2 is defined as 1, and finally as "a" squared.

Finally, $3 \times 4a = (3 \times 4)a$, where "$a$" again is defined as 1—the arbitrary unit of measurement.

Certainly the above point of view permits the separation of the units of measurement (labels) from the number operations used in the usual sense and as such merits some consideration in problem solving—the practical aspects of mathematics.

34 WHAT SKILLS BUILD PROBLEM-SOLVING POWER?

John W. Wilson

BEFORE YOU READ   Much knowledge regarding how children solve problems has been gained through research. A consistent finding is that pupils lack the ability to apply arithmetical operations correctly in problem solving. Mr. Wilson has identified three types of meanings for arithmetical operations. They are labeled (1.) mathematically pure, (2.) physical action, and (3.) socially significant. He then explores the implications of these meanings in regard to the problem of discrimination learning. In so doing, the author identifies a rationale for the use of arithmetical operations that is mathematically and psychologically sound.

   After reading the article the teacher should be able to differentiate between generalization and discrimination learning and describe the distinctions between mathematically pure, physical action, and socially significant meanings in problem solving.

How often have you heard pupils ask when faced with a verbal problem, "What do I do, add or subtract?" One of the children referred to the Diagnostic and Remedial Arithmetic Clinic at Syracuse University explained her procedure: "It's easy. When I see lots of numbers, I add. When there are two numbers and one is lots bigger, I subtract. If that doesn't work, I divide; and if it doesn't come out even, I multiply."

   Through the years much has been written on how to improve children's ability to solve verbal problems. The suggestions offered here, while not radically new, have been supported in two well controlled experimental studies (Pace 1959, Wilson 1964). The approach has subsequently been found exceptionally successful in improving the problem-solving ability of children referred to our clinic at Syracuse University. Classroom teachers trained to use this approach also report very satisfying results.

SEEING THE COMMON ELEMENT

Verbal problems describe social situations in which quantities are involved. Problem situations may vary with respect to the number domain involved,

---

Reprinted from *The Instructor*, vol. 76, no. 6 (February 1967), pp. 79–80. John W. Wilson is the Director of the Arithmetic Clinic of Syracuse University, Syracuse, New York.

the objects involved, the setting, the actions, the events, and so forth. For a particular set of problems, the child's major task is to see something common, something essentially the same, involved in all these variations. In problems which call for addition, the child must see a common element and respond by choosing addition as the appropriate operation. This the psychologist refers to as generalization learning—the capacity for giving a common response to the common element in otherwise dissimilar stimuli.

For effective problem solving, generalization learning is not enough. The learner must also be able to discriminate those problems for which addition is appropriate from those for which subtraction is appropriate. Discrimination learning is the capacity for giving different responses to different yet similar stimuli.

The common element embedded in any given verbal problem, regardless of the great variations in action, events, or objects involved, is the meaning of one of the four fundamental operations of arithmetic. Hence, the child must know the basic meanings of each operation, must be able to discriminate one meaning from another, and must be able to recognize each meaning when it is embedded in a variety of problem settings.

There are at least three types of meanings of arithmetic operations: *mathematically pure*, *physical action*, and *socially significant*.

MATHEMATICALLY PURE MEANINGS

All four arithmetic operations are what the mathematician terms "binary operations." Either addition or multiplication might be defined as an operation on a pair of numbers which yields a third number.

While such definitions are mathematically precise, they are psychologically inadequate for problem solving and too similar to facilitate discrimination. Nearly all one-step problems involve two numbers and we seek a third number. Mathematically pure meanings do not help a child decide which operation is appropriate.

The following verbal problems serve to compare the other two types of meanings, physical action and social significance:

A-1 John had 35¢. His father gave him 15¢ for raking the lawn. How much money did John then have?

A-2 Bill had some marbles. He lost 15 marbles to Jim. Bill then had 35 marbles left. How many marbles did Bill have to begin with?

S-1 Jim had 50¢. He spent 15¢ on a model airplane. How much did Jim have left?

S-2 Mary had 26 dresses for her doll. For Christmas, her mother gave her more pretty doll dresses. Now Mary has 40 dresses. How many dresses did Mary's mother give her for Christmas?

PHYSICAL ACTION MEANINGS

Ask most children what addition or subtraction means, and you will probably hear something such as, "Addition is putting things together. Subtraction is taking away or separating."

These action definitions focus on what is going on in the physical situations we often use as models for addition and subtraction. Subsequently, when a child reads a problem such as A-1 above, he sees a joining action is involved and thinks, "Addition is a joining action; therefore, I must have to add." In a problem like S-1 he sees the separating action which has been associated with subtraction. It is little wonder that problems such as A-1 and S-1 have traditionally been the easiest types of problems for children. Both have the actions emphasized in physical models used to develop the action meanings of addition and subtraction.

Action definitions are, of course, mathematically incorrect. Combining and separating are operations on sets—not on numbers. Also, despite the widespread use of these action-type meanings and the ease with which children acquire them, Wilson's study clearly demonstrated that the action meanings do not improve children's problem-solving ability. On the contrary, action meanings were shown to inhibit some children's ability.

It is not difficult to see why. The child who continuously associates a joining action with addition and a separating action with subtraction is severely handicapped when he encounters a problem such as S-2 above. In this problem a joining action is clearly involved, but the correct operation to use is subtraction. Many children try to solve this problem by addition. They are responding to the common element, the joining action. But in this case the element of action has led them astray.

Psychologically, the child who is equipped only with the action meanings of the operations cannot discriminate—he overgeneralizes. That is, he applies a generalized idea to situations to which the idea does not apply. Hence, he makes mistakes in problem solving by being unable to select the correct operation.

Action meanings of the operations, then, must be avoided. They are mathematically incorrect and, for problem solving, psychologically unsound.

SOCIALLY SIGNIFICANT MEANINGS

Concrete situations used as models for the operation have characteristics other than the actions involved. Analyzing these situations reveals that each operation has a unique purpose and a unique set of means for achieving that purpose. Such an analysis can lead to meanings of addition and subtraction such as the following. *Addition is an operation used to find a sum when we know the addends. Subtraction is an operation used to find an unknown addend when we know the sum and the other addend.*

In less sophisticated language, these meanings might be expressed as follows. *Addition is used to find the "size of the total" when we know the "size of each part." Subtraction is used to find the "size of one part" when we know the "size of the total" and one of its "parts."*

Any definition which emphasizes the purpose characteristic of an operation may be termed a *wanted-given definition.* Wanted-given definitions similar to the above can be made for multiplication and division.

On the basis of their wanted-given relationship, all one-step problems fall into one of four major categories. Subcategories of problem types can be made based on their social settings.

It is the unique wanted-given relationship embedded in all the problems in a particular major category that we must guide children to see as the element common to all the problems in that category. It is the guiding of children to see these wanted-given relationships which Pace's and Wilson's studies and the remedial work at the Arithmetic Clinic have found to be the most effective major approach to the improvement of children's abilities to solve problems.

SUPPORTING COGNITIVE SKILLS

This major approach should be supplemented with several supporting cognitive skills such as the use of equations to express wanted-given relationships, estimating correct answers, and having children make up their own problems. Certain elementary mathematics textbooks include these skills in the program of problem solving.

Perhaps the most important supporting approach, however, is to be sure children receive systematic teaching and practice in seeing wanted-given relationships in a wide variety of problems. Only a few mathematics textbook programs provide systematic teaching and practice.

The chart on pp. 290–291 describes and gives an illustration of each of the major types of one-step problems. Each falls into one of four categories according to the wanted-given relationship common to that category. Subtypes within a category differ in the sequence of events which the problem describes.

While texts will provide many examples for some types, a recent analysis revealed that in all but one or two series there are great gaps in the comprehensiveness and depth of coverage of many types of problems. However, by varying the number domain, the objects, and social context of each of the illustrative problems, you can construct a comprehensive set for teaching wanted-given relationships which are the heart of problem solving.

Practice Models for Problem Solving

ADDITION. Wanted: sum. Given: addends.

TO FIND	KNOWN	EXAMPLE
1. N of resulting set	N of each subset	Bill had 6 toy soldiers. His dad gave him 3 more toy soldiers. How many does he have now?
2. N of union set started with	N of subset removed and N of complement set	Bill had some toy soldiers. He gave 6 to Jim. Bill then had 3 left. How many did he have to begin with?
3. N of the greater set	N of lesser set and N of difference set	Jim had 6 toy soldiers. Bill had 3 more toy soldiers than Jim. How many did Bill have?
4. N of resulting set	N of each subset (no action)	Billy had 6 brown toy soldiers and 3 red toy soldiers. How many toy soldiers does he have?

SUBTRACTION. Wanted: addend. Given: sum and one addend.

TO FIND	KNOWN	EXAMPLE
1. N of subset left	N of union set started with and N of subset removed	Bill had 9 toy soldiers. He gave 6 to Jim. How many did Bill have left?
2. N of complement set	N of subset started with and N of resulting union set	Bill had 6 toy soldiers. His dad gave him some more toy soldiers. Bill now has 9 toy soldiers. How many did his dad give him?
3. N of set needed	N of set already has and N of desired union set	Bill has 6 toy soldiers. He would like to have 9 soldiers. How many more must he get?
4. N of difference set	N of greater and lesser sets (disjoint)	Bill has 9 toy soldiers. Jim has 6 toy soldiers. How many more does Bill have than Jim? How many fewer does Jim have than Bill? (comparison)
5. N of subset started with	N of subset joined and N of total set	Bill had some toy soldiers. After dad gave him 6 more, Bill had 9 toy soldiers. How many did Bill have to begin with?
6. N of subset removed	N of subset left and N of union set started with	Bill had 9 toy soldiers. Bill gave some to Jim. Then Bill had 6 left. How many did he give to Jim?
7. N of complement set	N of subset and N of universal set	Bill had 9 toy soldiers. Only 6 have rifles. The others have hand grenades. How many have hand grenades?
8. N of lesser set	N of greater set and N of difference set	Bill has 9 toy soldiers. Jim has 6 fewer soldiers than Bill. How many soldiers has Jim?

MULTIPLICATION. Wanted: product. Given: factors.

TO FIND	KNOWN	EXAMPLE
1. N of union set	N of disjoint sets and N of each set	John has 4 banks. There are 3 nickels in each bank. How many nickels does John have?
2. N of a set	N of another set and the ratio of that set to the unknown set	John has 12 pennies. He has 3 times as many nickels as pennies. How many nickels does he have?

| 3. N of cartesian set | N of each set | John has 3 shirts and 4 pairs of trousers. How many outfits does he have? |
| 4. N of union set | N of disjoint sets and N of each set | John put some coins into 4 banks. He put 3 into each bank. How many coins did he put in, in all? |

DIVISION. *Wanted: factor.*   *Given: product and one factor.*

TO FIND	KNOWN	EXAMPLE
1. N of equivalent sets	N of original set and N of each set	John had 12 pennies. He put a group of 3 pennies into each of several banks. How many banks did he use? (measurement)
2. N in each equivalent set	N of original set and N of equivalent set	John had some pennies. He put the same number of pennies into each of 4 banks. How many pennies did he put into each bank? (partition)
3. N of equivalent sets	N of resulting total set and N of each set	John put several groups of 3 pennies into a bank. Then he saw he had 12 pennies in the bank. How many pennies did he put in each time?
4. Ratio of one set to another	N of each set	John has 12 pennies and 4 nickels. He has how many times as many pennies as nickels? Or, he has what fraction as many nickels as pennies?
5. N of a set	N of another set and ratio of known set to unknown set	John has 12 pennies. He has 3 times as many pennies as nickels. How many nickels does he have?

35 OPEN SENTENCES—THE MOST USEFUL TOOL IN PROBLEM SOLVING

Louis S. Cohen

BEFORE YOU READ   The types of problems children are most often asked to solve are commonly called story problems, which may have a mathematical or applied basis.   In most cases the distinctive feature of the story problem is that the problem relationships must be translated into mathematical statements or equations.   In this article Mr. Cohen focuses on the development of mathematical statements in problem solving.   He also describes the parts of a mathematical statement and provides a rationale for their use.

   The information should enable the reader to gain insight into writing mathematical expressions and, in so doing, note some implicit suggestions for helping children develop equations to solve problems.   As a result of reading this contribution the teacher should be able to express problem relationships from a story problem in equation form, and subsequently solve the equation to obtain a numerical answer.

Open number sentences are useful in finding solutions of verbal problems. To write open sentences for problems, one must be able to translate verbal phrases and sentences into mathematical language. Mathematical sentences, much like English sentences, are made up of phrases and verbs. It is the combination of these phrases and verbs that will make the mathematical sentence complete.

NUMBER PHRASES

Since phrases are elements of the English sentence, let us first direct our attention to the number phrases that are elements of the mathematical sentence. Here are some word phrases typical of those occurring in problems, along with their mathematical translation.

Reprinted from *The Arithmetic Teacher*, vol. 14, no. 4 (April 1967), pp. 363–367. Louis S. Cohen is Mathematics Co-ordinator for Grades 1–12 for the Bloomington Public Schools, Bloomington, Minnesota.

The result of adding a number to 7 $7 + x$
The result of decreasing a number
  by 2 $\square - 2$
Five times some number $5 \times \Delta$

Seventeen divided by some number $17 \div y$ or $\dfrac{17}{y}$

Some discussion of the above examples might be helpful at this point in order to make the mathematical translations more meaningful. In each case, to transform the verbal phrase into mathematical language, it was necessary to introduce symbols, such as x, $\square$, Δ, y, or n, to stand for the unspecified number. Each of these symbols is called a *variable*. For the problems in this article, the replacement set for these variables will be thought of as the set of real numbers unless otherwise specified.

    Example 1

      The result of adding a number to 7 $7 + x$

Let us first observe that the phrases

$$7 + x$$

and

$$x + 7$$

are mathematically the same; that is, for any real number x,

$$7 + x = x + 7.$$

This follows from the commutative property of addition. However, the first phrase is the literal translation of the given verbal expression; and $x + 7$ would ordinarily be used to express the result of adding 7 to a number rather than adding a number to 7. In solving open sentences it is often useful to apply the commutative and other properties of the real numbers. At this point, however, we are simply translating English phrases directly into mathematical phrases. It is important to be precise in translating into mathematical phrases. This is illustrated in Examples 2 and 4 and later on in Examples 6 and 7, where the necessity of stating subtraction and division problems properly is shown. In addition, a precise translation may be essential to the solution of a more complex situation.

    Example 2

      The result of decreasing a number by 2 $\square - 2$

"Decreasing" implies subtraction, and it is "a number" that is being decreased; thus we have $\square - 2$. Let us note that

$$\square - 2$$

and

$$2 - \square$$

are *not* mathematically equivalent phrases. For example,

$$\text{when } \square = 5, 5 - 2 \neq 2 - 5.$$

In general, subtraction is *not* a commutative operation. (The symbol $\neq$ is read "is not equal to" and acts as a verb does in an English sentence. Symbols such as $=$, $\neq$, $<$, and $>$ are discussed in Table 35.1 at the end of this article.) A verbal phrase for $2 - \square$ might be "two decreased by some number," which is quite different from the expression, "some number decreased by two." This example points out the need for an accurate translation.

Example 3

Five times some number $5 \times \triangle$

"Times" implies multiplication. An equivalent phrase for

$$5 \times \triangle$$

is

$$\triangle \times 5,$$

since multiplication of real numbers is a commutative operation. For example,

$$5 \times 6 = 6 \times 5,$$

and

$$5 \times 17 = 17 \times 5.$$

However, the translation of the given expression is $5 \times \triangle$.

Example 4

Seventeen divided by some number $17 \div y$ or $\dfrac{17}{y}$

Division is the stated operation. Since 17 is being divided by some number, the phrase is $17 \div y$. Division, like subtraction, is not commutative. Therefore,

$$y \div 17$$

is *not* an equivalent phrase for

$$17 \div y.$$

Example 5

Two-thirds of some number $\frac{2}{3} \times n$

Multiplication is implied. An equivalent phrase for

$$\frac{2}{3} \times n$$

is

$$n \times \frac{2}{3}.$$

Following the notions developed in the prior examples, the most appropriate translation is $\frac{2}{3} \times n$.

Quite often the wording of certain verbal phrases can cause severe difficulties. For example, here are two, which will be stated and discussed in some detail.

Example 6

The difference between 10 and some number ...?

We know that "difference" implies subtraction. Could there be more than one possible translation of this expression? Could this phrase be represented either by

$$10 - y$$

or by

$$y - 10?$$

Since subtraction is not commutative, we know that these two phrases are not equivalent; but then which one should be used for the mathematical translation? We would find it difficult to justify either one of the translations over the other. The fact is that we have insufficient information to make a decision. This difficulty would be avoided if the verbal phrase included one of the following statements:

The result is to be positive, and $y < 10$.
    (Here $10 - y$ is the mathematical translation.)
The result is to be negative, and $y < 10$.
    (Here $y - 10$ is the mathematical translation.)
The result is to be positive, and $y > 10$.
    (Here $y - 10$ is the mathematical translation.)
The result is to be negative, and $y > 10$.
    (Here $10 - y$ is the mathematical translation.)

The difficulty is best removed, however, if the meaning is expressed un-ambiguously in the first place, as in the following:

The difference when some number is subtracted from 10
The difference when 10 is subtracted from some number

Example 7

The quotient of some number and 8 . . . ?
This can cause complications similar to those in Example 6. The term "quotient" suggests the operation of division. Is the mathematical translation

$$8 \div \square$$

or

$$\square \div 8 \, ?$$

Once again more information must be given to the reader before he can write a mathematical translation. From the discussion for Example 4 we know that the two possible translations are not equivalent, since division is not commutative. Some suggested alternatives of the verbal phrase:

Some number to be divided by 8
  (Then, in this case, $\square \div 8$ is the translation.)
Eight divided by some number
  (In this case, $8 \div \square$ is the translation.)

FOLLOWING INSTRUCTIONS

Going one step further in translations, let us begin by translating a verbal phrase to a number phrase and then write other number phrases related to this phrase.

1. Suppose a reference is made to some number. We can represent this number by Δ. Express mathematically the result of each of the following:

Five more than the number	$\Delta + 5$
Three less than the number	$\Delta - 3$
Four times the number	$4 \times \Delta$
The number divided by 6	$\Delta \div 6$ or $\dfrac{\Delta}{6}$
Twice the sum of the number and 5	$2 \times (\Delta + 5)$
Ten times three less than the number	$10 \times (\Delta - 3)$
The quotient obtained when four times the number is divided by 7	$\dfrac{4 \times \Delta}{7}$

For the most part, the example above displays operational procedure on a variable and is often used in "guess my number" drills.

2. Suppose a reference is made to Barbara's age. Representing Barbara's age today as n years, we can express each of the following in terms of Barbara's age now.

Barbara's age in 3 years	$n + 3$
Pat is one-half Barbara's age	$\frac{1}{2} \times n$ or $\frac{n}{2}$
Pat's age in 5 years	$\frac{n}{2} + 5$
Pat's age in 5 years is subtracted from Barbara's age in 3 years	$(n + 3) - \left(\frac{n}{2} + 5\right)$
Pat's age 8 years ago	$\frac{n}{2} - 8$
Barbara's age in 6 years added to Pat's age 8 year ago	$\left(\frac{n}{2} - 8\right) + (n + 6)$
Three times Barbara's age in 7 years	$3 \times (n + 7)$
Four times Pat's age 2 years ago	$4 \times \left(\frac{n}{2} - 2\right)$

Note that the difference between any two persons' ages remains the same throughout their lifetimes. However, it should be stated that if, at a given point in time, one person's age is a multiple of the age of another person, this multiple will not remain constant. For example, suppose that Barbara is 30 years old and Pat is 15 years old. The difference of their ages today is 15 years, and Barbara's age is two times Pat's age. In 5 years from now, Barbara will be 35 and Pat 20. The difference of their ages is still 15 years, but now notice the change in the multiple between their ages. In 5 years Barbara's age will be only $1\frac{3}{4}$ times Pat's age. In 30 years when Barbara is 60 and Pat is 45, Barbara's age will be $1\frac{1}{3}$ times Pat's age.

3. Wallace has some dimes	Δ
Joyce has 2 more dimes than Wallace	$\Delta + 2$
Express the value in cents of Wallace's money	$10 \times \Delta$
Express the value in cents of Joyce's money	$10 \times (\Delta + 2)$
Express the *number* of dimes Wallace and Joyce have together	$\Delta + (\Delta + 2)$
Express the *value* in cents of Wallace's money and Joyce's money together	$(10 \times \Delta) + [10 \times (\Delta + 2)]$

The last two sentences are quite different. The first involves the *number* of coins, while the second involves the *value* of these coins. If you stated that you had two coins, one could only guess at the amount of money you had. You might have 2 cents (2 pennies), 10 cents (2 nickels), 6 cents (one nickel and one penny), or even 200 cents (2 silver dollars). Do you see that the numeral used to represent the *number of coins* does not, in general, represent the *money value of the coins*?

NUMBER SENTENCES

In Examples 1 through 3 we pointed out typical word phrases and their mathematical translations. We will look at some word problems and write their appropriate mathematical sentences.

A complete mathematical sentence uses a symbol to represent certain key concepts. Consider the examples displayed below:

Table 35.1

Concepts	Symbol	Example of Use	Read
Equality	$=$	$\Box + 2 = 5$	Two added to some number "is equal to" five.
Inequality	$<$	$5 < 7$	Five "is less than" seven.
Inequality	$>$	$5 > 1$	Five "is greater than" one.
Similarity	$\sim$	$\triangle ABC \sim \triangle DEF$	Triangle *ABC* "is similar to" triangle *DEF*.
Congruence	$\cong$	$\triangle XYZ \cong \triangle JKL$	Triangle *XYZ* "is congruent to" triangle *JKL*.

These symbols are but a few of the mathematical "verbs" used in a mathematical sentence to express a complete thought.

For the moment, let us give our attention to statements of equality. A sentence that uses the equal symbol $(=)$ states that everything on the left-hand side of the equal symbol *is equal to* or *is another name for* everything named on the right-hand side. This type of sentence is called an "equation."

Since the main emphasis of this article is on the writing of mathematical sentences and not their solution, little or no mechanics will be given for the solution. We suggest that the reader, if interested, examine a few of the many algebra books available that do go through the techniques of solutions.

Checking for the truth of the solution is part of any word problem, and this we will do by going back to the original situation and noting whether or not the answer satisfies the given conditions. If we were to check the answer by using the open sentence, all we would be justified in stating is that the answer satisfied the mathematical sentence. It is possible to write incorrect sentences. Since we want to check to verify *both* the sentence and the solution set, we can do this only by going back to the original problem.

1. Situation
Louis had 15 baseball cards. David gave him some more. Now Louis has 32 cards. How many cards did David give to Louis?

Analysis
You do not know how many cards David gave to Louis. Let x represent the number David gave to Louis x

Number of cards Louis had at first   15

Number of cards Louis now has $15 + x$

It is also given that Louis now has 32 cards. Since "$15 + x$" and "32" name the same number, the sentence is $15 + x = 32$.

Solution
By an "educated guess" and a subsequent "substitution" you probably noted that the solution set for this problem is 17. If you were to read the mathematical sentence in words, you might ask yourself this question: "The sum of what number and 15 is 32?" The answer 17 is obvious. The truth set {17} indicates that David gave 17 baseball cards to Louis.

Check
Louis has 15 baseball cards   15

David gave him 17 more   17

Therefore, Louis should now have 32 cards, which agrees with the given information $15 + 17 = 32$.

2. Situation
James found 19 jacks that Marguerite had lost. Marguerite didn't remember how many she started with, but she does know she has 24 jacks left. How many jacks did she start with? (*Note:* Assume that James found all the jacks that Marguerite had lost.)

Analysis
You do not know how many jacks she started with. Let □ represent the number of jacks Marguerite started with   □

She lost 19 jacks   19

It is given that she has 24 jacks left. Since "□ $-$ 19" and "24" name the same number, the sentence is   □ $-$ 19 = 24.

Solution

"$\square - 19 = 24$" is read, "If 19 is subtracted from some number, the result is 24." What is the number? Another way to interpret this same sentence is "19 plus 24 is equal to what number?" The last suggestion comes from the definition of subtraction. The answer to both these statements is 43. The truth set {43} indicates that Marguerite started with 43 jacks.

Check

Marguerite had 43 jacks to begin with   43

She lost 19 jacks   19

She now has 24 jacks, which agrees with the given information $43 - 19 = 24$.

3. Situation

The Wizard from Squaresville has dwarfs and dragons. These creatures have 50 heads and 140 legs. How many dwarfs and how many dragons does the Wizard have?

Analysis

Some assumptions will have to be made about the given information. We will first assume that each of the dwarfs and dragons has a head and that each head is included in the 50 heads. We will further assume that each dwarf has two legs and that each dragon has four. You do not know the number of dwarfs, and you do not know the number of dragons, but you do know that there are 50 altogether. If there are 10 dwarfs, then there must be $50 - 10 = 40$ dragons. If there are 14 dwarfs, then there must be $50 - 14 = 36$ dragons. If there are 27 dwarfs, then there must be $50 - 27 = 23$ dragons. If there are x dwarfs, then there must be $50 - x$ dragons.

Let x represent the number of dwarfs x

Then the number of dragons is $50 - x$.

The other bit of information involves number of legs. If one dwarf has 2 legs, then the number of legs of x dwarfs is $2 \times x$.

Using the same reasoning for the dragons, the number of their legs is $4 \times (50 - x)$.

There are 140 legs altogether; therefore, the sentence is $(2 \times x) + 4 \times (50 - x) = 140$.

Solution

Through substitution one finds that the truth set is {30}. This indicates that there are 30 dwarfs, and from this information one can easily determine the number of dragons. $50 - x = 50 - 30 = 20$ dragons.

Check

There are 30 dwarfs	30.
There are 20 dragons	$50 - 30 = 20.$
Together	$20 + 30.$
They have 50 heads	$20 + 30 = 50.$
Total dwarf legs	$2 \times 30 = 60.$
Total dragon legs	$4 \times 20 = 80.$
Together	$60 + 80.$
They have 140 legs	$60 + 80 = 140.$

This agrees with the given information.

36 WORD PROBLEMS OR PROBLEMS WITH WORDS

Jerome Manheim

BEFORE YOU READ   There has been much discussion of the nature of verbal problems and how one solves them. In this article the author describes two types of such problems and the processes used to solve them. In reality his examples are more appropriate for secondary than for elementary school. Nevertheless, the elementary school teacher should be aware of three important constants regarding growth in problem solving. First, the role of language becomes increasingly important as pupils advance in school. Second, there is an increased use of variables and a decreased use of numerals as pupils advance. Third, the processes used by children to solve word problems are similar at all grade levels. This article lends additional support to the notion that a person develops problem-solving ability gradually over a long period of time.

As a result of reading this article the teacher should be able to describe three subtle differences between problem solving in the elementary school and in the secondary school.

The metamorphosis that "word problems" have undergone in our lifetime has resulted from psychological investigations into motivation. Evidence in support of the change comes from researchers and teachers, whenever they have asked about the "here and now" as opposed to the "there and then." Despite this major breakthrough, the "word problem" remains a generator of fear and frustration for many students. This article will be concerned with three aspects of elementary "word problems." If we cannot make them our welcome friends, it is hoped to remove at least some of the apprehensions traditionally associated with their appearance.

REAL AND IMAGINARY WORD PROBLEMS

We are accustomed to thinking of a "word problem" as "a problem with words" (excepting, of course, simple directions, such as "Solve for x," or "Find the roots of the following equations."). If we ask our students, or

---

Reprinted from *The Mathematics Teacher*, vol. 54, no. 4 (April 1961), pp. 234–238. Jerome Manheim is Dean of the College of Liberal Arts & Sciences of Bradley University, Peoria, Illinois.

ourselves, why such a problem is more difficult than a non-word problem, we are apt to find the difficulty attributed to "the nonmathematical nature of the problem." Ineptitude is frequently excused with the reminder that the solver is not, after all, supposed to be a physicist, social scientist, etc. How good or how poor this rationale is will emerge later. For the present we will distinguish between "real word problems" and "imaginary word problems."

A "real word problem" is one which employs English or other non-mathematical language to ask a question about a physical (chemical, economical, mathematical, biological, social, etc.) phenomenon, the laws governing the particular phenomenon being presupposed. The following are illustrative problems.

1. A train going east was overtaken in six hours by one leaving the same place two hours later and traveling sixteen miles per hour faster. Find the rate of each.[1]

2. An inductance of 1 henry, a resistance of 3,000 ohms, and a capacitance of 5×10^{-7} farad are connected in series with an e.m.f. of $100e^{-1000t}$ volts. If the charge and current are both zero when $t = 0$, find the current when $t = 0.001$ sec.[2]

3. Show that the sum of the roots of a quadratic equation with real coefficient is real.

To solve each of these problems we need to have prior knowledge about the relationships governing quantifiable words. In Problem 1 the relevant quantities are time, distance, and rate; in Problem 2 we must ultimately have access to the differential equation that describes the situation where the three circuit parameters are connected in series with an e.m.f.; in the last problem our prior knowledge is the quadratic formula. In each case, something external must be known or determined before the problem can be solved.

An "imaginary word problem" differs from a "real word problem" in only one respect, the governing laws, those which relate the quantifiable words, are explicitly enunciated. Here are some examples of "imaginary word problems":

A. The formula for changing degrees on a Fahrenheit thermometer to degrees on a centigrade thermometer is

$$C = 5/9(F - 32).$$

If $F = -22$, find the value of C.[3]

[1] J. C. Stone and V. J. Mallory, *A First Course in Algebra*, New Edition, (Chicago: Benj. H. Sanborn & Co., 1936), p. 228, Problem 30.

[2] H. W. Reddick and Frederick H. Miller, *Advanced Mathematics for Engineers*, 3rd ed., (New York: John Wiley & Sons, Inc., 1955), p. 90, Problem 40.

[3] J. C. Stone, *op. cit.*, p. 240, Problem 14.

B. A resistance coil has total resistance R. The coil is to be divided into two coils, which are then to be connected in parallel. If the resistance R_e, equivalent to two parallel resistances R_1 and R_2, is given by

$$\frac{1}{R_e} = \frac{1}{R_1} + \frac{1}{R_2},$$

how should the coil be divided to make R_e a maximum?[4]

C. The fundamental trantort unit on the western hemisphere of the planet Jaros is the fratezat; on the eastern hemisphere it is the caliope. The fratezat, F, and the caliope, C, are related by the formula:

$$C = 5/9(F - 32).$$

If $F = {}^-22$, how much is C?

A characteristic of these problems, as the reader has probably observed by comparing Problem A and Problem C, is that their solution is entirely independent of word interpretation and, hence, of physical meaning. No excuse about lack of training in the related discipline is valid in these cases. It is important for the student to understand this and then to exercise (for the particular problem) his prerogative to invent. After some encouraging, a student decided (Problem B) that a resistance coil looked like a square. When it was divided into two parts and connected in parallel, it looked like a corporal's stripes. Actually, these symbols are just as satisfactory as the accepted ones; neither looks anything like a resistance coil, nor is there any reason that they should.

We propose, then, to dispose of the "imaginary word problem" by deciding that it is not really a word problem after all. If the nature of such problems is explained to students, if they are taught to look for and focus on the intrinsic nature of the problem rather than the surrounding verbiage, most of the difficulty accompanying this type of problem should disappear.

It is true that the dichotomy is not so clean as we might wish. If we are willing to call the quadratic formula an external relationship (Problem 3), then what about the laws of arithmetic and algebra necessary to the solution of all the problems? These are not explicitly stated, and yet they are necessary. A practical means of resolving this semantic difficulty is to differentiate between language, axioms, and methodology on the one hand and derived results on the other. If a student does not know the language and rules of algebra, he probably should not have been exposed to the problem in the first place; if he does, our distinction is unambiguous.

---

[4] J. R. Britton, *Calculus* (New York: Rinehart & Co., Inc., 1956), p. 89, Problem 2.

THE TECHNICAL MECHANISM OF SOLVING
WORD PROBLEMS

If we have a "real word problem," then it is given entirely in the non-mathematical language (e.g., Problems 1 and 3 above), or it is easily transcribed into this language (e.g., Problem 2). The laws relevant to the solution can be similarly expressed. It is, however, the transcription from the nonmathematical tongue to the mathematical one that we seek, and since this is generally the more difficult, it is reasonable to inquire into the reason for the choice.

The reason we transform the expression of the problem from the nonmathematical tongue (e.g., English) to the mathematical tongue is that we have greater manipulative facility in the latter area. In fact, within mathematics itself we often effect transformations to facilitate solution. A problem that is presented in one coordinate system may be transformed to another. If the problem is topological in character, areas may be transformed into points, etc., as in the classical solution to the Königsberg Bridge problem. In differential equations we introduce operators because they assume an algebraic role, and we are more at home with algebra than with differential equations.

After the problem is solved in the transform language, we translate back into the original tongue to exhibit the answer.

Viewed another way, what is involved is a double mapping. The problem originally given in one space (e.g., English) is mapped into another space (mathematics). Transformations within this latter space are made according to established rules. At the proper point the inverse mapping, from the mathematics to the English (or the x' to the x, or the algebra to the solution of the differential equation), is effected.

This tells us why we use mathematics to solve word problems; it doesn't tell us how to express the problem mathematically.

OBTAINING THE SOLUTION

If all goes well, then the chronology for solving a word problem will read:

1. The problem is understood.
2. The laws relevant to the situation are selected.
3. The general laws in statement 2 and the corresponding "words" in statement 1 are made to interact in order to get mathematical expressions that are mappings of the word data.
4. The mathematical symbols are manipulated according to an accepted methodology.
5. The manipulation ceases when transformation of the solution is obtained.
6. The inverse mapping occurs, and the answer is exhibited.

A number of things may happen which can disrupt or delay this program. Numerous writers have discussed problem solving in general. We shall restrict our examination to some difficulties that arise specifically from the word nature of the problem.

Choosing the laws relevant to the situation   For definiteness of approach we will focus on the train problem above, though the discussion has general applicability. We really have two problems here: how do we select a law for consideration, and how do we know when to cease looking for more laws?

As we read over the problem, those words that are amenable to quantification are selected; these are clearly distance, time, and rate. (We may have some ambivalent feelings about the word "east" because this refers to direction, a concern that is frequently relevant to a problem. This shall be kept in mind.) We now cast about, among our store of preinformation, for laws relating some or all of the quantifiable words. Either we know that "distance = (rate)(time)," or we don't. If the formula is entirely foreign to us, i.e., it is not part of our preinformation and is not derivable from known data, then we will not solve the problem, and the excuses based upon the nonmathematical character of the problem are clearly valid here. If, on the other hand, we know the formula, then we have forfeited all rights to this excuse, as we shall see later. Assuming that we do know the formula, we lay it out (write it down) for consideration. This answers the first part of our question.

We must next decide when to stop looking for formulas relating the quantifiable words. There is no complete set of universal rules here, but there are useful suggestions. In the first place, we want enough laws exhibited so that all the relevant quantities are mentioned at least once. We have a law relating distance, time, and rate; at this point, we must make up our mind about "cast." Although it is possible to develop a metarule that will tell us about the necessity of including a rule about a direction, it will be of limited applicability; it will not resolve corresponding difficulties that arise in other problems, where "hotter," "richer," "heavier" occupy the questionable role. Nonetheless, the decision must be made. Assuming the absence of a semantic problem, the decision about the relevance of a word is essentially a mathematical one. "How does the word 'east' affect the structure of the problem?" Once we have decided that "east" is a mathematical dummy, we will be in a position where all the relevant words in the problem that are concerned with magnitude appear in the chosen set of law(s)—in this case, "$D = rt$." Although this fact does not, of course, guarantee that we need not seek additional governing laws that are external to the problem, it suggests that we *may* have sufficient law(s) for the problem. Barring prior familiarity with the problem type, we won't know whether or not we need additional relationships until we have proceeded further with the problem—either solving it, in which case it is clear that we had employed sufficient law(s), or failing of a solution in a manner indicating that we need additional relationships.

Generally speaking, we should proceed with the solution as soon as we have sufficient laws to relate all the relevant words. For, in most elementary problems where not enough laws have been used, the evidence for this will appear early in the attempted solution in the guise of a deficient set of equations. The alternative choice of seeking additional relationships can be dangerous, especially for the novice. The main danger is that laws not independent of the preceding ones will be chosen. For example, in the present problem the solver might propose

$$\text{rate} = \frac{\text{distance}}{\text{time}}$$

as a new relationship. In the absence of error, he is then likely to show that distance = distance or $0 = 0$, a tribute to his impeccable arithmetic but of zero value to the problem at hand.

Instances of the laws   The next step is the interaction between the statement of the problem and the law(s) that have been selected. This generally means that special instances of the law(s) are exhibited to reflect the particular conditions of the problem. These are adjoined to the set of equations that are mathematical expressions of the relationships enunciated in the statement of the problem. If we let subscripts distinguish the two trains, this latter set of equations is:

$$D_2 = D_1$$
$$r_2 = r_1 + 16$$
$$t_1 = 6$$
$$t_2 = 4.$$

After making the substitutions in the law, the following set of equations can be added:

$$D_1 = r_1 6$$
$$D_2 = (r_1 + 16)4.$$

The technical operations   It is now time to manipulate. As every teacher knows, blind manipulation is not mathematics and will seldom lead to the solution. Even more important in mathematics than knowing how to do something is knowing what you want to do in the first place. If the present problem has been understood, the student knows that he is seeking values for r_1 and r_2. His manipulation must proceed towards this end, and his proficiency in achieving the goal is a measure of his manipulation ability.

Exhibiting the answer   If the solver knows where to stop the manipulation, it is only because he has the interpretation of the symbols constantly before him. There will not be any problem concerning the inverse mapping, i.e., once he has decided that he is going to cease manipulation, when he has expressions for r_1 and r_2:

$$r_1 = 32$$
$$r_2 = 48,$$

he will have no difficulty in stating: "The velocity of the first train is 32 miles per hour, and the velocity of the second train is 48 miles per hour."

The above treatment undoubtedly has limitations. For one thing, not every problem is as amenable to analysis as the illustrative example. Variations and failures will occur. But the author has successfully employed the general approach to reduce the tensions usually associated with "word problems." It is not proposed that the teacher should discuss psychology or mappings with an elementary algebra class. However, much of the apprehension that "word problems" induce can be dissipated if the essential nature of word problems is discussed: (a) when they are "word problems" and when they aren't; (b) when they become problems that require proficiency in the discipline of mathematics and cease, thereby, to be problems of physics, economics, sociology, etc.; and (c) what kinds of decisions the potential solver must make that are not required in a nonword problem. With the current emphasis on logical analysis and the study of structure, the role of the "word problem" should be re-evaluated. Carefully presented, it can be a ready complement to this emphasis, an ample justification for its retention.

37 PROBLEM SOLVING— PROGRAMMING AND PROCESSING

Herbert Hannon

BEFORE YOU READ   Nearly everyone can recite steps to be followed in solving a problem. What is often not clearly identified is the relationship between how a pupil develops a plan for solving a problem and how he executes the plan. In this article Professor Hannon describes a programming and processing aspect for solving verbal problems. The article contains numerous implicit suggestions for teaching problem solving in the elementary school.

By contrasting this article with the previous one by Jerome Manheim, the teacher can gain additional insight into the dimensions of verbal problem solving in the schools. More specifically, as a result of reading the teacher should be able to identify the essential features of both programming and processing as dichotomized by Professor Hannon and illustrate each phenomenon with an example appropriate for use with children.

To the writer it would seem that there are just two basic ingredients in problem solving: "programming" or sketching the solution, and "processing" or performing the necessary computations. A student may have success or failure at either of these two levels. In order to help the student in his problem solving, it would seem to be desirable to analyze these steps to determine the necessary ingredients for each.

In order to program a solution, certain symbols are needed and the problem solver must choose one or more from each of the sets listed below as needed.

Number Symbols	*Grouping Symbols*
$\{0, 1, 27, \frac{4}{7}, 2\frac{1}{2}, \ldots\}$	$\{(\ ), [\ ], \ldots\}$
Operation Symbols	*Relation Symbols*
$\{+, -, \times, \div, \ldots\}$	$\{=, <, >, \neq, \ldots\}$
Place Holder Symbols	
$\{N, \square, \bigcirc, \Delta, \ldots\}$	

Reprinted from *The Arithmetic Teacher*, vol. 9, no. 9 (January 1962), pp. 17–19. Professor Hannon is in the Department of Mathematics at Western Michigan University, Kalamazoo, Michigan.

By combining elements from these sets, it is possible to get a number sentence which says in symbolic form just what the description of the problem situation said in words. The problem is solved, of course, when the place holder symbol has been replaced by a number symbol (a numeral) which it represents in the sentence. We then say that the sentence is true. Other number replacements would obviously lead to a false statement. As an example:

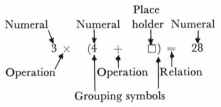

Since word sentences are written in a horizontal manner, it would seem to be desirable to write our number sentences in the same manner also. Here, programming the solution implies that the entire solution is sketched out before any computation is done.

Problem solving in the lower grades always begins with problem types which require but one step, or computation, for their solution. In such problems, grouping symbols will not be needed as they are used to establish the order in which the operations or computations are to be done if a certain order is necessary.

The following sentence patterns are characteristic of these one step problems:

Addition Patterns

$$4 + 3 = \square$$
$$\square - 3 = 4$$

Subtraction Patterns

$$11 - 6 = \square$$
$$6 + \square = 11$$
$$11 - \square = 6$$

Multiplication Patterns

$$4 \times 3 = \square$$
$$\square \div 3 = 4$$

Division Patterns

$$10 \div 5 = \square$$
$$\square \times 5 = 10$$
$$10 \div \square = 5$$

No attempt should be made to force a problem solution to fit a certain pattern since the sense of the problem must determine the pattern. Students can be made very familiar with the above patterns, however, by means of concrete situations involving counting procedures in which the interrelationships between the processes are noted carefully.

Problem solving situations should be allowed to "flow" into one of the patterns previously discussed. One should not try to force all problems involving a given operation into one type of representation. It is here that the desirability of the horizontal form—the use of a number sentence becomes evident. For example:

> After John had given away 3 candies, he had 4 candies left. How many had he at first?

The form to be used is shown by the number sentence $\square - 3 = 4$. This number sentence is implied from the structure of the physical situation and the solution should never be forced into the addition pattern, $3 + 4 = \square$. Thus, the number sentence is always established first (the programming of the solution), then the process is recognized by the pattern obtained, that of addition in this case. A variety of approaches may be used in rationalizing the solution. Certainly vertical forms are desirable for computation since they make it possible to employ the place value implication of the number symbols to promote ease of computation.

Another example will help to establish the concept.

> John had some candies. He divided them equally among his 5 friends and found that each of them had 6 candies. How many candies did he have in all?

The "flow" pattern is suggestive of $\square \div 5 = 6$.

The student must recognize this pattern as one of multiplication. "Processing," using the symbols, now calls for the use of a multiplication fact.

Many problem types may be recognized where one or more steps in the solution are involved.[1] It is not the purpose of this paper to develop these types. Perhaps it is not desirable to even suggest that a complete list can be formulated since it is the description of the problem situation as a number sentence that is important.

As an example, then, we might look at the programmed solutions suggested by the following two step problems:

> After John had mowed 4 lawns at $3.00 each, his father gave him a bonus of $2.00. How much money did John then have?

> During the 4 weeks they were on vacation, John mowed the lawn for his two neighbors. For one lawn he received $3.00 per week and for the other $2.00 per week. How much did he earn altogether?

---

[1] Hartung, M. L., Van Engen, H., Knowles, L., and Gibb, G., *Charting the Course for Arithmetic* (Chicago: Scott, Foresman and Company, 1960), pp. 170–72.

In these word sentences the same numbers appear in the same order. Obviously the number sentences or programmed solutions do not look alike. The patterns exhibited are listed below:

$$(4 \times 3) + 2 = \square$$
$$4 \times (3 + 2) = \square$$

Grouping symbols become essential in formulating the solutions since it is quite important that the right number values be grouped and the operations of multiplication and addition be performed in a certain order.

Finally, students should have practice in devising problem situations to fit a suggested pattern. For example, the following pattern might be used to develop a problem:

$$4 + \frac{\square}{2} = 8$$

This might lead to the developing of a problem situation such as:

John has saved $4.00. How much more must he earn to buy a basketball which costs $8.00 if his father says that he may spend only half of what he will earn toward the ball?

SUMMARY

The examples listed recognize that the structure of the physical situation (putting together of sets of objects, the taking away of a subset of objects, etc.) determines the number sentence. In this paper the development of the number sentences has been called "Programming the Solution," while the actual performing of the computations has been called "Processing the Numerals," or number values. Good practice requires the complete programming of a solution before any of the computation is performed. The solution is thus sketched out in number sentence form with elements from the appropriate sets (listed in the first part of the paper) used to combine the ideas involved in the problem. Certainly such an approach to problem solving should prove to be interesting to both student and teacher alike.

SECTION VII

The Case for Teachers: Facilitating Professional Decisions

"Method is like packing things in a box; a good packer will get in half as much again as a bad one."

—Richard Cecil

Introduction

313

INTRODUCTION

There is unquestionably a relationship between teaching and learning. That is not to say that learning does not take place without teaching, yet every day that schools are in session a teacher makes professional decisions that provide direction which helps children develop cognitive skills and affective values. To do this means that teachers must make intelligent decisions regarding the experiences likely to maximize learning.

The past decade has seen the operation of several forces which exerted dramatic pressures in changing the role of teachers. Two are easily discernible. Most obvious is the accelerated growth of knowledge. In elementary school mathematics this has manifested itself in the need to know more about the subject and to grasp this knowledge from a structural, rather than factual, point of view. Second, not unrelated to the first, is the reaffirmed focus on the learner as an individual, and the concomitant pressure to "individualize" all instruction. The resultant new role for teachers in this setting is no longer that of having a task to perform but rather of having a role to play. This role requires, in addition to being a substantive scholar, that the teacher function as an information manager and organizer, administrator and stimulator of learning. While certain current organizational schemes—such as staff differentiation, continuous progress, and utilization of paraprofessionals—may alter a specific setting slightly, a teacher must ultimately make the crucial professional decisions that assure an effective instructional program.

Not all elementary teachers are confident in their ability to deal with the substance of mathematics, and it is unreasonable to expect each to be a specialist in this field. In view of the emerging role of the teacher however, it is reasonable to expect that teachers be specialists in mathematics instruction.

Of paramount importance to success in teaching mathematics will be the decisions to be made as the immediate learning environment is organized. The latter process is one of deciding how to tailor the total educational environment to the needs of children. For the practitioner of integrity this "tailoring the educational environment" is a complex operation. The teacher must possess the requisite knowledge to form and test hypotheses regarding: (1.) what kind of learning is involved or desired; (2.) what environmental arrangements are most likely to promote that kind of learning; and (3.) what kinds of interaction will promote the most productive involvement of a given learner or group of learners with selected content or courses of action.

Today professional decisions must be made from an ever-widening range of existing alternatives, and viable alternatives must be developed when appropriate ones do not seem available.

Each of the articles in the following Section presupposes that a teacher's primary task remains the development and facilitation of an "active" learning environment appropriate to all children in his charge. This is compatible with the responsibility to develop an acute sensitivity to needed change rather than to seek the accommodation of stability. In a true sense the largest failing of teachers, often believed found in unexplored questions and alternatives not pursued, may lie in their inability to take decisive action.

The concluding Section of this book identifies five larger areas of continuous teacher involvement where increased teacher autonomy has resulted in increased teacher responsibility. Few would deny that teacher decisions regarding early mathematics education of children, meeting individual needs, accessing what has been taught, testing historical or present curricular assumptions, and selecting new instructional materials are among the most crucial professional decisions an elementary teacher can make. These areas provide the direct focus for Section VII.

38 MANAGING MATHEMATICS IN THE EARLY EDUCATION OF CHILDREN

G. Schlinsog

BEFORE YOU READ   The early education of children has been investigated for many years.   In truth, research response from young children has often guided learning theory and practice.   Now, in this space age and with the advent of more sophisticated research methods, newly discovered knowledge is generating a clearer understanding of how young children develop, both emotionally and intellectually.

The writings of Bloom, Bruner, Hunt, and Piaget, among others, have made it clear that the early years are crucial periods for both language development and for acquiring fundamental quantitative and spatial ideas.   Yet these discoveries have proven inimical to our traditional concept of readiness.   Consequently, this new knowledge is being accepted slowly, because teachers fear its logic will not provide children with "appropriate skills and right conclusions."   As an example, not many of us are willing to sit back and do essentially nothing except provide sufficient time for young children to devise alternate solutions to real problems, even when improved problem-solving techniques are stated as an objective.   The teacher has a professional choice, a decision to make.

This article suggests a model, together with some illustrative implementation, for an environment that will enhance the mathematical development of young children.   Although the affective domain enjoys a prominent role, it is not at the expense of cognitive development.

After reading the article, the teacher should be able to list mathematical ideas appropriate for young children, and illustrate, with one example for each, four steps necessary to develop a sound instructional program.

Our concepts of early childhood education are being altered rapidly by those active in the study of child growth and development.   The established fact that a major portion of the shaping of the intellect takes place before a child reaches the age of seven [1] is startling, and it imposes tremendous responsibility on those interested in teaching young children.   Equally crucial and influential as it relates to the mathematics education of young children has been the enunciation of three distinguishable stages [2] along

---

Original material written especially for this volume.   Professor Schlinsog often contributes to professional journals on this topic.

the continuum of quantitative cognition. The early years are crucial in the development of such aspects as language ability, personality, intelligence, and the ability to think. The growth of a child's thought processes depends upon his having something to think about and upon his opportunities to have appropriate new experiences. What he is able to assimilate from those experiences depends partly on the thinking processes he has already developed. Patterns of abstract thought emerge slowly as the child encounters new ideas, reacts to them, and incorporates them into his own intellectual behavior.

The 1960's saw the beginning of a number of projects under the general heading of compensatory education. These projects have focused attention on the lasting effects of deprivation during a child's early years. Experimentation and research are providing insights into the possibilities of arresting and even reversing the effects of cultural, social, or experiential deprivation. Carefully planned kindergarten and preschool programs are being used to encourage language development, to stimulate the growth of cognitive abilities, and to guide the formation of selected concepts in the minds of young children. [3]

All of these events have contributed to the accumulating evidence that the environment and experiences of the infant and young child are more crucial or decisive in developing his *capacity* to function as an adult than all his later years of schooling. Altogether, these changing emphases would seem to point to new types of kindergarten and preschool programs in mathematics. To the conventional concern for cognitive development must be added a refurbished dimension, a realistic concern for the affective development; that is, the establishment of values, interests, appreciations, and attitudes. The latter deals with emotions; that is, feelings, awareness, individual learning styles, and pupil acceptance of the learning environment.

Present evidence points to the emergence of new early childhood programs having language development as their core. [4] Within these programs, there is a definite place for mathematics as a prerequisite for perceiving, discussing, reasoning, and accepting the quantitative aspects of life. There are key mathematical concepts, important for later learning, which have significance and interest for children five, six, and seven years of age. Work with geometric, numerical, and quantitative ideas becomes a form of play, and the fascination frequently continues until formal written work and pressure for conformity begins to dull the child's interest.

APPROPRIATE MATHEMATICAL CONCEPTS FOR YOUNG CHILDREN

It is appropriate at this point to raise a question as to what mathematical concepts are suitable for development at the early age of four to seven years. Although it might decrease the readability of this article, a list of possible concepts is suggested below. To conserve space they are presented in outline form.

Concepts and skills in early mathematical development
I. Prenumber concepts
    A. Longest = shortest
    B. Tallest = shortest
    C. Biggest = smallest
    D. Thickest = thinner
    E. Narrow = wide
    F. Thin = thick
    G. Highest = lowest
    H. Heavier = lighter
    I. More = less
    J. Far = near
I. Number concepts
    A. Counting
        1. Rote
            a. One's
            b. Five's
            c. Ten's
            d. Two's
        2. Rational
            a. One's
            b. Five's
            c. Ten's
            d. Two's
        3. Identification—"Which group has four objects?"
        4. Reproduction—"Please give me five sticks"; "Draw a picture of three boats."
        5. Comparison—"How many more black boats than white boats are there?"
        6. Recognition of groups—"· · · able to identify number in a group *without* counting."
    B. Numerals
        1. Recognition or identification of
        2. Writing of
    C. Invariance or conservation of number
    D. Ordinal property of number
    E. Problem solving—*verbal* problems involving simple operations

        Example:

$$2 + 2 = \underline{\hspace{2cm}}$$
$$3 - 2 = \underline{\hspace{2cm}}$$

    F. Recognition of terms
        1. Square
        2. Circle
        3. Triangle
        4. Rectangle
    G. Identification of coins
        1. Penny
        2. Nickel
        3. Dime
        4. Quarter
        5. Dollar
    H. Relative value of coins—"Which is more, three pennies or a nickel?"
    I. Comprehension of fractional terms—1/2, 1/4, 1/3.
    J. Place value
    K. Right versus left

MATERIALS AND METHODS FOR DEVELOPING MATHEMATICAL CONCEPTS

Having identified a list of appropriate concepts, the next question is how to go about teaching or developing these concepts. Unfortunately, words have no precise and absolute meaning. Teaching mathematics in the kindergarten or preschool may mean one thing to one person and something entirely different to another. *The position taken here is that mathematics instruction at this level is not incidental, does not rely upon workbooks or papers and pencils, and is not to be confused with drill or the formal instruction frequently associated with traditional arithmetic instruction.*

    Instead, a good program is conceived of as consisting of a large number of widely varied experiences, each aimed at helping children develop specific concepts, ideas, or skills. While the activities may be extremely informal, the planning and preparation behind them should be done carefully and systematically. Games, concrete materials, manipulative devices, songs, stories, exploratory experiences, and planned activities make up the program. Teacher incentives include exploration, doubt, bafflement, and surprise in a climate where children are encouraged to take a calculated risk and receive support.

    One of the first functions of the teacher is that of screening the children to determine which skills or concepts need developing or refining. His task then becomes one of selecting, creating, or devising experiences which lead the child to the desired understanding.

    All of this is easier said than done, and perhaps the best way to convey an image of what is meant in the preceding paragraphs is to provide some illustrations. The following are offered, not as models to be imitated but as examples of activities that some teachers have found effective. An important point is that each activity is planned with specific children or groups of children and specific concepts in mind.

Let us say that a teacher has identified a group of children who can count by rote but cannot count rationally. He will then provide a large number of interesting experiences in which these children will count sets of blocks, tools, children, crayons, or other objects. In the beginning the teacher will count with them. The children may need to touch or pick up each object as it is counted in order to coordinate the thought processes with the physical processes.

One teacher working with four-year-old preschool children has five chairs at each table. When milk time comes, one child from each group has the privilege of distributing the proper numbers of napkins. One napkin is needed for each chair. There is much trial-and-error, much counting together, and much learning, for after a few months the same children can go to the kitchen and return with five cartons of milk, six cartons of chocolate milk, and four cartons of orange juice. The counting experiences in the room are not limited to milk and napkins. Other reasons for counting are used.

Another teacher, working with five-year-old kindergarten children, found some could count rationally to ten, to twenty, and some even further. Some were showing an awareness and recognition of the numerals (symbols), and others wanted to learn them. Having accepted the thesis that one can help children develop mathematical concepts without resorting to formal instruction, the teacher devised a set of experiences, including free play with some commercial materials made of wood or plastic and marketed under various names. The materials are designed so the children match objects or patterns with appropriate numerals. Some are interlocking and some may be put together only in consecutive order.

Further experiences with recognition of numerals were obtained through the use of a walk-on number line made of individual pieces of carpet on which the numerals had been spray-painted. These were laid end to end on the floor, and the children soon learned that their magic carpets didn't work if they were not in the proper order.

The teacher and children created "fun-type" of activities, such as the following: "Can you walk your age?" "Where am I?" "Walk forward two, walk back three; where are you?" "Can you walk the number of tables we have in the room?"

During the year the teacher made many other uses of the number line, but the ones described here developed skill in rational counting and recognition of the numerals. When not in use the individual pieces of carpet were stacked easily in a cupboard. Other walk-on number lines may be made from a variety of materials. They may be chalked, taped, or painted on the floor; or they may be purchased from commercial sources.

Several different stages or steps have been identified in the process through which a child learns to count. These are named in the list of concepts cited previously. The fourth stage is reproduction, when a child is able to "reproduce" a given quantity as in the directions, "draw a picture of five boats" or "bring me three sticks."

One teacher wished to give her group of preschool children continued experience with rational counting and, at the same time, focus on the reproduction aspect of counting. She cut triangles, rectangles, squares, and circles from felt. Scattering these around the room, the teacher started the game by saying, "Can you find two circles?" "Can you find one triangle and two squares?" In addition to providing experience with rational counting and reproduction, the game helped develop an awareness and knowledge of basic shapes. The teacher also used the game to foster recognition of colors, by saying, "Can you find one red triangle and one blue circle?" Other children were involved by being asked to verify the results.

The invariance or conservation of quantity is a difficult concept for young children. A small child may be satisfied with a tall, narrow glass of milk, yet protest that he is being cheated when the same quantity is given to him in a wider, lower glass. He has not yet grasped the concept of conservation. Some teachers approach this concept by allowing children to experiment, using sand or water, with jars, bottles, and containers of various sizes and shapes.

All of the foregoing are simple, relatively informal, planned activities. Each of the examples involves the use of concrete materials and requires the "active" engagement of children. While many materials may be made by the teacher, an ever-increasing variety of helpful gadgets and equipment is available from commercial sources. Catalogues from companies such as Responsive Environments Corporation, Childcraft Equipment Company, Creative Playthings, and Judy Company list many useful materials. [5]

SUMMARY

Our changing views on the nature of the development of a child's intellectual capacity have highlighted the crucialness of his early experiences. New programs are emerging which take this into consideration. In these, mathematical experiences have a role to play, both in the child's immediate world and as a foundation for later learning. The development of a sound and effective program seems to depend on certain essential or key steps:

1. Identification of concepts appropriate for and relevant to the children with whom one is working.
2. Screening and evaluation of children relative to each specific concept.
3. Selection or creation of games, materials, and experiences which help children develop specific concepts, that is, active engagement.
4. Following up with further evaluation and continued experiences as necessary.

322 THE CASE FOR TEACHERS: FACILITATING PROFESSIONAL DECISIONS

REFERENCES

1 Bloom, Benjamin S. *Stability and Change in Human Characteristics* (New York: John Wiley & Sons, 1964).
2 Flavell, John H. *The Developmental Psychology of Jean Piaget* (Princeton, N.J.: D. Van Nostrand Co., 1963), pp. 327–341.
3 Passow, A. Harry, "Early Childhood and Compensatory Education," in *Designing Education for the Future. No. 2: Implications for Education of Prospective Changes in Society*, Edgar L. Morphet and Charles O. Ryan, editors (New York: Citation Press, 1967), pp. 77–97.
4 *Ibid.*
5 Childcraft Equipment Co., Inc., 155 East 23rd Street, New York, New York 10010; Creative Playthings, Princeton, New Jersey 08540; The Judy Company, 310 North Second Street, Minneapolis, Minnesota 55401; REC, Learning Materials Division, Responsive Environments Corporation, 200 Sylvan Avenue, Englewood Cliffs, New Jersey 07632.

39 SOME WAYS TO INDIVIDUALIZE INSTRUCTION

J. Fred Weaver

BEFORE YOU READ   Classroom organization—that is, the grouping of children for optimum teaching-learning effectiveness—is a present and constant challenge. Historically, children have been assigned to teachers on an age-grade basis. Within this basis, classroom organization has ranged from large, whole, group instruction (heterogeneous grouping) through recitation involving several small groups of children of similar abilities (homogeneous grouping) to "social" groupings where children work with classmates. Teachers are currently being asked to "individualize" their mathematics instruction, which has often been unfortunately interpreted as "teaching each child separately," a task which often results in frustration as well as sterile instruction.

Evidence indicates that pupil success in mathematics is dependent upon variables more crucial than within-class organization. Certainly it is now clear that children learn mathematics best through active engagement with relevant material under the guidance of a skillful teacher. After considering all of the components of the instructional setting, each teacher must ultimately make his own decisions about classroom organization.

As a result of reading this article the teacher should be able to enunciate a personal philosophy for individualizing instruction and describe three broad dimensions of flexibility for within-class organization.

PROLOGUE

Miss Arnold was satisfied that Maria, José, Kevin, and Billie Jo were now ready to work together on the problem situation that she had outlined to them and illustrated with several examples. She glanced at each of the other centers of classroom activity. The children, for the most part, appeared to be almost unaware of her. For instance:

Sammy and Alan were engrossed in helping each other.

The pupils who had worksheets like Patty's were in no way dawdling.

This is an original draft of a manuscript published in an abbreviated, edited form in *The Instructor*, vol. 76, no. 6 (February 1967), p. 75, under the title "Are You Ready to Individualize Mathematics?" Professor Weaver is at the University of Wisconsin, Madison, Wisconsin.

Sue was less fidgety than she is most of the time—and she was not discouraged with her activity. ("I 'goofed' again yesterday," mused Miss Arnold, a bit provoked with herself, "and thought that Sue could handle her work. Why do I so often misjudge her?")

The children working with Tim were progressing without hesitation. ("A bit later I'll talk directly with them and find out just how well they sense the relationships that should come from their work. I don't think that they will disappoint me in this.")

And, as expected, Carmen was proceeding eagerly and with confidence along the special path provided for her. ("She really keeps me on my toes!")

Miss Arnold was glad for the talk she had had with Mr. Bernardo, her principal, concerning the wide range of ability and performance levels among the children in her class. And Mrs. Copeland, the mathematics consultant, was equally helpful with her specific suggestions for differentiating instruction effectively, based on individual pupil background, abilities, and needs.

("Hmmm. Patty seems to be hesitating with her worksheet. Maybe I . . . oh, good for her! She's come a long way in sensing how to help herself when uncertain about something.")

As Miss Arnold moved over to talk with the children working with Tim, she passed slowly and observingly by Patty—just to be sure that she had not misjudged *this* situation.

Miss Arnold recalled how she had introduced the operation of multiplication in the not-very-distant past. She was pleased with the effectiveness of her approach—thanks to Mrs. Copeland's suggestion—which was based on the fact that for two counting numbers m and n, their product $m \times n$ may be defined as the number of elements in an m-by-n array.[1] Specifically, for instance, the product of 5 and 3 was associated with the number of elements in a 5-by-3 array (*see* Figure 39.1), and the product of 4 and 6 was associated with the number of elements in a 4-by-6 array (*see* Figure 39.2).

Figure 39.1 A 5-by-3 array illustrating that $5 \times 3 = 15$

[1] For a discussion of this and other characterizations of multiplication *see* J. Fred Weaver, "Multiplication within the Set of Counting Numbers," *School Science and Mathematics*, vol. 67, pp. 252–270 (March 1967).

▽ ▽ ▽ ▽ ▽ ▽
▽ ▽ ▽ ▽ ▽ ▽
▽ ▽ ▽ ▽ ▽ ▽
▽ ▽ ▽ ▽ ▽ ▽

Figure 39.2 A 4-by-6 array illustrating that $4 \times 6 = 24$

It was not at all surprising that these children soon showed marked differences—in their understanding of the underlying concept, in their ability to associate symbolic statements with specific instances of multiplication, in their ability to sense properties and relationships that are characteristic of this operation, in the rate at which they achieve "automatic recall" of basic multiplication "facts," and so on. It was because of these and other expected differences that Miss Arnold found herself to be the director of the play, with its intricacies of plot and characterization, which is now in progress as the curtain rises on . . .

Act N (in simultaneous scenes)

Scene 1   Maria, José, Kevin, and Billie Jo have displayed sets with 7, 9, 11, and 12 members respectively. Each child is making as many different rectangular arrays as possible, using all members of his collection of objects. Maria has succeeded in making just two arrays: a 7-by-1 and a 1-by-7 array. She is drawing a representative "picture" of each and will name it appropriately (hopefully!). Kevin has been able to make three arrays: a 3-by-3, a 1-by-9, and a 9-by-1 array. These children will continue at this work until they have explored sets of 2, 3, 4, 5, 6, . . . , 24, 25 objects.

(This in effect will lead eventually to partitioning the set {2, 3, 4, 5, 6, . . . , 24, 25} into a subset of *prime* numbers [{2, 3, 5, 7, . . . , 19, 23}] and a subset of *composite* numbers [{4, 6, 8, 10, . . . , 24, 25}], based on the kinds of arrays that can be constructed.)

Scene 2   Sammy and Alan are gaining additional needed experience in associating a number sentence with an array. Each child has several sheets of this form:

△ △ △ △ △ △ △ △

△ △ △ △ △ △ △ △

△ △ △ △ △ △ △ △

This is a _____ -by- _____ array.

It has _____ members.

It shows that _____ × _____ = _____.

Figure 39.3

These pupils profit from completing, exchanging, and checking such sheets with each other, and from sharing the ways used to find the number of members in the various arrays.

Scene 3   Patty and some other pupils are completing worksheets such as:

$$2 = \underline{1} \times \underline{2} \qquad 3 = \underline{1} \times \underline{}$$
$$2 = \underline{2} \times \underline{} \qquad 3 = \underline{3} \times \underline{}$$

$$4 = \underline{1} \times \underline{} \qquad 5 = \underline{} \times \underline{}$$
$$4 = \underline{2} \times \underline{} \qquad 5 = \underline{} \times \underline{}$$
$$4 = \underline{4} \times \underline{}$$

$$6 = \underline{} \times \underline{} \qquad 7 = \underline{} \times \underline{}$$
$$6 = \underline{} \times \underline{} \qquad 7 = \underline{} \times \underline{}$$
$$6 = \underline{} \times \underline{}$$
$$6 = \underline{} \times \underline{}$$

and so on.

They are working toward the same ultimate purpose that Maria, José, Kevin and Billie Jo are, but at a higher level of understanding and symbolic representation. The groups eventually will compare their findings.

Scene 4   Sue is working independently with study cards of the form:

$$7 \times 4 = \square \qquad\qquad 7 \times 4 = \boxed{28}$$

Front   Back

which she is sorting into several piles—such as, "Know for Sure," "Can't Remember," and "Wrong"—for further appropriate consideration.

(Yesterday Sue had trouble responding quickly and confidently when working with open sentences such as $6 \times \square = 30$ and $\square \times 8 = 24$. She understood well enough how to "figure out the answers," but she needed greater proficiency in her "automatic mastery" of many "basic multiplication facts" in order to work with such open sentences efficiently. Later she will be introduced to the operation of division and its application in such instances.)

Scene 5   Miss Arnold now has reached Tim and his coworkers. Suddenly . . .

The curtain falls on Act N of our play, before we were able even to glimpse some of the remaining scenes that were going on simultaneously with the preceding ones.

EPILOGUE

Miss Arnold's increasingly skillful direction of this ongoing play is guided by some sound conclusions she has reached from her own classroom experience;

from discussions with Mr. Bernardo, Mrs. Copeland, and with her fellow teachers; and from various forms of in-service education, including attempts to untangle the maze of professional literature pertaining to differentiated instruction.[2]

(1.) *Individualization* is a necessary condition for truly effective mathematics instruction. This does not mean that each child must or should be "taught separately," but it does mean that instruction must be planned and implemented on the basis of the unique needs and abilities of individual pupils.

(2.) There is no plan of school organization, no plan of inter- or intraclass grouping that has been "proved" to be best for all elementary-school situations. However, individualization is facilitated by plans that permit *flexibility* in the assignment of pupils for instruction. It is inhibited by plans that lead to rigidity and permanence of such assignments.

(3.) Any plan of school-class organization is but a means to an end: effectively individualized instruction. No such plan "guarantees" that instruction will be individualized, nor does it make such individualization "automatic." Individualized instruction must be effected through variations in *each* of three broad dimensions, *no one of which is sufficient alone.*

(a.) There must be variation in instructional time, taking into account pupils' individual learning rates. But in our eagerness to enable some children to move along at a more rapid pace than others, we must be careful not to promote unbridled acceleration which may lead to superficial learning.

(b.) There must be variation in methods and materials of instruction. There simply is neither a given method nor a given set of materials that is equally appropriate for all children and for all facets of mathematical learning. Any attempt to "standardize" either of these things is antithetical to the very nature of individual differences and individualized instruction.[3]

(c.) There must be variation in the kind and level of mathematical content studied. This dimension, and particularly its latter aspect, was very evident in Act *N* glimpsed above. There are times when individualization more-or-less dictates that different children will be

[2] For a relevant presentation and extensive bibliography *see* J. Fred Weaver, "Differentiated Instruction and School-Class Organization for Mathematical Learning within the Elementary Grades," *The Arithmetic Teacher*, vol. 13, pp. 495–506 (October 1966).
[3] For a significant critique of "discovery" as *the* method of learning and instruction *see* Lee J. Cronbach, "The Logic of Experiments on Discovery" in *Learning by Discovery*, L. S. Shulman and E. R. Kieslar, editors, Skokie, Ill.: Rand McNally & Company (1966), pp. 77–92.

working with different kinds of mathematical content. But there are many other times when individualization is accomplished more advantageously through variation in the level at which common content is approached. This, coupled with variation in previously mentioned dimensions, makes for effective individualization in terms of *level or depth of learning*.

Providing optimumly individualized mathematics instruction is a challenge to be welcomed. Through our understanding of children, our understanding of the learning process, and our understanding of mathematics we can meet that challenge with a high degree of confidence.

40 ARE YOU A TEACHER OR A TESTER: EVALUATING MATHEMATICS INSTRUCTION

C. W. Schminke

BEFORE YOU READ   Teaching generally assumes a continuous, ascending commitment to developing understanding. This professed commitment is nowhere more popular than in the mathematics programs of our public schools. Especially within the past decade there have been attempts to upgrade the mastery of mathematics, particularly through new curricula. But the introduction of new programs and new approaches to learning has made the process of effective evaluation even more elusive than it formerly was. Talks with teachers indicate that many current evaluation practices designed to measure mastery have not kept pace with the increasing sophistication of the total curriculum. Within the process of functional evaluation judgments relating to the merits of response cannot be avoided. These judgments are basically professional decisions; decisions the teacher will use to redirect instruction and redesign learning sequences. The essence of the plan which follows is the way in which it unifies teaching strategy and assessment in a relevant and functional manner.

As a result of reading this article the teacher should be able to contrast the strengths and weaknesses of three commonly used procedures for evaluating mathematics instruction, and illustrate with an example at least three types of evaluative data that may be collected for mathematics folders.

We must assume a relationship between teaching and assessment. Effective assessment (1.) reveals what the child knows and can do; (2.) indicates what he knows that he has not had an opportunity to reveal; (3.) illustrates the capability and potential for divergent thinking; and (4.) determines the pace individual learning styles can accommodate.

Arithmetic is both a mathematical and mental process. Whether or not a child can add 23 and 27 is much easier to determine than (1.) whether

---

This article is a revision of a manuscript originally printed in the *Curriculum Bulletin* of the School of Education of the University of Oregon, in the fall of 1963. Professor Schminke is head of the Department of Curriculum and Instruction at the University of Oregon, Eugene, Oregon.

or not he knows in a certain situation that 23 and 27 are the numbers to be combined, (2.) whether he has an efficient thought process for combining the numbers, (3.) whether he recognizes that this combining action results in no new quantity, and (4.) whether he understands that the order of the combination will not affect the resulting new notation. Checking to see if pupils learned what has been taught is thought to be uncommonly easy in arithmetic. A careful rereading of the previous statement may illustrate why this is not the case.

Three commonly used methods of evaluating learning in arithmetic are the use of (1.) standardized tests, (2.) text and workbook tests which accompany the commercially produced arithmetic series, and (3.) informal teacher-made tests.

Standardized tests perform many valuable functions, when used as an aid in planning the instructional program. They may help us to determine groups of superior children, typical children, and retarded children for various educational purposes. They may help reveal a lack of individual and group progress and thus spot inadequacies in curriculum offerings. Standardized test results can also serve as a focal point for productive parent-teacher conferences. Their objectivity, ease of administration and scoring, national norms, and the accompanying manuals for interpretation and use of results can be considered advantages. They have a place in the overall educational program of a school for the many purposes they serve.

Where, then, are the limitations of standardized arithmetic tests for the classroom teacher? Oddly enough they are present in those things claimed as advantages. Consider objectivity—what this really means is that scores, to a large extent, depend on "exact" answers. For example, multiplication fact knowledge may be determined solely by the "correct" response (recognition items) to 9×6, the product of which is only a case of remembering what was presented in instruction and may not be indicative at all of the depth of understanding of the fact or of the process. Not only may a "correct" or "incorrect" response be independent of understanding the process, this same objectivity prevents an accumulation of evidence regarding a pupil's resourcefulness in attacking new problems. Ease of administration and scoring are not always the advantages to the classroom teacher that they seem to be, when one considers the total effect of modern methods of machine scoring. In most cases individual diagnosis is not possible because teachers are frequently not permitted to compare test booklets with scored answer sheets for follow-up instruction. In addition, there is often a resulting loss of enthusiasm and a lack of stimulation because of the temporal distance between the examination period and availability of results to the teacher. The reporting of results on "national norms" has often led us to place more confidence in this procedure than may be warranted. Rather than truly national, "norms" may simply be representative of those schools willing to participate in the standardization procedures.

Even if all norms were national, one might ask the value of comparing the achievement of a superior group of children in a favored community with a national average. It cannot be presumed that any group is doing satisfactory work because they appear to be "up to the norm." It should be pointed out that this criticism is being overcome somewhat by those schools and districts who prepare their own norms based on the actual achievement of their pupils over a period of years in addition to the use of the national norms. Finally, most standardized tests employ the common language and form used in instruction. They provide little opportunity to appraise the thought process used in computation, and do not appraise all the content presently included in a variety of enriched instruction programs.

Many of these limitations hold for textbook tests as well, and place a premium on remembering facts as presented a short time before. If the tests are located in the pupil's text they have the added disadvantage of being available for pupil scrutiny before they are actually used in evaluation.

Teacher-made tests have many of the same limitations if not thoughtfully and carefully constructed, although they have the obvious advantage of the opportunity to place special emphasis where desired, and are not usually available to pupils before they are used.

Performance on the material just described can at best indicate achievement in a narrow sense. Yet all of this is not intended as a sweeping indictment of standardized testing or other present practices. The disadvantages were reviewed in some detail to emphasize that commonly accepted forms of testing are only one means of obtaining evidence of pupil learning in arithmetic, thereby placing them in their proper perspective and relegating them to those phases of the educational program for which they are best suited.

Good teachers accept the desired outcome of evaluation as continuous improvement in learning and teaching. This position implies that separate instruction and evaluation cannot be done effectively without loss to one or the other. Thus evaluation may be defined as a series of professional techniques by which *useful* information is obtained concerning how well pupils are learning and have learned the desired outcomes of instruction. In arithmetic this means not only a child's ability to answer a quantitative situation and the determination of his behavior in meeting a new quantitative situation but also the pupil's ability to explain work done, suggest other procedures for finding correct solutions, show a solution is correct, and evaluate the suggestions of others. It is safe to add that a major accomplishment for any teacher is to conduct an evaluation program in such a way that pupils realize it is for the purpose of learning, and that learning is not for the purpose of evaluation.

What specific steps may a teacher systematically perform in evaluating arithmetic learning to overcome some of the obvious difficulties previously mentioned? The single most important procedure recommended here is that the teacher establish a systematic procedure (arithmetic folder) for regularly making essential observations in order to evaluate the complete arithmetic behavior of pupils. Within this framework the *crucial* procedure is the basis upon which this useful and essential information will be collected. Inherent in the following illustrative technique will be suggestions for improving teacher inquiries, the key feature of which is the requirement that pupils make use of an underlying principle in order to respond.

The collection of useful information for the arithmetic folder may be greatly enhanced by skillful and frequent use of questions during instruction. The following examples are best used during the discussion aspect of whole-group instruction and are primarily of non-pencil-and-paper variety.

(1.) "Gerald, which of the numbers that I am going to say is nearest 34?" (19, 43, 31, 39)

(2.) "Tom, why is the quotient figure 8 placed above the dividend figure 0 in this example—$40/\overline{320}$?"

(3.) "Peter, if $5 + 3 = 8$ is a true number sentence, why is $3 + 5 = 8$ also a true number sentence?"

(4.) "John, can you show us another way to solve $\dfrac{5}{10} + \dfrac{475}{1000}$?"

(5.) "Sherry, if you did not know how to divide, could you think how to solve $36 \div 12$?"

(6.) "Martha, can you explain why we might say a sheet of paper is a better representation of a plane than your desk top?"

(7.) "Kent, how many ways can you think of to solve this example— $3 \times 4 = 12$?"

The information revealed by pupil responses to these oral inquiries is, in the opinion of the writer, crucial to the teacher's effective evaluation of arithmetic instruction, and is not obtainable in any other manner. Here are illustrative examples of the kind of statement the teacher may record in the arithmetic folder as a result of the above inquiries:

(1.) Gerald has a well-developed concept of ordinal number.

(2.) Tom did not understand the regrouping principle in division as this introductory stage of work with 2-digit divisor.

(3.) Peter understands the role of commutativity in basic addition.

(4.) John does not as yet understand the basic relationship of common and decimal fractions.

(5.) Sherry is unable to use serial subtraction to solve a division question.

(6.) Martha intuitively grasps the "limitlessness" and "flatness" notions of planes.

(7.) Although Kent seems to know the multiplication facts he lack insight into the relationship between addition and multiplication.

Equally useful information may be obtained with thoughtfully constructed questions which require pencil and paper but which are of the short-answer variety. Often these responses can be placed directly in the arithmetic folder, or they may be interpreted in the anecdotal manner illustrated above.

(1.) The value of the circled ② is how many times the value of the under-lined 2 in two hundred twenty-three? (② 2 3)

(2.) Write the largest number you can with the digits 5, 9, 6, and 7.

(3.) Write a sentence which tells why we move the second partial product one place to the left when we multiply by 4 in this example—485 × 48.

(4.) Which of the following represents a point—(●, ●, •)?

(5.) The sum of four numbers is 60. What is the average?

(6.) Write a division situation described by the division question $4\overline{)13}$ in which the left over part must be interpreted as the next whole number.

(7.) Show in several ways that the answer to this number sentence is true—7 × 9 = 63.

(8.) Make a drawing to show that a flower bed 15 feet long contains 180 square feet.

There is another type of pencil-and-paper activity of a somewhat more extended nature which provides equally useful information and which can conveniently be passed on to the child's teacher for the following year.

(1.) A pupil composition summarizing how a new process was learned. For example, "How I Learned How to Divide a Whole Number by a Fraction," or "How We Learned to Estimate Quotient Digits."

(2.) A systematic year-to-year growth of understanding may often be determined by the increasing maturity of a pupil's responses to the vocabulary of arithmetic. For example, in successive semesters or years the teacher simply says, "Write all you can about the meaning of this word in arithmetic." A variety of words may be used, such as partial product, remainder, fraction, or quotient.

(3.) Prevailing individual and group attitudes toward arithmetic may be revealed by using the following simple instruction: From the list of six school subjects on the board, write the numeral 1 above the one you like best and the numeral 6 above the one you like least. Now place a 2 above the one you like second best and a 5 above the un-marked one you like the least. Continue in this manner until all subjects are marked by a numeral.

Because of the importance attached to these informal techniques by the writer, their advantages are worthy of review in some detail. Initially it may be noted that they require no special planning. They are simple observations which intelligent and alert teachers would make daily when employing techniques representative of the best kind of instruction in arithmetic. The procedures contain few of the limitations inherent in the usual evaluation program in regard to time and space, to say nothing of the mental health of the pupils. In regard to the latter, it should be noted that activities are constructed to determine what pupils *do* know rather than what they do not know. Through this approach it is possible to observe arithmetical behavior in all its functional relationships. Faulty thinking can be noted, as well as the prior and accompanying errors which led to faulty thinking. Essentially, then, the evidence is obtained when it can be used to best advantage; and perhaps most important, the kind of evidence secured, both group and individual, is that which cannot be determined by the usual testing procedures.

Wouldn't you rather be a teacher than a tester?

4^{1} WANTED: CLASSROOM TEACHERS TO DO RESEARCH ON BASIC PRACTICES OF ELEMENTARY SCHOOL MATHEMATICS

H. Clifford Clark

BEFORE YOU READ   Teachers probably do not often think of themselves as occupying a pivotal position in the research enterprise, much less *engaging* in classroom research endeavors. This is unfortunate because it has resulted in a passive role for teachers. Others have initiated and guided the research action. Consequently, instructional decisions are made daily based on conclusions in which teachers have no investment.

Lack of teacher involvement in research is equally unfortunate in another important way. Much research has been done which involves teachers, but more often·than not the research examines such things as (1.) professional background, (2.) role perception, (3.) substantive qualifications, and (4.) value systems—among other things. Such studies of teacher characteristics are not fruitful as change agents. They are irrelevant to some extent. Investigation needs to center around what teachers *do* when they organize, assign, diagnose, and prescribe the learning environment for children.

The assumptions suggested for testing in this paper are to be viewed as a challenge to creative teachers. With little added investment of time and at no expense, the suggested activities, and others like them, can become a part of a teaching style. After the style is developed, instructional decisions can hold special importance because of their basis in experience rather than emotion.

As a result of reading this article the teacher should be able to distinguish two roles in research for the classroom instructor, and show the relationship between action research and improved teaching. It should also be possible to state an original assumption related to teaching, and describe an accompanying activity appropriate for testing the assumption.

An original manuscript written especially for this volume. Professor Clark teaches preservice and in-service classes in mathematics education at Brigham Young University in Utah.

Many ideas concerning the teaching of elementary school mathematics are accepted as axioms. Few have been adequately tested. Too often, the basic assumptions for the teaching of mathematics are developed as a result of the intuitive hunches of curriculum innovators or textbook writers rather than upon field-tested studies.

In the recent past thousands of elementary teachers have modified their instructional methods in an attempt to keep pace with current trends. Methodology now places a greater emphasis on understanding the mathematical processes of arithmetic. Scores of new teaching models, manipulative materials, and supplementary aids have found their way into the classroom.

In a period of such activity it is appropriate to examine carefully many of these teaching practices and materials. Intuitive hunches regarding instructional procedures need to be replaced by field-tested research activities and studies.

A major burden of this applied research responsibility rightfully falls to the classroom teacher. No other person is in a position to fulfill this role. Hundreds of elementary classroom teachers are needed to engage in creative research activities to test the validity of recent notions that are accepted practice in teaching elementary school mathematics.

In the past the typical role of an elementary teacher, with regard to research, has been somewhat dull, routine, and passive. For the most part he was never consulted during the conceptualization stage. He has primarily been asked to answer questionnaires; carry out prescribed treatments; administer tests; or perform other, similar, though predetermined, routine tasks. His creative role in designing relevant research has been limited. Few elementary teachers have actually been encouraged to design and execute a researchable idea in their classrooms. In short, the teacher has not been an accepted partner in the research enterprise.

The word "research" has often frightened elementary teachers. Sophisticated researchers have emphasized the need for precision in sampling theory and research design. Complicated statistical procedures have made many elementary teachers feel inadequate and incapable of conducting useful research in their classrooms. Nonparametric measures are viewed with disdain. As a consequence, little applied research is accomplished and many ideas, useful and otherwise, in teaching elementary school mathematics go unchallenged for want of someone to bring them under scrutiny.

While basic research certainly has a place in elementary school classrooms, teachers should be actively engaged in many applied research activities as a natural consequence of their desire to improve instruction. A creative problem-solving approach involving informal activities is often helpful in building a foundation for more formal research. Suppose, for example, that as a fifth-grade teacher you devise an alternate approach to teaching the division of common fractions. You may then develop a set of trial exercises and, if well satisfied with their effectiveness, submit them to a more rigorous examination.

The classroom teacher must continue to provide the laboratory for formal research initiated by the local district or an outside educational agency. Still, confident teachers should play a more active and direct role in determining priorities for effective instruction in mathematics.

There is yet another manner in which teachers may play a significant research role from their classroom positions. In many cases original research is limited to small samples from isolated areas. Therefore, questions arise as to the generalizability of these studies to other classrooms or school districts. There is a critical need for many studies to be replicated under varied circumstances to establish a broader applicability. With some ingenuity teachers can contribute much by repeating selected procedures with students, keeping a record of the results, and comparing the findings with those reported earlier. When a teacher finds a difference in results between his class and those reported in the literature a more extensive and carefully controlled study might ensue in order to verify the findings.

It was stated earlier that a careful examination is needed of many current teaching practices and materials which have been introduced in elementary school mathematics. Specifically, what are some key practices and basic assumptions common to contemporary programs that might be questioned through classroom research?

To answer this question an examination of professional textbooks, periodicals, and other writings relative to mathematics education was made. A large list of statements was compiled, condensed, and carefully edited. From the many assumptions generated, four have been selected for illustrative purposes. Each of the four appears below, together with one suggestion for a classroom research activity. Some of the assumptions are based on considerable research, while others are more indefinite. Each appeared repeatedly in the literature. Teachers can scrutinize these statements carefully, test them in the manner suggested, and consider additional ways in which these and other assumptions that can be devised might be tested.

Assumption no. 1   If an increased emphasis is placed on providing children with meaningful experiences in arithmetic, there is less need for separate practice of the drill type.

Activity no. 1   Select a topic to be introduced for systematic study in the third-grade class; for example, regrouping in subtraction. Design learning activities to occupy four class periods. Spend the same amount of time on arithmetic as normal. However, spend an increased amount of time within the period developing appropriate illustrations with pupils, manipulating relevant materials, and exploring alternate solutions. Spend a decreased amount of time on drill activities. At the end of the four class periods give the children the test usually employed for this topic. The assumption is made that the test contains exercises normally used for drill purposes. Compare what the children achieve with what they normally accomplish on similar topics. A further comparison of the achievement with the previous group of children who took the test may be made.

Assumption no. 2 Rules and relations in mathematics which are discovered by learners are retained longer and are related more readily to similar concepts.

Activity no. 2 Will first graders who learn their basic addition facts through a discovery approach retain them longer than those who learned them only by rote-learning methods?

Two first-grade teachers might cooperate to explore this question. Instructor A teaches a given set of basic addition facts using only rote-learning methods. Immediately following the instruction the students are tested. No further instruction on these facts is given for two weeks, at which time a retest is given to determine retention.

Instructor B teaches the same set of basic addition facts using a discovery approach which provides opportunity for the students to generalize and discover the facts for themselves. Following the instruction the same testing procedures used by Teacher A are followed by B. A comparison of the results for each group is made to determine which method has the better retention power.

Assumption no. 3 Elementary school children are capable of learning more mathematics than has been taught in the past, and can understand subtle mathematical concepts previously thought too difficult to be learned in the elementary school.

Activity no. 3 To test this assumption encourage the students to gain a deeper understanding of some specific mathematical topic. This may require some additional learning on the teacher's part. One such topic might be the coordinate plane. Become familiar with the process of using ordered pairs to name points on the coordinate plane. Develop some lessons designed to teach this skill to the pupils. When the teacher feels the pupils have been adequately taught how to use ordered pairs to name points, and how to write an ordered pair which corresponds to a given point, he gives them a test that:

(1.) contains a coordinate plane;
(2.) provides ordered pairs which the pupils are to locate and connect with line segments;
(3.) requires them to name, when appropriate, the geometric figure they have constructed.

Now the test results are analyzed to determine the extent to which pupils were capable of learning this concept. If students did well, there is less reason to question the validity of the assumption stated above. If the students did poorly, additional research might be undertaken to test this assumption further.

Assumption no. 4 Improved techniques of teaching, and the use of supplementary aids, can make it possible for pupils to learn more in less time.

Activity no. 4   Contemporary math programs have focused a great deal of attention on specific new techniques for teaching certain mathematical concepts. A third-grade teacher might develop a specific procedure using array cards to teach his class beginning concepts of multiplication and division. An accurate record of the time spent is kept and compared to previous methods to determine if this newer technique can be taught as effectively in less time. The same procedure might be used to test any number of supplementary aids and manipulative materials. A more extensive and carefully controlled study might follow to verify the findings.

42 WHAT LIES AHEAD: EXERCISING OPTIONS WITH EMERGING PROGRAMS

Norbert Maertens

BEFORE YOU READ   It is customary in elementary school mathematics to have children gain competence by working through commercially prepared programs—textbooks, workbooks, or other instructional material. The choices made in selecting instructional programs are crucial because of the implications for their potential to restrict or extend the quality of mathematics education for children.

The frustrations of the recent past in trying to adjust to a new era of mathematics education are a barometer for what lies ahead. When an ideal program appears to have emerged, we can be reasonably sure it will not remain ideal for long. New knowledge stimulates teachers and curriculum innovators; thus, continuous demands for change remain. The professional teacher, in order to remain secure during such shifts, must have clearly formulated criteria for assessing change and the materials that accompany it. These criteria must, in turn, be in concert with contemporary thought and need.

Currently, some appropriate criteria revolve around the potential of the changing material (1.) to be relevant to mathematics as a system of ideas, (2.) to stimulate pupil initiative and self-reliance, (3.) to accommodate exploratory response, and (4.) to encourage unique teaching styles.

Intelligent application of selected criteria requires an awareness of what exists. The teacher will play an increasingly prominent role in decisions regarding selection of programs for instruction. Professor Maertens' article will serve to make the teacher conversant with several programs that are likely to exert a significant influence on elementary school mathematics in the seventies.

Upon completion of this article the teacher should be able to provide a description of five contemporary instructional programs, enumerating the special features of each.

Elementary school mathematics has been in ferment for a considerable period of time. The sweeping changes suggested by the experimenters of

---

An original manuscript written especially for this volume. Professor Maertens is at the University of Oregon, Eugene, Oregon.

the Ball State Program,[1] the Educational Research Council of Greater Cleveland (G.C.M.P.),[2] and the University of Maryland Mathematics Project (U.M.Ma.P.)[3] of the late fifties and early sixties simply added dimension to problems that have been of concern to educators for years. Change was needed and changes were made! Now many educators assume that elementary school mathematics is entering a period of adjustment the hallmark of which will be stability. They do not anticipate influences and change as widespread as was previously generated. Comforting as the latter thought may be to some, it is clearly unrealistic, perhaps even undesirable.

The changes of the recent past may be more realistically viewed as the forerunner of what lies ahead. Experimental programs are more prevalent now than ever before, and their implications for change are much broader. In addition, industry has entered the education business. Industrialists expect changes to be revolutionary; further, they expect them to be profitable. Keeping this in mind, let us examine a few of the many experimental programs in existence today.

THE NUFFIELD PROJECT

Based on the developmental psychology of Jean Piaget, the Nuffield Project offers an approach different from that normally found in the elementary classroom. Through the use of carefully worded assignment cards, along with a variety of concrete materials, teachers encourage children to use their natural creativity as they approach mathematics.

The Nuffield Project demands that teachers make changes in their classroom organization, as well as in their methods of presenting mathematical ideas. Usually the classroom is divided into groups of from two to four persons. This arrangement is flexible, and the teacher may use all the pupils for some lessons or encourage an individual to pursue some interesting area by himself, if it appears worth while. Normally, groups assemble around tables arranged throughout the room. Each table contains a variety of provocative concrete materials to be used that day or during the next several days. The role of the teacher is twofold: to provide adequate, interesting materials and challenging assignments; and to help children discover the characteristics and patterns to be found through manipulation of the materials. Assignments must be carefully structured so that adequate prerequisites have been learned, and assistance is limited to pointing out unseen avenues of possible investigation. Teachers do not show children how to find solutions. To do so would interfere with the motivating effect that accompanies true discovery, and would interpose teacher values on child behavior.

---

[1] Published by Addison-Wesley, Palo Alto, California.
[2] Published by Science Research Associates, Inc., Chicago, Illinois.
[3] Published by Holt, Rinehart and Winston, Inc., New York, N.Y.

As they solve problems, children must often make use of authentic measuring instruments common to skilled tradesmen. They make use of surveyor's tapes, compasses, spring balances and scales, and so on. Such instruments lend an aura of excitement to the work, as well as serving to familiarize the children with tools of measurement. Other materials may be constructed by the teacher or by students.

Properly executed, the Nuffield materials strive for student independence and accountability. Each of several tables set up throughout the room contains materials needed by a child or group of children, and each has an assignment card posing the problem of the day. Assignments such as the following are common:

> Fold a square so that each half fits exactly on the other half. In how many ways can you fold the square so that this occurs?

Each group of children works with the materials on the table to discover that the squares could be folded as shown in Figure 42.1, and one of the children records results.

Figure 42.1

As each group finishes its work, the teacher introduces the term "axis of symmetry" and assigns additional work enriching this concept. Throughout the lesson teacher involvement is kept minimal.

The methods and materials of the Nuffield Project may be added to any on-going program. Nuffield proponents suggest that the program be incorporated gradually, since use of the materials requires that teachers reorient their approach to instruction. Since the project requires precise instruments, initial expense might be high, and so a carefully planned, gradual change appears most efficient.

THE UNIVERSITY OF ILLINOIS ARITHMETIC PROJECT

Under the direction of Professor David A. Page, the University of Illinois Arithmetic Project has attempted to devise materials to make mathematics interesting to children. The Illinois materials are not designed as a complete course but rather as enrichment materials to extend and deepen a child's understanding of the basic principles of mathematics. Certain of the materials are sequential, and it is suggested that the entire sequence be used in introducing and working with a particular topic.

Unlike many experimental programs, which assume some degree of mathematical sophistication on the part of the teacher, these materials are prepared with two objectives in mind: (1.) to develop materials appropriate to children, and (2.) to assist the teacher in learning the mathematical principles which are important to his teaching. Each of the exercises supplies appropriate amounts of drill on topics previously learned, and presents materials necessary to the learning of a new concept or generalization. Throughout the entire series of materials the role of mathematical vocabulary is de-emphasized. Professor Page believes ideas to be more important than vocabulary, and his materials are designed to assist children in exploring and discovering these ideas, rather than in learning terminology. Although not ignored, the emphasis of the program is not on computation but on having children discover mathematical principles.

The Illinois Project has become known for its new ways of using materials; for example, showing addition as cricket jumps on a number line, or using frames to write mathematical sentences. When using the number line children are told that a plus cricket will always jump toward the right, but that a minus cricket always jumps toward the left.

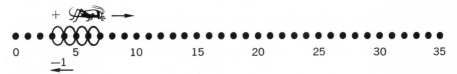

Figure 42.2 A + cricket starts at three and takes four more jumps. Where is he?

Children are led to see that $3 + 4 = 7$, and are shown the number sentence describing that action. The number line is also used to show children the undoing of addition by having a minus cricket start at 7 and take four jumps. The question is then asked, "Where is he?" The relationship of subtraction to addition is thus graphically demonstrated. Multiplication and division are received as extensions of the actions taken in addition and subtraction. Rather than having a cricket take jumps of one space each time, the size of the jump is determined by having a plus cricket take a given number of jumps, and then determining where he is. Division is shown in the same manner using a minus cricket.

Another interesting innovation of the Illinois Project is the use of frames through which children are led to find solution sets to given problems. As teachers get ready to work with frames, they suggest the rule that frames of the same shape used more than once in a number sentence must all contain the same number. Frames of differing shapes are variable. They may have the same number as other shaped frames, but may also represent other numbers. For example, the problem $\square + \square = 8$ may only be answered $4 + 4 = 8$. However, the problem $\square + \triangle = 8$ may be solved by the following:

$$1 + 7 = 8$$
$$2 + 6 = 8$$
$$3 + 5 = 8$$
$$4 + 4 = 8$$
$$5 + 3 = 8$$
$$6 + 2 = 8$$
$$7 + 1 = 8$$

The use of frames of various shapes suggests to children a desired class of variable; thus, these configurations are more closely tied to past experiences than algebraic letters.

The examples shown above are representative of the University of Illinois Arithmetic Project. Used wisely, these materials can help the classroom teacher to enrich his program and greatly expand not only the student's perception of mathematics but his own as well.

INDIVIDUALLY PRESCRIBED INSTRUCTION

Begun in Pittsburgh in 1964 by the Learning Research and Development Center, the Individually Prescribed Instruction (IPI) project has as its goal the preparation of an individualized program of instruction for every child. Programmed instruction by itself did not seem to permit such individualization. Each student encountered a sequence of material which had been structured so that particular objectives were attained. If a student had trouble on a particular exercise he had to stop and seek assistance. Normally, early programs did not provide such help. The same was true for those students having a superior background. They encountered the same material as others. Effort was not made to assist children in skipping a sequence. Programmed instruction was simply a highly sequenced set of instructional material on a given topic.

With this in mind a group of teachers and subject matter specialists from the University of Pittsburgh carefully prepared a series of objectives for instruction written in behavioral terms. These objectives were ordered for the total mathematics program, and the total program was broken down into thirteen subareas ranging from numeration to geometry. Identifiable levels of competence contained within the program allowed pupils to be assigned to levels, depending upon their scores on a battery of diagnostic instruments.

Following diagnosis, each child is given a prescription delineating the material to be learned for a specified period of time. A child then takes his prescription to the materials center and is given the material he needs to attain an objective. When he completes his work it is corrected by a teacher aid, and a new prescription is written. The teacher's role is to write the initial prescription, look over the corrected worksheet completed by the child, and then to prescribe additional work. When the child completes a unit, he is given a diagnostic achievement test to determine areas needing additional stress and the future areas of instruction. Careful records are kept of each child's progress through the programmed sequences, and frequent diagnostic tests are given to determine whether these records reflect true performance.

Although not exclusively so, the IPI materials tend to be oriented toward paper-and-pencil work. Manipulation of materials is not required to complete many of the worksheets. Teachers are urged to use a variety of manipulative devices in helping children attain and expand concepts. Because the materials are carefully programmed, teachers spend much of their time prescribing sequences of material rather than teaching as is normally conceived. Children who need assistance raise a small flag. The classroom teacher or an aid then helps the child with his particular problem.

The IPI program has objectively set about defining the goals of elementary mathematics, levels of competence, and instructional sequences. Their materials are continuously examined, and with time should become even more precise.

THE MADISON PROJECT

Under the direction of Professor Robert B. Davis and Mrs. Beryl Cochran, the Madison Project has designed many methods and materials needed to carry out a supplementary program in modern mathematics. Concurrent with the regular arithmetic program, the Madison Project materials are to be used for approximately one hour per week. As teachers become familiar with the materials they can gradually be worked into the regular arithmetic program, and in fact might serve as the vehicle through which total curriculum reform in mathematics is implemented.

The emphasis of the program is on creative, informal exploration by children. Rote drill is not a part of the work, since practice of necessary skills is accomplished as children explore and discover. Unlike adults, who tend to comment that they haven't learned a particular skill yet, students will eagerly attack a problem, often in a creative and logically structured manner. As they attain success children often discover new ways of attacking a problem, as well as perceiving relationships between problem-solving methods.

The Madison Project attempts to teach basic concepts of algebra, arithmetic, and coordinate geometry to children in the elementary school. The rationale for including such material is that children of elementary age are far more likely to explore and seek alternative solutions to a problem than are high school students. They also tend to remember successful solutions which are principles of mathematics and which they may use to solve other, more complex problems.

As the child uses generalized principles of mathematics to solve problems, he becomes familiar with them and is no longer concerned by them. They become vehicles to use in unlocking more abstract problems, and need not be memorized. While the child gains experiences, he gains readiness in attacking new problems. For example, his understanding of quadratic equations is based on a myriad of experiences, not memorized generalizations. Through this variety, children develop the background of essential experiences which allows them to cope with more formal abstract mathematics. Typical Madison Project materials include Machines in Geometry. Through a series of problems, such as those listed below, children derive machines (formulas) which help them to solve problems in mathematics.

$3 \times \square = 15$ Find the truth set for this open sentence.

(Answer: 5.)

$a \times \square = b$ Make up a "machine" to solve each equation.

(Answer: ba.)

Through a series of these and other experiences children are led to discover a formula for the area of a rectangle. They are then led to generalize their formula to a parallelogram, so that $A = b \times h$ is seen as the correct form for any parallelogram. From this children see how this learning is related to that needed to find the area of a triangle. Finally they derive the formula $A = 1/2(b \times h)$. How many adults fully understood the relationships of the area of a triangle to that of the area of a rectangle or to that of a circle? If there are few it is because they were not told about the relationship. Their learning of geometry was fragmented, probably completely divorced from their learning of other kinds of mathematics, and composed of association rather than meaningful responses. With the Madison program students are challenged to seek order consciously through construction of mathematical principles.

THE ENGELMANN PROGRAM

The teaching methodology advocated by Siegfried Engelmann is vastly different from that espoused by nearly every other program in the country, either experimental or commercial. His methods are deductive rather than inductive—discovery learning is not advocated. As he works with children Mr. Engelmann carefully defines the objectives desired for each day's activity; he isolates components of the task to be learned, and carefully teaches each of these components. Precise, painstakingly conceived examples are given, so that children do not confuse one mathematical principle with another. Little use is made of manipulative materials, and when such materials *are* used, their purpose is for elaboration of mathematical learning which has been presented deductively, rather than to have children discover a relationship for themselves.

Mr. Engelmann holds teachers accountable for the performance of children in their rooms. He contends that failures in arithmetic are directly related to inadequate instruction. Mental and physical inadequacies do not alter what must be taught if a child is to achieve a specific criterion of performance. For example, he feels that a diagnosis of perceptual deficiency or immaturity is useless in solving a teaching problem, and that the only meaningful emphasis available to the teacher is a concentration on specific teaching techniques designed to prevent failure for such children.

Teachers using the Engelmann materials generally work with children in small groups. Mr. Engelmann suggests that children be assembled into three groups containing from four to seven persons in the low group, seven to twelve in the middle group, and the remaining children in the high group. Thirty minutes of daily arithmetic instruction is suggested for each group; and when instruction is not being conducted with their groups, children work under the direction of an aid or complete an assignment. An essential reason for grouping is that teachers will receive immediate feedback as they present a lesson. In this manner they can make changes in presentation during the conduct of the lesson, and, more important, provide immediate knowledge of results to children who have responded in class. Rewards for correct responses are generally verbal ones, which are given immediately. Mr. Englemann's rationale is that when the poorest student learns, all students will learn.

Proponents of the Engelmann method suggest it is crucial that the teacher be able to isolate concepts to be learned. There must be one, and only one, possible interpretation of a demonstration. If the concept is not isolated, it is subject to misinterpretation by the child. Teachers are urged to explore ways in which the most naïve child could misinterpret a demonstration, and then either alter it or provide further demonstrations to rule out the possibility for misunderstanding. When given a choice the simplest demonstration of a concept is always used. If the task to be learned is complex, the elements making up the task are broken down into their components, which are then taught individually. After competence is attained on the isolated parts, the teacher demonstrates to the children how these parts are related and how they form a mathematical principle.

Teachers are advised to spend no more than five to eight minutes working on a particular series of tasks. Mr. Engelmann suggests that three or four different exercises be scheduled for each half-hour period, and that dissimilar exercises follow each other. Teachers are encouraged to concentrate on those aspects of the curriculum which can provide the most rapid progress. For example, he suggests that learning of multiplication facts cannot be appreciably speeded by additional work. Since this is so, he advises that time be spent on helping children to apply their knowledge in multiplication rather than in seeking increased competence with multiplication facts. A rule to be followed is not to delay a child until he masters a skill, unless that skill is essential to what is to come.

Mr. Engelmann's instructions to the teacher are very specific. Typical is his suggestion of how number pairs, such as those shown below, should be taught:

$$1 + 1 =$$
$$2 + 2 =$$
$$3 + 3 =$$
$$4 + 4 =$$

The series of number pairs should be presented in this order through $10 + 10$. Statements should be presented in a rhythmical manner, with the teacher clapping hands three times between each statement.

In summary, the Engelmann program relies heavily on the ability of a teacher to project enthusiastic acceptance of children, to be outgoing and vivacious, and to be extremely well-oriented to the task and instructional sequence of each day's lesson. By its very nature the program is oriented to the teacher, relying almost exclusively on methods which are deductive; and because of this teachers are responsible for carrying out the total program. It might be said that teachers *are* the program, for a task left unlearned will not likely be discovered through manipulation. Children's successes are teacher's successes; but unfortunately children's failures must likewise be viewed as teacher's failures. This is the harsh responsibility of the Engelmann method.

IN SUMMARY

The programs cited are only a partial compilation of the many experiments currently under way. They serve to point up the great divergence in today's experimentation. For example, the Nuffield Program places great emphasis on manipulation of concrete materials so that children may discover mathematical principles for themselves. In contrast, Siegfried Engelmann suggests that children should be taught mathematical principles by first isolating their components, teaching them, and then showing children how these components form generalizations Discovery processes are not used. Both of these differ from the IPI materials, which are carefully structured so that each child works individually on a program that has been prescribed to his potential. Other programs, such as the Madison Project and the University of Illinois Arithmetic Project, are supplemented in nature and make extensive use of guided discovery. Through carefully planned and executed sequences of instruction they lead children to discover important mathematical principles.

Despite their apparent divergence these programs have certain similarities. Each places great emphasis on sequential instruction, whether through guided discovery or expository teaching, and each clearly defines its objectives. Take note of this, for as these and other experimental programs gain emphasis, the teacher's task will be to evaluate their utility for a particular group of students objectively. Without clear objectives and a knowledge of how to sequence instruction, the teacher's task will be difficult, if not impossible.

CASTING A FURTHER GLANCE

Intriguing as they are, the aforementioned programs are only the forerunners of much greater changes to come. With the great expansion in computer technology, coupled with improvements in display screens, it may well be that instruction as we now know it will soon be obsolete. The many problems encountered in computer-assisted learning are being solved; and with the entry of corporate industry into the educational media field it appears only a matter of time until computer-assisted learning will become a part of nearly every classroom in the country. Teachers must begin to take a more active interest in the experimentation presently going on in mathematics education. By ignoring change, as teachers have done in the past, they may effectively turn the education of students over to industrialists whose primary motive in educational wares is that of profit.

How can teachers better prepare for change? They can examine programs which are in experimental stages of development to determine their underlying philosophies, and gradually employ the new and effective techniques which are evolving. They can be aware of the structure of the mathematics being taught. They can investigate other techniques of teaching and try them with students. They can evaluate and make obvious adjustments themselves, so that they become thoroughly familiar with these techniques They can find areas where instructional sequence is inadequate for a given child and introduce instruction to remedy that inadequacy. Above all, they can be aware of change and be open to change, for this is a certain and desirable constant in the education enterprise. The change that lies ahead may even be revolutionary.

ILLUSTRATIVE EXPERIMENTAL CENTERS

(1.) Engelmann Arithmetic Materials; contact Engelmann Follow Through Program, Clinical Services Building, College of Education, University of Oregon, Eugene, Oregon.

(2.) Experimental Teaching of Mathematics in the Elementary School; contact Patrick Suppes, Institute for Mathematical Studies in the Social Sciences, Stanford University, Stanford, California.

(3.) Individually Prescribed Instruction; contact Learning Research and Development Center, University of Pittsburgh, Pittsburgh, Pennsylvania.

(4.) Madison Project; contact Madison Project, Webster College, St. Louis 19, Missouri.

(5.) Minnesota School Mathematics and Science Teaching Project (Minnemast); contact Minnesota School Mathematics and Science Center, University of Minnesota, Minneapolis, Minnesota.

(6.) Nuffield Mathematics Project; contact John Wiley & Sons, Publishers, New York, New York; or the Nuffield Foundation, Mathematics Teaching Project, 12 Upper Belgrave Street, London, S.W.1., England.

(7.) School Mathematics Study Group; contact SMSG, School of Education, Cedar Hall, Stanford University, Stanford, California.

(8.) University of Illinois Arithmetic Project; contact Education Development Center, 55 Chapel Street, Newton, Massachusetts.

INDEX